Butrint

ARCHAEOLOGICAL HISTORIES

Series editors: Thomas Harrison, Duncan Garrow and Michele George

An important series charting the history of sites, buildings and towns from their construction to the present day. Each title examines not only the physical history and uses of the site but also its broader context: its role in political history, in the history of scholarship, and in the popular imagination.

Avebury, Mark Gillings and Joshua Pollard
Carthage, Sandra Bingham and Eve MacDonald
Dura-Europos, J. A. Baird
Hadrian's Wall: Creating Division, Matthew Symonds
Knossos: Myth, History and Archaeology, James Whitley
Pompeii, Alison E. Cooley
Stonehenge: A Brief History, Mike Parker Pearson
Tarquinia, Robert Leighton
Troy: Myth, City, Icon, Naoíse Mac Sweeney
Ur: The City of the Moon God, Harriet Crawford

Butrint

At the Crossroads of the Mediterranean

Richard Hodges

BLOOMSBURY ACADEMIC
LONDON · NEW YORK · OXFORD · NEW DELHI · SYDNEY

BLOOMSBURY ACADEMIC

Bloomsbury Publishing Plc, 50 Bedford Square, London, WC1B 3DP, UK
Bloomsbury Publishing Inc, 1385 Broadway, New York, NY 10018, USA
Bloomsbury Publishing Ireland, 29 Earlsfort Terrace, Dublin 2, D02 AY28, Ireland

BLOOMSBURY, BLOOMSBURY ACADEMIC and the Diana logo are trademarks of Bloomsbury Publishing Plc

First published in Great Britain 2025

Copyright © Richard Hodges, 2025

Richard Hodges has asserted his right under the Copyright, Designs and Patents Act, 1988, to be identified as Author of this work.

For legal purposes the Acknowledgements on p. xvi constitute an extension of this copyright page.

Cover image: Aerial view of Butrint. Butrint Foundation Archive
Photographer: Alket Islami

All rights reserved. No part of this publication may be: i) reproduced or transmitted in any form, electronic or mechanical, including photocopying, recording or by means of any information storage or retrieval system without prior permission in writing from the publishers; or ii) used or reproduced in any way for the training, development or operation of artificial intelligence (AI) technologies, including generative AI technologies. The rights holders expressly reserve this publication from the text and data mining exception as per Article 4(3) of the Digital Single Market Directive (EU) 2019/790.

Bloomsbury Publishing Plc does not have any control over, or responsibility for, any third-party websites referred to or in this book. All internet addresses given in this book were correct at the time of going to press. The author and publisher regret any inconvenience caused if addresses have changed or sites have ceased to exist, but can accept no responsibility for any such changes.

A catalogue record for this book is available from the British Library.

A catalog record for this book is available from the Library of Congress.

ISBN: HB: 978-1-3505-4864-0
PB: 978-1-3505-4860-2
ePDF: 978-1-3505-4861-9
eBook: 978-1-3505-4862-6

Series: Archaeological Histories

Typeset by RefineCatch Limited, Bungay, Suffolk
Printed and bound in Great Britain

For product safety related questions contact productsafety@bloomsbury.com.

To find out more about our authors and books visit www.bloomsbury.com and sign up for our newsletters.

To Iris

CONTENTS

List of Illustrations viii
Preface xi
Acknowledgements xvi

1 In the Footsteps of Aeneas 1

2 A Mediterranean History 15

3 Butrint, Corfu and the Trojan Myth 35

4 Caesar's Legacy 59

5 Early Christian Butrint 91

6 Byzantine and 'Despotic' Butrint 117

7 *Insula Botentro*: Corfu's Protector and Right Eye 139

8 Tangled Web: Archaeology, Politics and Economic Revival 157

Notes 167
Further Reading 175
Glossary 177
Dramatis Personae 181
Bibliography 183
Index 193

ILLUSTRATIONS

Figures

From the Butrint Foundation archives unless stated otherwise.

0.1	View of Butrint looking west towards Corfu	xii
0.2	Luigi Ugolini at Phoenicê, *c.* 1926	xiv
0.3	A reconstruction of the principal archaeological sites at Butrint	xv
1.1	A map showing the location of Butrint and the boundaries of the Butrint National Park	2
1.2	A vertical photograph of Butrint's Hellenistic and Roman Theatre	3
1.3	A view of Butrint in its 'Homeric landscape' from Mount Mile	6
1.4	The changing environmental context of Butrint	9
1.5	Cover of *L'Antica Albania*, by Luigi M. Ugolini, 1927	13
2.1	Cyriacus of Ancona	16
2.2	Ali Pasha of Tepelenë drawn by Louis Dupré	19
2.3	Edward Lear's view of Butrint from Cape Stillo, 1857	21
2.4	Ugolini's excavations of the Theatre, 1928	23
2.5	Ugolini and his team in the Theatre, *c.* 1930	26
2.6	Nikita Khrushchev and Enver Hoxha at the Lion Gate, May 1959	30
2.7	Dhimosten Budina (centre right) and Kosta Lako (in cap), Butrint, *c.* 1970	31
2.8	Conservation training on the Vrina Plain excavations	33
3.1	Shepherd huts on the acropolis, 1924	35
3.2	Upper Palaeolithic flints from Xarra found by Luigi Cardini, 1930s	37
3.3	Surveying the cyclopean south wall of the acropolis	39
3.4	A reconstruction of the Hellenistic sanctuary and Theatre	43
3.5	View of Kalivo from the air	44
3.6	Map of Phoenicê	45
3.7	The Scaean Gate before excavation, 1924	49
3.8	Excavation of the Hellenistic Theatre, 1931	52
3.9	A manumission from the 'Tower of Inscriptions'	55
3.10	The archaic and later Hellenistic fortifications at Çuka e Ajtoit	56
3.11	Butrint and the Vrina Plain looking east	57

4.1	Bust of Agrippa found by Ugolini in the Theatre excavations	62
4.2	Reconstruction of Roman Butrint, *c.* AD 100	66
4.3	A section of the Roman bridge	67
4.4	A plan of the Roman forum excavated by the University of Notre Dame	68
4.5	View of the buildings in the north-east corner of the Roman forum in 2013 (courtesy of David Hernandez)	69
4.6	View of the Theatre and its stage building, the *scaenae frons*	70
4.7	Igino Epicoco's reconstruction (for Ugolini) of the Roman Theatre's *scaenae frons* from Carlo Ceschi's plan	70
4.8	The Hellenistic figurine of Pan found on Mount Mile	72
4.9	A reconstruction of the centuriation on the Vrina Plain south of Butrint	76
4.10	A plan of the mid-first- to second-century maritime villa at Diaporit	81
4.11	A sculpture discarded in a third-century drain in the Roman forum	85
4.12	A diagram showing the impact of the fourth-century earthquake on the lower town at Butrint	88
4.13	Ugolini on the acropolis, spring 1928	89
5.1	Reconstruction of the Roman houses and later Triconch Palace	93
5.2	A view of the Triconch Palace under excavation, 2002	95
5.3	A window frame from the Triconch Palace	98
5.4	A copper tag (obverse and reverse views) with an apotropaic motif from the Triconch Palace	100
5.5	A view of the Great Basilica and Lake Butrint beyond	101
5.6	The Baptistery with its sixth-century mosaic pavement	106
5.7	A detail of the mosaic from the fifth-century Vrina Plain Basilica	111
5.8	A reconstruction of the sixth-century pilgrimage centre at Diaporit	114
5.9	A mid-sixth-century infant's grave from the Triconch Palace	115
6.1	A view of the excavations in the western defences Tower 1 showing the red layer of ninth-century burning and destruction	121
6.2	Local ninth-century pots from Tower 1 in the western defences	122
6.3	A selection of glass waste (lamps) found in Tower 1 in the western defences	123
6.4	An aerial view of the post-built ninth-century dwelling made in the Vrina Plain aristocratic settlement	124
6.5	Four lead seals from the aristocratic house	125
6.6	A map of the new eleventh-century town of Butrint	127
6.7	A post-built eleventh-century dwelling found in the Triconch Palace excavations	127

6.8   A gold nomisma of Basil II (976–1025) found in the Triconch
      Palace excavations (obverse and reverse views)   128
6.9   A Byzantine hoard dating to *c.* 1204 from the Triconch Palace   130
6.10 A photogrammetric record of the Medieval and Venetian
      defences at the Water Gate   131
7.1   The image of a lion (the 'lion of Saint Mark') on sherds of a
      sixteenth-century maiolica jug found during excavations in
      Butrint   140
7.2   A map of fifteenth- to sixteenth-century Butrint in the
      Venetian period   148
7.3   A view of the sixteenth-century Venetian Tower in the lower
      town at Butrint   151
7.4   Aerial view of Ali Pasha's early nineteenth-century castle   153
7.5   The seventeenth-century Triangular Fortress   154
8.1   View of the Triconch Palace after conservation, 2005   162
8.2   Visitors looking at the Roman forum and Theatre   163
8.3   Telemack Llahana (left) and Lords Sainsbury (centre) and
      Rothschild (centre right) discuss conservation with the author
      (right) at Butrint, 1995   165
8.4   The Butrint team, 2002   166

Table

2.1   The archaeological periods of settlement at Butrint, *c.* 1300 BC
      until the twenty-first century   17

PREFACE

Butrint owes much to Roman court poet, Virgil, and the courtier's desire to flatter the Emperor Augustus, master of an immense Roman realm. Its place in history was seized upon by the poet and sealed in aspic as a mythic place on the voyage to found the eternal city of Rome. Luigi Maria Ugolini, the Italian excavator who, as we shall see, made huge excavations in Butrint in the 1920s and 1930s, lyrically explains that, as he read Virgil's *Aeneid* on the acropolis at Mycenae in 1925, he dreamed of giving new form to the legend of *Buthrotum* in the service (we read between the lines) of Italy's then Fascist government. That dream, rightly or wongly, has made Butrint as eternal as Rome.[1]

Ugolini's huge excavations at Butrint belonged to a pioneering age, launched by Heinrich Schliemann's legendary nineteenth-century digs at Mycenae and Troy. He had to contend with the wildness of this place on Albania's new frontier as well as the constant problem of waterlogging in his trenches.

Archaeology in the 1920s and today could not be more different. In the 1920s it was at the disposal of a European history fashioned by the classics and chronicles; today we seek to challenge and comprehend the context of those same chronicles. So, Ugolini's testament, *Butrinto. Il Mito d'Enea* (Butrint. The Myth of Aeneas, 1937) describes his personal odyssey and seeks to situate his discoveries in terms of a past filled with conquerors and invaders. This present book starts from Ugolini's legacy and self-consciously follows the footsteps of Aeneas, but being the results of the Butrint Foundation's enquiry, it seeks to promote a very different odyssey.

First and foremost, it is a history shaped by the ever-changing forces of nature over a long period, what the French historian, Fernand Braudel, called *la longue durée*.[2] Next, it takes account of the interaction between the Mediterranean world and the community at Butrint. As we shall see, this community changed continually until the Venetians brought some constancy in the later fourteenth century. Lastly, it offers some scope, from time to time, for re-visiting the history of events which touched Butrint. My aim, too, in humble emulation of Ugolini, is to offer not only a contemporary description of Butrint as a microcosm of Mediterranean archaeology (a century after Ugolini dreamed of digging here), but also to signpost the modern challenge to protect this mythic place in the face of the need to build an enduring European Albania.

FIGURE 0.1 *View of Butrint looking west towards Corfu.*

Today, the UNESCO World Heritage Site of Butrint prospers because of its location. It has long been recognised as Albania's premier cultural heritage asset. After Tirana, the capital, it is possibly the best-known place in Albania, attracting 300,000 visitors a year. Then, again, although a tourist destination for Albanians and Kosovans, its bread-and-butter revenue comes from tour boats from Corfu. In 2022 over 75,000 visitors took the hour-long journey from Corfu to Saranda to see the ancient ruins. Ancient cities in the Ionian Islands such as Corfu and Lefkada can match Butrint's history, yet no other archaeological site in this region summons up the past in such a timeless landscape. 'Visiting it today (John Julius Norwich wrote in 1999) must be very like visiting Ephesus or Baalbek a hundred years ago: no car parks, no souvenir stalls, no sound but the sound of birds and the ever-busy crickets. If you yearn to lose yourself in romantic meditation, alone among the ruins of a once-great city, then Butrint is the place for you'.[3]

Why Is Butrint Special?

In 1991 the first democratic elections were held in Albania after the fall of the communist government that had been in power since 1944. A period of chaos ensued as the country's government manoeuvred to deal with the transition from a command economy to a modern pluralist one. New elections were forced, and punctuated by episodes of great unrest (notably the uprisings caused by the pyramid schemes in January to March 1997), Albania has effectively put its past behind it and displaying the energy of a long-dormant creature, propelled itself towards being an European country.

In 1992 Albania joined UNESCO as a member state and almost immediately the World Heritage Centre, acting on behalf of the Albanian government, inscribed Butrint as its first World Heritage Site.

Why Butrint? As we shall see, being so far from Tirana and close to the border, Butrint was not as well known as other major Graeco-Roman sites in Albania, such as Apollonia. Moreover, the Illyrian city of Berat and the Ottoman museum-town of Gjirokastra had greater status within Albania. The choice of Butrint was probably a compromise made during the extreme turmoil of 1991–2. As much as anything it reflected a foreigner's choice because Butrint was close to the gateway of Saranda into the country with attractively disposed ruins and a palpable Mediterranean appearance.

From its inception in 1993 the Butrint Foundation, established as a British charity by Lord Rothschild and Lord Sainsbury of Preston Candover, set as much store in protecting and conserving the landscape around the site as in researching the archaeology of Butrint itself. The reasons were obvious. The previously state-owned coastline was phenomenally valuable. Lending such a coastal zone an identity in the form of the timeless, global prestige of a UNESCO site associated with the myth of Troy, made it especially attractive to developers. As we shall see in Chapter 7, the fact that many of these projects were economically unviable and therefore not in the country's interests, mattered little.

When, in April 1998 the Butrint Foundation in partnership with the Getty Grant Program and UNESCO held a workshop on the future management of the site, the invited Albanian officials and scholars were asked to define why Butrint was special. The Butrint Foundation's team anticipated that the replies would concentrate upon the ancient heritage – Butrint's Theatre or its Baptistery, for example. In fact, the four workshop teams came to the one common conclusion. Butrint was special because it was magical. As one approached down the narrow, twisting coast road, the sudden discovery of the ancient city in its unspoilt 'Homeric' landscape lent an air of mystery to the place. This mysteriousness was increased by the disposition of the monuments within the thick woodland (a wood largely belonging to the post-war period). Upon quizzing, the workshop members recalled how a foreign ministry permit was required to pass beyond the military post stationed on the road at the north end of Lake Butrint. The archaeological remains, in short, were considered off limits in a militarized frontier zone, close to Greece. Indeed, further quizzing revealed that before the road was built for Nikita Khrushchev's visit in May 1959, Butrint was hard to reach. The simplest route was by a poor track running to the east of Lake Butrint to the border villages of Xarra, Mursia and Konispoli. From Xarra the track passed on to the collective farm at Vrina and then to Butrint itself.

Paradoxically, then, the spirit of isolation and magic rather than the spectacle of truly great monuments are Butrint's precious assets. Yet, the history of these monuments is a Mediterranean one, shaped by its accessibility and connectivity. The alchemy of this curious contradiction is made even richer by the story of Butrint's rediscovery and excavation.

This book illustrates thirty years of fieldwork at Butrint supported by the Butrint Foundation in partnership with the Packard Humanities Institute. This story is described through twenty-first-century eyes, drawing upon the rich archives of the site – including the unpublished records of Luigi Maria Ugolini's Italian Archaeological Mission in the 1920s and 1930s – as well as major new excavations and many surveys made in collaboration with Albania's Institute of Archaeology. New methods have been harnessed to new thinking, making it possible to interpret Butrint not strictly in terms of Virgil's enduring story, but so that visitors and scholars, seduced by its limpid beauty, can place it within the long, ever-fascinating ebb and flow of Mediterranean history.

Butrint, Albania's first UNESCO World Heritage Site, is Albania's most celebrated place. Several million visitors have made a journey since 1991 that, during the Cold War, seemed unthinkable. As the gateway to this embryonic republic, wrestling with the transition towards being a European Union member state, it is a story that is far from finished.

FIGURE 0.2 *Luigi Ugolini at Phoenicê, c. 1926.*

FIGURE 0.3 *A reconstruction of the principal archaeological sites at Butrint.*

ACKNOWLEDGEMENTS

This book is a reworking that updates and enlarges an earlier book, and assembles the results of an indefatigable and remarkable team.[4]

The late The Lord Jacob Rothschild and the late Lord John Sainsbury founded the Butrint Foundation as a British charity in 1993. That same year they kindly persuaded me to excavate at Butrint, serving as the foundation's scientific director. I have not only benefited immensely from their generous support, but I have had an inestimable and unforgettable education in the process. My thanks, too, to the late Drue Heinz, and to her Trust that has given us wholehearted support to work on the rich archives of Butrint. I also wish to record my debt to the foundation's successive directors, Sir Patrick Fairweather (1997–2004), Daniel Renton (2004–6), Rupert Smith (2006–8) and Brian Ayers (2008–).

David Packard, President of the Packard Humanities Institute, urged me in 1998 to think more ambitiously, enlarging the scope of our work in Albanian archaeology and at Butrint, in particular. With his encouragement, I hope that in this book I have gone some way towards realizing what he had in mind.

Without doubt our work at Butrint has been facilitated by the gracious and thoughtful encouragement of Professor Muzafer Korkuti, as well as the great friendship I have enjoyed with Lorenc Bejko, Ilir Gjipali, the late Kosta Lako, Telemack Llahana, Nevila Molla, Diana Ndrenika, Erjona Qilla and, above all, Iris Pojani.

As will be very evident I owe a great debt to Will Bowden, the late Riccardo Francovich, Oliver Gilkes, David Hernandez, Sally Martin, John Mitchell and the late Klavs Randsborg who at one time or another offered wise counsel on the excavations and the cultural heritage strategy. Special thanks to David Hernandez who has pursued excavations in the forum supported by the University of Notre Dame and published groundbreaking reports on Butrint. Thanks also to Sarah Leppard, who prepared most of the illustrations from the Butrint Foundation archives.

My debts extend well beyond this list and in some ways selecting names means that many may be forgotten, but to the thousand or so who have excavated with the Butrint Foundation, my warmest thanks. I should like to recall my particular thanks to Martine d'Anglejan and Emmy Rothschild, who played such a crucial part in the early years of our project.

1

In the Footsteps of Aeneas

We had soon put the cloud-capped citadels of Phaeacia down below the horizon and we coasted along Epirus until we entered the harbour of Chaonia and then walked up to the lofty city of Buthrotum.

VIRGIL, *AENEID* III[1]

Butrint, ancient *Buthrotum*, sits at the crossroads of the Mediterranean. It is tucked off to the east side of the Straits of Corfu, directly opposite Corfu's mountainous north coast. 'Corfu lies like a sickle beside the flanks of the mainland', Lawrence Durrell reminds us in *The Greek Islands* (1978), 'forming a great calm bay, which narrows at both ends so that the tides are squeezed and calmed as they pass it'.[2] From this extraordinary setting, Butrint commands the sea routes up the Adriatic Sea to Venice, across to Sicily and Spain, and south through the Ionian islands to the Aegean. Like ancient Dyrrhachium (Epidamnos in the seventh century BC; modern Durrës) to the north, it also controlled a passage into the mountainous Balkan interior. Here began a route to Thessalonika and, beyond, Constantinople, modern Istanbul. Today, the abandoned ancient and Medieval port is located 3 kilometres inland from the Straits of Corfu surrounded by a Homeric landscape.

For nearly three millennia Butrint has occupied a low hill on a sharp bend in the Vivari Channel, which connects the Corfu Straits to the inland lagoon of Lake Butrint. The walled city, designated as a UNESCO World Heritage Site in 1992, covers an area of *c.* 16 hectares; but the Butrint Foundation's surveys (as I shall describe them in Chapter 3) on the eastern side of the Vivari Channel show that at times in antiquity Butrint covered as much as 30 hectares. The walled city comprises two parts: the acropolis and the lower city. The acropolis is a long narrow bluff, approximately 200 metres long and 60 metres at its widest, rising up to 42 metres above sea level at its east end. Its sides are accentuated by a circuit of walls that separate it from the natural and artificial terraces gathered around the flanks of the hill. The lower city waxed and waned through the centuries and occupies the lower-lying contours down to the edge of the Vivari Channel. Remains of a

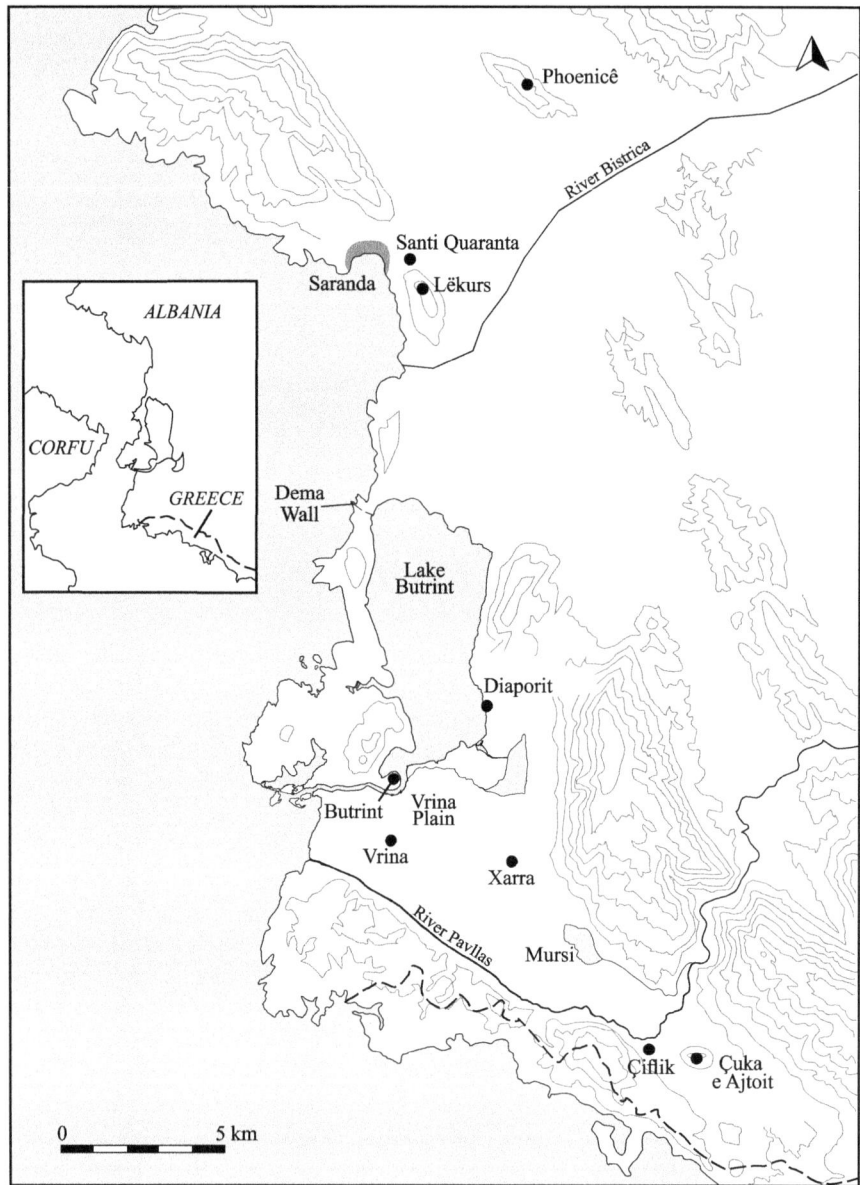

FIGURE 1.1 *A map showing the location of Butrint and the boundaries of the Butrint National Park.*

FIGURE 1.2 *A vertical photograph of Butrint's Hellenistic and Roman Theatre.*

cemetery are recorded on the rocky spine of the hill running west from the acropolis, but its extent is unknown. The most obvious monument outside the city walls, on the opposite side of the channel, is the Triangular Fortress, which after 1572 (when the Venetians formally designated the town as deserted) became the nucleus of the early modern settlement. Butrint is a rare example of an ancient name that has survived from antiquity. Moreover, since the visit of the Renaissance antiquarian, Cyriacus of Ancona in 1435, it has always been associated with Aeneas.[3]

Butrint's setting is seductively from another age before charmless vacation resorts. The place seems to belong to the world of Achilles, Odysseus and, of course, Aeneas. Being unspoilt, sometimes one might imagine Virgil's poetic hero, Aeneas arriving today. A narrow plain, formerly a marsh, separates the Straits of Corfu from rolling hills to the south, along which runs the frontier between Albania and Greece first fixed at the Treaty of London in 1913. Immediately east of Lake Butrint, an imposing range of hills and low mountains – white-capped in winter – rise up to 824 metres, forming a protective barrier around the ancient city and its inland lake. The lake is about 6 kilometres long and approximately 2.5 kilometres wide with depths ranging from 3.5 to 14 metres.

Butrint is a natural harbour, with sufficient depth in the Vivari Channel for most pre-modern vessels. More importantly, it is a safe anchorage. Vessels ploughing the frequently difficult currents north of Corfu, and then entering the 3-kilometre-wide Straits, could find shelter at Butrint from both northerly and southerly winds. *The Mediterranean Pilot* (1880) says that Butrint Bay affords the best anchorage on the coast abreast Corfu, and that the Vivari Channel can only be entered by small boats because a sand bar lies across its mouth. A second, though less protected, anchorage lies in Ksamil Bay, immediately east of the northern mouth of the Straits of Corfu. As I shall explain, the bay lay within the Hellenistic territory of Butrint as well as, much later, the early modern Venetian enclave. It is no surprise, then, that remains of Roman and early modern cargoes have been found here by amateur divers.

Less obvious to the modern eye is its position on the network of Balkan roads. The present road from Saranda (the nearest modern port, 20 kilometres to the north) to Butrint was constructed for Nikita Khrushchev's visit in May 1959. Otherwise, the artery looks towards Tirana, the capital of modern Albania, with the tarmacked roads running from Saranda, north to Vlora and east to Gjirokastra. Butrint, in other words, seems like a terminus. This was not the case when it flourished as a port in antiquity and the Middle Ages. We learn something of this from the Arab geographer al-Idrisi in the mid-twelfth century AD.[4] The coastal route he describes starts at Dyrrhachium (modern Durrës) and proceeds south to *Lablôna* (modern Vlora, near ancient Apollonia), then to *Dzimâra* (modern Himara); next to *Budrout*, a populated centre with bazaars (Butrint); then to *Fâsko* (opposite the Ionian island of Paxos) and then to *Bondisa* (modern Vonitsa, east of ancient Nicopolis). The route probably owes its origins to antiquity and a version of it appears on the fourth-century AD Peutinger Table, a road map denoting key roads and stations. From this ancient arterial highway, roads into the interior commenced. The inland route from Butrint passed by way of Konispoli (followed by multilingual mobile Vlach shepherds until the Second World War), then leads to Ioannina – the capital of Epirus, little more than 100 kilometres to the east – and, after the snows have melted, on to Thessaly and Macedonia.

Butrint, then, belongs to the geography of Epirus, a region which today forms north-west Greece, but in antiquity spread as far north as Vlora Bay in central Albania. Yet much of Butrint's history is tied to the Ionian islands and to Corfu, in particular. Corfu lay at a marine crossroads in the Mediterranean, and being close to it, Butrint was often caught up in its political and economic circumstances.

Corfu was first colonized by the Eretrians on their way to Italy in the eighth century BC. They were soon expelled by the Corinthians in 734 BC who established a successful colony based on maritime trade. Known as Corcyra, it soon began founding colonies of its own, some independently of its mother city, Corinth and some as joint foundations with her, both in Italy and on the coast of Illyria. Corcyra's growing economic power brought her into conflict with Corinth, however, and what the historian, Thucydides records as the first sea battle in Greek history was fought between the two cities in 664 BC. The animosity persisted and in the late seventh century BC, the Corinthian tyrant, Periander, conquered the island, which only regained its independence after his death in 585 BC. In the ensuing period Corcyra prospered.

By the time of the Persian Wars in the early fifth century BC, Corcyra had a fleet second only to Athens. Her problems with Corinth continued and in 432 BC the Corcyreans called on Athens for help against Corinth over their joint colony Epidamnos (Roman Dyrrhachium; modern Durrës). The subsequent sea battle precipitated the Peloponnesian War, during which Corcyra was riven with bitter internal conflicts between democrats versus oligarchs.

Weakened and depopulated, the island's safe harbours nevertheless made her a rich prize, and her ensuing history reflects this. After the Battle of Chaeronea in 338 BC she was taken by Philip II of Macedon and in 299 BC the island was given to Pyrrhus, king of Epirus, as a wedding present. Regaining her independence some twenty or so years later Corcyra surrendered voluntarily to Rome in 229 BC. During the subsequent two centuries the island prospered once more, as the Romans gave it autonomy in exchange for the use of its harbours. Octavian (who would become the Emperor Augustus) assembled his fleet here before the battle of Actium in 31 BC where he defeated Cleopatra and Mark Antony. Corfu's sympathies had been with the defeated side and Octavian penalized the island, precipitating a long period of decline. In AD 395, when the Roman Empire was split between East and West, the island of Corfu became part of the Eastern (Byzantine) Empire and by the ninth century, the city of Corfu was known as Korypho after its new location from the sixth century on the 'Twin Peaks', the later Medieval Venetian *Palaio Frourio* (Old Fortress). The city evolved steadily around the peaks until the sixteenth century, when its unplanned *borgo* took shape. Thenceforth, Venetian maps chart the shaping of the first stages of the present town, initially around these peaks, then in an elegant, gridded arrangement on the rolling land to the west.

Epirus, by contrast, was the shadowy realm of the savage Echetus in the *Odyssey*, but also the great kingdom of Pyrrhus and the scene of legendary battles between Julius Caesar and Pompey, then Octavian (later the Emperor Augustus) and Mark Antony (with Cleopatra). Here, in the first century BC the distinguished Roman knight, Titus Pomponius Atticus maintained a great estate with slave scribes copying Cicero's texts.

Later, Epirus boasted its own Despotic kingdom upon the fall of Constantinople to the Franks in 1204. The region then only interacted episodically, as we shall see with Corfu and its quintessential Mediterranean anchorage in the Ionian passage between the Adriatic and Aegean – under Venetian, French and British hegemony. Finally, during the Napoleonic era Epirus enjoyed a moment of legendary fame under the tyrannical Ali Pasha of Tepelenë when it became the limits of Asia.

Homeric Landscape

Epirus is composed of a series of steep, sub-parallel and relatively tall mountain ranges, which divide the region into areas of coastal lowlands and a series of basins. This striking landscape, the result of intense folding and over thrusting, is a direct consequence of the dynamic tectonic history of the region. The geo-tectonic units trend NNW–SSE, parallel to the Ionian coastline, forming the external Ionian subzone. The position of these belts is indicated by the present-day Ionian Islands. Butrint is one of many micro-regions of coastal Epirus.[5]

The landscape of the Butrint National Park, created in 2000, covers not only the main archaeological site but also a tract of land running from the Straits of Corfu to the east side of Lake Butrint. The Park is dominated by a rugged inland mountain range and a smaller, denuded coastal range of steeply inclined beds of limestone, dolomite and sandstone, dissected by numerous small streams. The two ranges are separated by a large valley, up to 2 kilometres wide and infilled by a succession of Quaternary and Holocene deposits. Lake Butrint, occupying the valley centre, is fed by rivers from the north and exits into the Ionian Sea through a gap in the coastal range, flowing westwards around the limestone spur that projects inland from the Ksamil peninsula upon which the ancient city of Butrint is located.

The modern alluvial plain stretches away from Butrint to the south-east and contains the occasional outcrop of limestone, such as the striking hog-backed hill of Kalivo (formidably fortified in the Bronze Age and again in the earlier Hellenistic period), bordering the southern margin of the lake, and hilltop village of Shën Dëlli. The widespread and dynamic nature of the fluvial regime within the valley during the Pleistocene is evident from the large relic gravel terraces which form a ridge along the south-eastern edge of the valley. These much-denuded deposits stretch from the modern village of

FIGURE 1.3 *A view of Butrint in its 'Homeric landscape' from Mount Mile.*

Mursia (10 kilometres east of Butrint) towards the head of the valley in a line reaching Kalivo. Similar fluvial deposits abut the southern flanks of the limestone outcrops upon which the modern villages of Shën Dëlli and Vrina are located, and it is likely that these relic outcrops form a sediment trap, their presence diverting the flow of down-cutting channels.

Two rivers dominate the plain around Butrint. The Bistrice (Lumï Bistrica) runs from the Mali Gjerë mountains southwards to the northern margins of Lake Butrint for about 11 kilometres. Here in 1959, as part of a reclamation project, it was diverted westwards through the man-made Çuka Channel to Saranda Bay. The Pavllas river (Lumï Pavla) is probably the most complex system, originally flowing along the plains of Butrint where in ancient and pre-modern times it appears to have meandered considerably, resulting in a braided channel network. Until the 1950s one channel joined the Vivari Channel at Butrint's (Venetian) Triangular Fortress. Following an irrigation project, it was diverted south-westwards along the side of the Korafit Hills to reach Butrint Bay.

The landscape around Butrint was significantly transformed by large-scale irrigation, drainage and land reclamation schemes beginning in the late 1950s. These schemes, some undertaken under Chinese bilateral supervision, resulted in the drainage of marshes and the removal of all clumps of woodland. Despite these changes, the low intensity of land-use, which predominates in this sparsely populated area, has preserved a wide range of species-rich habitats.

Foremost of these habitats is Lake Butrint. Today it covers an area of 16 square kilometres and is linked to the Straits of Corfu via the Vivari Channel. The limnology of the lake is divided into two distinct layers. The upper layer (approx. 8 metres in depth) is rich in oxygen (8–9 mg/lit) and supports a diverse marine culture. The salinity of this layer changes seasonally from 15 gr/lit in winter to 33 gr/lit in summer. The lower layer (approx. 14 metres in depth) lacks oxygen and is sulphurous. The lake is rich in fish species including mullet, eel and bream. Mussels are the predominant mollusc and have been farmed in the lake since the 1960s. The north and south shores of the lake are flanked by saltwater marshes with associated amphibian, reptile and bird populations. To the south-east of Lake Butrint is the much smaller Lake Bufi. This covers an area of 83 hectares and has an average depth of 1 metre. Fed by freshwater springs, it originally drained into Lake Butrint but is now connected by a cut channel that allows water to flow either way between the lakes. As a result, saline water from Lake Butrint has increased the salinity of Lake Bufi (5 gr/lit).[6]

Close to the seaward entrance of the Vivari Channel lies Lake Armur. This is a saltwater lagoon partially cut off from the Straits of Corfu by low salt-marsh-covered islands. The lagoon is rich in migratory fish and shellfish, especially mussels.

The lagoonal landscape appears timeless, but this is an illusion. The marshes have changed dramatically since 1991 when the state collective farms created in the 1960s ceased operating. From this moment the network of drainage ditches was no longer maintained. Increasingly the landscape is returning to its previous condition, as it was in Medieval, Venetian, Ottoman periods and even when the British Royal Air Force photographed it from the air in November 1943.

Perhaps the most startling discovery, however, has been the history of Lake Butrint itself – a history that has inevitably not only determined the landscape around the archaeological site but also the history of Butrint itself. The changing configurations of the lake, of course, are intricately linked to a series of sea-level changes since prehistoric times.

Sea-level change has been well studied in the Mediterranean basin thanks to the negligible tides, favourable geomorphological settings and the abundance of historical records and archaeological sites at coastal locations like Butrint. Unfortunately, due to a widely varying sea-surface topography (up to 50 metres difference between East and West basins and 20 metres between the North and South Adriatic) and basin dynamics and the tectonic settings of localized areas, it is impossible to produce a sea-level curve representative of the Mediterranean basin as a whole. However, the general trend in sea-level change since the height of the last glacial maximum, *c.* 13,000 BC at which time sea levels were *c.* 150 metres below their present level, can be seen from the sea-level curve from Preveza, at the southernmost point of Epirus. This shows a rapid rise in sea level up to around *c.* 4,000 BC, reaching levels approximately 5 metres below the present level, followed by a much slower, more stable increase.

Comprehensive data on specific aspects of coastal changes in Albania comes from the lagoonal landscape at Karavasta in central Albania, approximately 200 kilometres north of Butrint. Here the preserved shoreline – a so-called palaeo shoreline from the last glaciation – approximately follows the current bathymetric depth of -100 metres. Around Butrint, this would have resulted in a large coastal plain, and a shoreline extending well to the west of Corfu. The rapid rise in sea level, marking the terminal phase of the Pleistocene, is known to have reached its maximum height sometime around 6,000 BC.

Coastal studies at Karavasta also show tentative evidence of a corresponding Holocene palaeo-shoreline along the landward limit of the current coastal plain. A similar Holocene sea-level high 'stand' has been proposed at Butrint up until a seismic event of *c.* 1500 BC, in which the low-lying area surrounding Butrint would have formed a large coastal embayment of which Lake Butrint and Lake Bufi represent a remnant phase. It is not currently known how far this body of open water extended along the inland valleys.

From the time of the high sea 'stand', a complex pattern of fluvial sedimentation within the embayment would have dominated the geological formation of the coastline as the shoreline progressed westwards in a reversal of Late Pleistocene conditions. This process has continued to the present day and is very evident after heavy spring and autumnal rains which flush mud-filled water out into the Ionian Sea. However, local tectonic activity plays an important role in controlling relative sea levels and has dramatically influenced how deposits occurred. A multi-disciplinary investigation of ancient sea-level indicators making use of radiocarbon dating concluded that there have been two periods of tectonic uplift on the island of Corfu. The first occurred in the period between about 750–350 BC; the second occurred more recently. Of the eight sites investigated on Corfu, all but one show uplift between 1–1.5 metres. Most coastal sectors showed Holocene uplift taking place between the mid-fourth and mid-sixth centuries AD. This has been referred to as the Early Byzantine Tectonic Paroxysm and is very apparent in the excavations within Butrint (see Chapter 3). Scientists have concluded that the Early Byzantine Tectonic Paroxysm was associated with seismic activity at the edge of the Mediterranean creating the so-called accretionary wedge and subduction trench – a deep underwater trench –

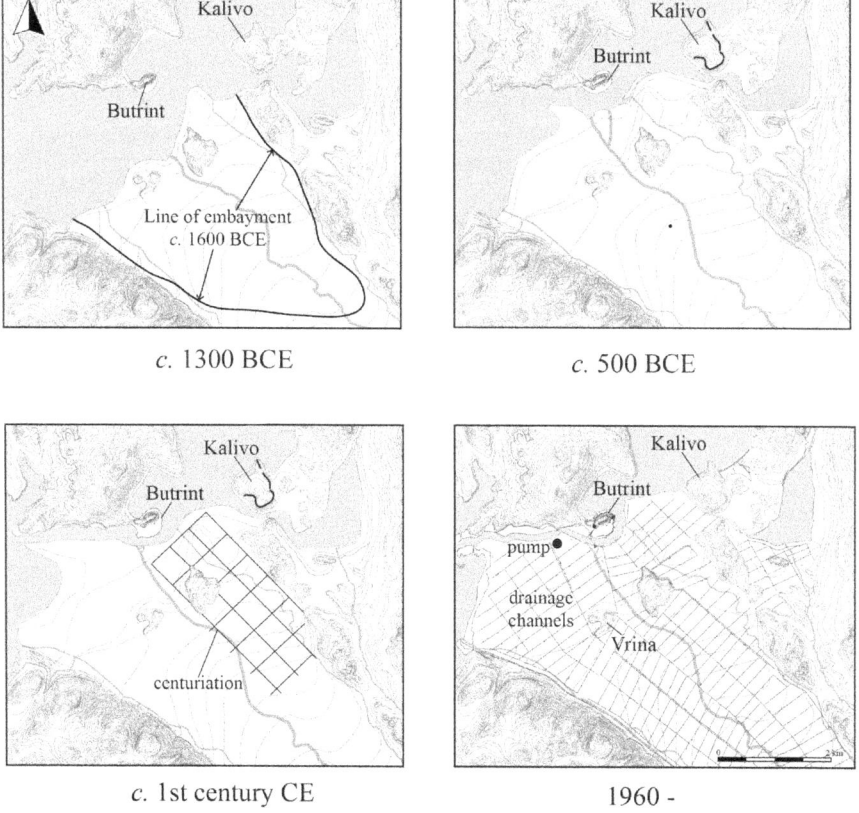

FIGURE 1.4 *The changing environmental context of Butrint.*

that run in a north–south direction alongside the west of the southern Balkans.[7]

Today Butrint and its micro-region appear to be undergoing subsidence, leading to a steady rise in sea level. Each year the ancient city is subsiding by a centimetre or more. This is best illustrated by the submergence of Roman (and earlier) levels beneath the current water level. It is not yet clear whether this is due to the differing formations of the deposits on the coastal plain warping the geological formations as a result of pressure or seismic episodes. Climate change and seismic issues are sure to put the lower city of Butrint in grave danger of submersion by the later twenty-first century if not before.

So, as I shall describe, the earliest occupation of the acropolis coincides with the upper date for the tectonic uplift measured on Corfu. In Hellenistic times, Lake Butrint formed part of a navigable waterway to the interior, effectively giving the Chaonian tribal hilltop capital of Phoenicê (north of Saranda) access to the Ionian Sea. It is likely that access became more and more restricted by the build-up of sediment eroded from surrounding slopes, altering forever the relative strategic and economic positions of Butrint and Phoenicê. The foundation of the C(olonia) I(ulia) Buth(rotiensium) on Julius Caesar's instructions in 44 BC probably relates to the lowest sea level in recent human history hereabouts. His keen eye spotted the rich agrarian potential of the erstwhile marshes. This certainly determined the development of the city, as we shall see in Chapter 4. Likewise, the re-configuration of the Roman town in the later fourth or fifth centuries was inextricably connected to the environmental consequences of the so-called Early Byzantine Tectonic Paroxysm.

Butrint and its lagoonal landscape, therefore, provide a particular laboratory for benchmarking environmental change affecting a long-occupied city and its activities. Today it feels timeless, hence with reference to the town's mythic association with Trojan exiles, this landscape has often been described as Homeric.

The Rise and Fall of Epirus

Butrint lay on the western fringe of the region of Epirus, a region known for its pastoral economy. Its high pastures and deep valleys provided grazing for cattle. Pindar makes this point in his fourth *Nemean Ode* (ll.51–3) in the 470s BC: 'far-reaching Epirus where cattle-pasturing hills slope down from Dodona to the Ionian Sea'. Aristotle ascribes the great size of the cattle and the high yield in milk to the fine pasture that was available all year round. Not surprisingly, the bull appears on a Hellenistic coin issue of Epirus and of the great Hellenistic city of Kassope in south Epirus. The bull, of course, is also associated with Butrint. Epirote sheep were also famous for their size. Varro, writing in the first century BC, mentions that one shepherd tended a flock of a hundred animals with fine fleeces. The mountain dogs that guarded livestock were also celebrated. Virgil praised the horses of the region.[8] Fish and fowl too get many mentions from ancient, Medieval and early Modern writers. Butrint was effectively a fish-farming enclave from the sixteenth century onwards. Butrint was also renowned for its hunting. In the early nineteenth century Ali Pasha of Tepelenë led hunting parties around Lake Butrint. Mussolini's son-in-law, Count Ciano, did the same in the 1930s.

The wealth of the region meant that it sustained large populations since the Upper Palaeolithic. As we shall see, Neandertal hunter-gatherers assembled around the fringes of Lake Butrint from *c.* 100,000 BC leaving conspicuous lithic (flint and stone) debris. Luigi Cardini, the prehistorian attached to the Italian Archaeological Mission at Butrint in the 1930s (see Chapter 2), identified similar signs of early hunter-gatherer activity at many points along the coast between Butrint and Vlora Bay. Neolithic and earlier Bronze Age communities are less conspicuous, but in evidence, as the recent Albanian–American excavations at the Konispoli Cave near Butrint demonstrated.[9] Here, an early Neolithic pastoralist community was making use of the high-altitude cave just as if it was a peasant group of modern times. By Hellenistic times, as the written sources emphasize, Epirus was a mixture of towns and small farms.[10] The British ancient historian, N. G. L. Hammond rationalized the motive for this as follows: 'The chief function of the Epirotes was to hold the frontier of the classical and Hellenistic world against the Illyrians, and their finest achievement was to evolve an original form of political organisation which was particularly well adapted to the geographical and ethnographical conditions of Epirus'.[11] Whatever the geopolitical conditions (described in Chapter 3), there is no doubt that the region defined itself in terms of its peers to the south and north.

The heartland of Epirus in this age was governed by the Molossian tribe.[12] The tribe prospered in the fourth and third centuries BC when its family had aspirations to be a supra-regional power. So, the mother of Alexander the Great was a Molossian princess. The Molossians today are best known from the large sanctuary of Dodona, lying in low hills 15 kilometres south of Ioannina in central Epirus. Its large theatre, built primarily for pilgrims to visit their oracle by the tall oaks, was larger than the Dionysiac theatre at Athens and is said to have accommodated over 20,000 people. Such numbers also feature in the written sources, though these must be treated with caution. Polybius writing in the second century BC describes, for example, how 150,000 Molossians were enslaved by the Roman army of Aemilius Paullus after he conquered the region in 167 BC. Such numbers are far from improbable. The scale and size of the cities in the region – of which Butrint was relatively modest – can only be interpreted as a sign of affluence. Such large populations contrast markedly with the region in early Modern times. In 1930 the population of the Greek part of Epirus was only 300,000; doubtless southern Albania numbered comparably fewer. As Hammond concluded in his classic monograph on ancient Epirus (1967):

the centuries of Turkish occupation saw a deterioration in husbandry and agriculture of all kinds, and many of the peasants of Northern Epirus in particular are, through no fault of their own, ignorant and illiterate and incapable of winning more than a meagre subsistence from the soil. It is doubtful if any part of modern Europe is as backward . . .[13]

Epirus and indeed southern Albania today are seen through a modern prism. The wealth and status of the region in antiquity and even during the Middle Ages was gradually dissipated as it lay on the far fringes of the Ottoman Empire. William Martin Leake and François Pouqueville surveying the region in the early nineteenth century on behalf of the British and French governments, respectively, provide some sense of this. Leake describes – writing in the 1830s – the abundant fish and explains that these were

. . . salted on the spot, and the greater part sent to Corfu . . . for its supply of fish during its long fasts of the Greek church. . . . From hence also Corfu is chiefly furnished with firewood, and with staves to make casks for its oil and wine. These circumstances explain the importance which Venice always attached to the possession of Butrint. Good timber for ship-building was to be found here too.[14]

Pouqueville, in fact, damningly recalls in his autobiography the uncomfortable conditions here: 'The air of these lakes, and consequently of Butrinto, is now as pestilential as that of the famous Pontine marshes of Italy. The effects of this air are dreaded even across the sea in Corfu . . .'.[15] But the stark destitution into which the region had fallen was to be masked by Romantics like the poet, Lord Byron who effectively idolized the chieftains of the region as noble savages. Ali Pasha of Tepelenë – much admired by Byron – was undoubtedly a remarkable figure. His military architecture (at Gjirokastra, Ioannina, Porto Palermo, and Tepelenë) as well as his fascination for antiquity, however, should not blind us to his often savage, autocratic grip of his people.[16]

The abject poverty was much in evidence by the late nineteenth century and, to some extent, fuelled the Albanian nationalist movement. The Balkan Wars, however, in 1912–13 were short, horrific harbingers of the coming First World War. So, although the Greek army seized Epirus from the Ottomans, it was compelled by the Great Powers after the Treaty of London in 1913 to cede much of Northern Epirus to the new republic of Albania (see Chapter 6).[17] Many Greeks in Epirus were angry about this, and in August 1923 assassinated the Italian General Tellini as he inspected and determined the line of the southern frontier near Kakavia, east of Butrint. This incident induced Mussolini, newly at the helm of Italy's government, to bomb Corfu as a reprisal, arrogantly seeking reparations from the Greeks. The Greek government prevaricated until the League of Nations prominently intervened and ordered Greece to negotiate with Italy. The outcome left the

FIGURE 1.5 *Cover of* L'Antica Albania, *by Luigi M. Ugolini, 1927.*

boundary where it is today. Butrint, in effect, was in a borderland while Saranda and its Greek-speaking Epirotes remained inside a new country.[18]

The Italian government doubtless calculated upon the political chasm that had been created between the newly created Albania and Greece and despatched an innocuous archaeological mission to establish an inconspicuous foothold in the area. Following in the footsteps of Aeneas, founder of Rome, Luigi Maria Ugolini and his colleagues arrived at Butrint in 1924 after a demanding odyssey from Skhodra. Ugolini's landscape photographs of Butrint from that visit and his later missions capture a deserted borderland. Fascinated by the ethnography of the region, Ugolini took every opportunity to pose either an Albanian in his fez or a shepherd in front of an ancient wall or peering into the far distance. So, he published photographs of shepherds, fishermen, village women at their weaving and children in traditional costumes. None of these elegantly charged souvenirs could conceal the fact that the destitution, if anything, had deteriorated since the nineteenth century.[19] It was to shock N. G. L. Hammond when, as a student at the British School at Athens, he hiked through the mountains to visit Ugolini's excavations in 1930.[20]

Though close to Corfu and its smarter, sea-borne society, southern Albania fared poorly under the new Albanian government as it was far from the capital at Tirana. The achievements of the Italian mission did little to mitigate this sense of a forgotten place that millennia before, as Ugolini's popular book, *Il Mito d'Enea* (The Myth of Aeneas, 1937) illustrated, had been an epicentre in a region celebrated for its historical prowess. The stated aims of the communist government that came to power in 1944 was to create a 'paradise on earth'. Southern Albania, after initial deprivation as the country embarked on five-year plans in harness with the Yugoslavs then the Soviets then the Chinese, began to enjoy an equilibrium that brought equanimity to the lives of its predominantly peasant community. Yet, when the travel-writer Eric Newby visited Butrint in the 1970s on an arranged coach tour (described in *On the Shores of the Mediterranean* [1984]), he was shocked by the repellent inequality. In an acerbic passage he describes party officials enjoying the leisure of the beach at Ksamil while peasant destitution prevailed with an air of profound gloom.[21]

When in 1991 Albania ended a communist saga that had started with the 'great partisan war' against the Germans in World War Two, Epirus and Butrint, in particular, began to embark, as we shall see, on a voyage of rediscovery, reconnecting with its Mediterranean roots. Being Albania's premier tourist destination, the newly inscribed UNESCO World Heritage Site profited from its proximity to the archetypal Mediterranean resort island of Corfu.

In short, to understand Butrint we must unfetter ourselves from the geopolitics of the end of the Ottoman Empire and the Albanian and Greek nationalism this fostered. As we shall see, for much of its long history, the port owes its status to its Mediterranean connections. Central to this maritime story was its association with the myth of Aeneas because it lay on the main routeway to Rome.

2

A Mediterranean History

Butrinto, anciennement Buthrotum, capitale de la Chaonie, n'offre plus que des ruines qui n'ont jamais été bien reconnues; dans des temps plus hereux pour la Grèce, et sous un regime moins barbare, l'on verra sans doute un jour cette contrée explorée avec fruit, et ses richesses archéologiques sortir de la nuit qui les couvre depuis tant de siècles.

LOUIS DUPRÉ[1]

The Rediscovery of Butrint

Luigi Maria Ugolini (1895–1936), the Italian excavator of Butrint, liked to associate himself with Cyriacus of Ancona – the Medieval Pausanias, as some have described the first antiquarian to visit Butrint. Cyriacus and Ugolini were from the region of Emilia Romagna; both had tireless curiosity. But there the similarity ends. According to one of the many letters written by Cyriacus during his voyage down the Dalmatia coast and onto the Peloponnese in a bireme, a two-banked galley, he visited Butrint on 26 December 1435 because there was plague at Corfu. Possibly he was familiar with the work of Cristoforo Buondelmonti, writing in 1420, who described the mountains of Epirus, '*in quibus Heleni propinqua matre Troiaque, et Butroto nunc panditur ultro*' ('Among whom, the mother of Helen, a native of Troy, is now to be found at Buthrotum'), and recalled the foundation of the city by the Trojan, Helenus. Certainly, Cyriacus in his letter describing his visit follows suit: '*Bothrotum, antiquam in Epiro Troiani Heleni urbem*'. After a brief pause, he sailed south to Parga and Nicopolis (in southern Epirus).[2] He returned briefly the following May.

Apparently, Cyriacus recorded two inscriptions which he quite probably removed, as well as drawing sketches of the ruins. The Corpus of Latin Inscriptions lists these as follows: a funerary inscription to Titus Pomponius Lupercus, probably a freedman in the Roman colony, and a dedication to the third-century emperor, M. Iulius Filippus (Philip the Arab) and his wife, the empress Marcia Otacilia Severa. Butrint at this time was a Venetian port, already as best we can tell, failing as a seaport and in the process of being transformed into a loose collection of fish-houses maintained by Corfiots (see Chapter 5). Cyriacus, we might imagine, would have visited the castle on the acropolis and found a gaggle of stone dwellings clustered around the slopes and less substantial timber houses occupying parts of the waterlogged skirt alongside the Vivari Channel.[3] Any antiquities, as Ugolini was to discover, would have been either re-used in the churches and townhouses, or else deeply buried.

The will to document antiquities went hand-in-hand with the Renaissance desire to map their world. Drawing upon the long Italian merchantmen tradition of cartography, the Venetians proved to be exceedingly exacting

FIGURE 2.1 *Cyriacus of Ancona.*

TABLE 2.1 *The archaeological periods of settlement at Butrint, c. 1300 BC until the twenty-first century*

Period	Dates	Settlement
Bronze Age	*c.* 1300–1050/1000 BC	Hilltop encampment
Iron Age	*c.* 1050–650 BC	Abandonment?
Archaic Greek	*c.* 650–525 BC	Corfiot emporium
Archaic Greek	*c.* 525–500 BC	Small *polis*
Classical Greek	*c.* 500–475 BC	Construction of Acropolis wall
Classical Greek	*c.* 475–350 BC	Abandonment
Hellenistic	*c.* 350–167 BC	Small *polis* – sanctuary
Roman Republican	*c.* 167–31 BC	Fortified sanctuary town
Roman Imperial	*c.* 31 – *c.* AD 400	Colony, sanctuary and town
Late Roman	*c.* AD 400/450–625/50	Town and bishopric
Mid-Byzantine	*c.* AD 625/50–825/50	*Kastron* in abandoned town
Mid-Byzantine	*c.* AD 825/50–975/1000	*Kastron* on the Vrina Plain; town abandoned
Mid-Byzantine	*c.* AD 975/1000–1204	New Byzantine town and bishopric
Byzantine Despot & Angevin	*c.* AD 1205–1350	Town and bishopric
Venetian	*c.* AD 1350–1572	Venetian town and fishery
Venetian	*c.* AD 1572–1797	Town abandoned; Venetian fortified fisheries
Ottoman	AD 1798–1913	Fortified fisheries
Italian Archaeological Mission	AD 1928–41	Research site and tourist destination
Albanian Archaeological Mission	AD 1959–91	Research site and tourist destination
Butrint National Park	AD 1999–	A national park and tourist destination

mapmakers. And it is from their work, harbingers of the better known British and French nineteenth-century hydrographical maps, that we learn much about Butrint. One of the first attempts to chart the coastal and interior topography of Butrint and its hinterland was made by Giovanni Camotti in the late sixteenth century. This was part of a general survey of Venetian territories around the Adriatic Sea. Camotti's 1:200,000 scale maps include a chart of Corfu and Butrint. Camotti's work was continued by his successor Vincenzo Coronelli, who from 1685 served as Cosmographer to the Venetian Republic. Coronelli mapped almost every one of the Republic's possessions in the Adriatic, sometimes re-working plans produced by Camotti, or undertaking new surveys of sites, such as the detailed plan[4] of the so-called enclave of Butrint, nestling in what had become an Ottoman continent. His great work *Golfi, Isole Spiaggi dell Istria, Albania, Epiro* (1706), remained the basic handbook for the navigation of the Adriatic until the Napoleonic Wars. His maps also appear to have formed the basis for the important survey of Butrint made in 1718 (see Chapter 6).[5]

The Napoleonic War brought an increased interest in the area on the part of the British, Austrian and Neapolitan governments. Corfu and its straits were a strategic seaway that needed to be known and controlled. Interestingly, in 1818 a combined venture by the British, Austrian and Neapolitan governments led to a new survey of the Albanian coastline under the command of Capt. W. H. Smyth. The result was Smyth's admiralty map, *Chart of the Channels of Corfu with the Adjacent Coast of Albania* (1825). At exactly the same time an Austrian and Neapolitan atlas, *Idrografia Generale del Mare Adriatico*, was published. Smyth's chart was updated in 1840, when full soundings were taken in Butrint Bay, and again in 1863 when Commander A. L. Mansell of *HMS Firefly* undertook an extensive new survey. The 1863 expedition also despatched surveying parties inland to create the first true topographic survey of Butrint and its immediate environs. These charts remained the basis of all subsequent revisions until after the Second World War. Further data was included in volume III of the admiralty's *Mediterranean Pilot*, which provided the basis for the description of Butrint in many subsequent journals and books. Despite their keen interest in the area, the French never undertook a comprehensive survey of southern Albania. The 1826 *Carte Physique Historique De La Grèce* of Comte Guilleminot, with an inset map of Butrint, was based partly on the observations of French Grand Tourists and partly on military data collected during the short-lived late eighteenth-century French occupation of the Ionian islands (see Chapter 6).[6]

The maps, of course, provide a sense of the geographical character of Butrint and its enclave, but little of the historical personality of the place. This changed when Butrint became inadvertently caught up as a minor sideshow in the political scheming behind the Napoleonic War. In 1804, with Napoleon's ascendancy in Europe at its zenith, control of the Adriatic Sea became of strategic importance. The British set out at once to stop succour

FIGURE 2.2 *Ali Pasha of Tepelenë drawn by Louis Dupré.*

to their French enemies while every effort was made to enlist new allies. This was the context for Colonel William Martin Leake's visit as a plenipotentiary to the court of the irascible Ali Pasha of Tepelenë, by this time a powerful force in what had been Epirus. Leake was an artillery officer who had been seconded to the Ottoman army to train its gunners and then accompanied the Turkish army to Egypt as they marched to confront Napoleon. His experience made him an excellent candidate for the British government's military mission to Epirus, and the opportunity afforded Leake the time to indulge in his passion for ancient Greece. His French counterpart was François Pouqueville. Like Leake, he had been to Egypt and on leaving he had been captured by pirates. Imprisoned first in Tripoli then Constantinople, he took the opportunity to learn ancient Greek. On being released, the Napoleonic government despatched him to Epirus as its consul general.

Both, by coincidence it might seem, visited Butrint in 1805. Both, no doubt, were instructed to record its strategic value, but both, steeped in classics, made copious notes about its antiquity.

Leake arrived by boat from Saranda, and describes his arrival at Butrint thus:

> As we approach Vutzindró (Butrint), the water becomes muddy, and in the bay is almost fresh. This bay is very shallow on the northern side, and the bar at the mouth of the river will even now, when the water is still at

the highest, but just admit of the entrance of καΐκια, or small coasting vessels. We row three maybe 4 miles up the river, through a plain once perhaps the property of Atticus, a friend of Cicero, and now peopled with horses from the neighbouring village. We then arrived at the Vivári, or more vulgarly Livári; that is to say, the principal fishery, which is on the left side of the river, at its exit from the lake, nearly opposite to the peninsula which, was anciently occupied by Buthrotum. The only buildings at the Livári are a ruined house of Venetian construction, and near it an old triangular castle, occupied by a dirty bilibásh (representative) of the Vezír, and fifteen or twenty soldiers.[7]

François Pouqueville described Butrint thus:

... on the south side of the channel, communicating between that lake and the sea, is constructed the modern Venetian fortress of Buthrinto, and on the opposite side are the ruins of old Buthrotum ... These ruins show an acropolis or citadel, and the Roman town enclosed within a double wall, containing fragments of both Greek and Roman architecture. But, in the walls of the acropolis are preserved foundations of the highest antiquity, consisting of vast blocks without cement. Between the hill Megalongi and the mouth of the Simois is the road-stead of Geroviglia ... nearly two English miles broad and long, is cut asunder in the middle by a barrier of strong reeds, to enclose the fishing grounds, leased out yearly together with the Lake and customs.[8]

Both spies must have known of Butrint from the increasing numbers of Grand Tourists who were now venturing south of Italy to explore Greece and the Levant. One such anonymous tourist inscribed his initials and a date, *AD 1796 P. A. M.*, on a Byzantine fresco on the acropolis. In 1819 the French artist Louis Dupré visited in the company of the British High Commissioner on Corfu, Sir Thomas Maitland, in order to meet Ali Pasha. Unimpressed, he dismissed it as follows: 'The fortress, if one can really apply that term to such a miserable tower, is armed with three cannon of mixed calibre . . .'.[9] Nevertheless, Dupré took the opportunity during a duck hunt to sketch the octogenarian Ali Pasha in his brightest coat being rowed through the reeds at the edge of the Lake Butrint.

Thereafter a steady stream of tourists and artists made the short trip from Corfu. The best-known artist of this time to record Butrint was the painter Edward Lear. Lear excluded Butrint from his famous 1848 itinerary, but during his residence on Corfu during the 1850s visited several times, sketching Butrint on 7 January and again on 7 March and again in April 1857.

Other visitors of this era included regular parties of huntsmen and tourists. The remarkable Irish aristocrat Arthur MacMurrough Kavanagh – a paraplegic – visited on a number of occasions in his yacht, *Eva*. One such

FIGURE 2.3 *Edward Lear's view of Butrint from Cape Stillo, 1857.*

trip in 1862 was sufficiently memorable to prompt him to write a book, *The Cruise of the R.Y.S. Eva* (1865). Like Lear, his party put ashore at Ksamil and employed local beaters to flush game birds and boar out of the thick undergrowth. Despite being born without arms or legs, the adventurous Kavanagh was a crack shot and an eager early photographer. His book is illustrated with lithographs made from the photographs taken on this occasion, the earliest known photographs of the immediate environs of Butrint.

The Italian Mission

The story of Butrint really took shape after 1924 when Luigi Maria Ugolini brought his energy and intellectual drive to search out the legend of Aeneas. In many ways, the Butrint we see today was configured by Ugolini, a romantic who belonged to an inter-war generation striving to justify Italy's Fascist revolution. A sketch in his posthumous book, *Butrinto. Il Mito d'Enea. Gli Scavi*, shows a man with a large head, high cheek-bones and soft, penetrating eyes.[10]

Luigi Maria Ugolini was born in 1895 in Bertinoro, close to Bologna. His early interest in antiquities and fossils led him to study classics and agronomy at the University of Bologna. His thesis, not unnaturally, was on the prehistory of his hometown, Bertinoro. The First World War disrupted his studies, and he enlisted in the Alpine Mountain corps, suffering a wound to his kidneys that would eventually prove fatal. After graduation in 1921, he attended the school of specialization in classical archaeology at Rome University. His background and qualifications – coming from the heartland of Benito Mussolini and having served with distinction with military élan – made him the perfect choice of the new regime to undertake an archaeological reconnaissance of Albania for the Italian Ministry of Foreign Affairs. The Italian government was concerned to enlarge its influence over the fledgling state of Albania and was accordingly alarmed by the presence of a French archaeological mission at the Graeco-Roman city of Apollonia close to the country's oilfields. The Italian government also wanted to exploit the political gamble it had taken in August 1923 when – after its general, Tellini, surveying the south Albanian border had been assassinated – it had bombed neighbouring Corfu to win reparations. Such matters doubtless were discussed when Ugolini met the Italian prime minister, Benito Mussolini, at Bertinoro in November 1923.

Ugolini's meandering journeys in Albania began in Skhodra and, arriving by boat, ended at Butrint. In two days he saw three ancient cities: Butrint, Kalivo and Mount Aetos (Çuka e Ajtoit). He followed the Vivari Channel from the Ionian Sea to Lake Butrint and energetically clambered over the extensive fortifications as well as the Venetian and Turkish castles *'poeticamente rivestiti di edera'*.[11] From the beginning he had no difficulty in identifying the ruins with those of ancient *Buthrotum*. Virgil's description of the city lent itself to the ruins. Yet the topography troubled him: the acropolis seemed insufficiently elevated to be Virgil's 'lofty city', his thoughts perhaps echoing those of William Martin Leake who had tartly observed: 'Virgil had a most imperfect idea of the place, when he applied to it the epithet of lofty, and its resemblance to Troy is very like that of Monmouth to Macedon'.[12] Some measure of Ugolini's initial uncertainty about Butrint is apparent in his first book, *Albania Antica* I (1927). Butrint is described in only two pages and allotted only one illustration ('the hill on which the ruins of Butrint rise'); by contrast the nearby Hellenistic capital of Phoenicê occupies fourteen pages with eight photographs. Thus, his later memory may have been inexact for he recounts how in 1925 on the acropolis at Mycenae he dreamed of excavating at Butrint to trace the archaeology of Virgil. Instead, following his Albanian excursus, in 1926 he launched a major project at Phoenicê, 30 kilometres north of Butrint, just beyond the ancient limit of Lake Butrint. Perhaps Phoenicê as a Hellinistic capital was better suited to the political aims of the Ministry of Foreign Affairs. Here in 1926–7, Ugolini excavated the Hellenistic 'treasury', several Roman cisterns, and an early Christian basilica, as well as recording standing Roman remains within the village at the foot of the hill. But on 12 December 1927 Ugolini sent a formal letter to the Albanian Ministry of Education, notifying them that the Italian Archaeological Mission proposed to explore Butrint in 1928.[13]

FIGURE 2.4 *Ugolini's excavations of the Theatre, 1928.*

The next three years were perhaps the apogee of Ugolini's archaeological career. A whirlwind of excavating, lecturing and touring followed. Beginning on 8 February 1928, a tent and ten cases of preserved meats, released from military stores, were sent ahead to Albania. The same month a film crew from the Istituto Luce in Rome was despatched to Butrint to make the most of the propaganda value of the project. By Easter of his first season his team had discovered the great eastern gate (later named by Ugolini as the Scaean Gate), a Roman mosaic (in the *frigidarium* of the forum baths), a sacred spring dedicated to Junia Rufina (by the Lion Gate) and the great polychrome mosaic of the Baptistery. By June Ugolini was excavating in the Theatre (though as yet he did not realize this) where he reported the discovery of several statues. A further year was to pass before he had convinced himself that he had in fact discovered the Theatre. Soon the well-preserved *cavea* and stage were apparent, associated with which were more Roman statues and Greek manumission inscriptions.

Equipped with water-pumps and a permanent team of twenty labourers who drained the trenches, the excavations proceeded at a staggering pace. The young Ugolini was a driven man. The triumphs and difficulties were evocatively summed up in his own account of finding the head of the 'Goddess of Butrint':

> ... during the excavation of the Theatre, in fact when we were intent on liberating the *scaenae* of the Theatre from the earth, a workman

announced from his section that there was 'something rounded' in the middle of the quagmire of the excavations. I leapt into the trench, convinced that it was a piece of sculpture and replaced him in the delicate task of extraction. I began the work full of expectancy – it really was a head, and one that appeared to have a perfect profile! The Albanian workmen who were all around me were visibly fascinated and congratulatory, for it was the first such head to be found at Butrint.

I washed the sculpture continuously, the better to see it during the delicate work of extraction and revealed a beautiful head whose fine and clear marble contrasted with the lead-coloured mush of the surrounding mud, enhancing its appearance. To our eyes was revealed a natural cameo, or perhaps more appropriately, the head of Persephone as it rose above the earth.

The head was intact: 'It even has a nose! It even has a nose!' cried one of the Albanians who was also fired up with that fervour only to be comprehended by those who ply the pick to the earth. Those who have this passion plunge their hands into the womb of mother earth to retrieve her lost secrets and restore to the light of the world those marvellous treasures that have been buried for uncounted centuries.

Our anxious experience was not a delusion, as it was one of the crowning moments of our work. The head was a Greek original of the best work; the head of the 'Goddess of Butrint'.[14]

The 'Goddess of Butrint' quickly became a symbol of the excavation and began to acquire a life of its own. The most persistent story was that the Italian mission stole the finds from Butrint and that the Goddess of Butrint was given by King Zog to Benito Mussolini to cover up this theft. A later (communist) newsreel of 1948, for a film entitled *New Albania*, claimed excitedly that 'The fascists destroyed the antique sculpture, and stole the marble heads found in various temples before they left the country.' Yet another story features Ugolini coveting the statue to the extent that he concealed it in a crate destined for Italy. Happily, so the story goes, a zealous customs officer insisted upon opening the crate and denounced Ugolini. A major diplomatic incident should have followed but, as relations between King Zog and Benito Mussolini were much improved, the Albanian king graciously donated the 'goddess' to the Italian leader in order to conceal the scandal. There it remained until 1982 when the Italian government, in a gesture to normalize relations, returned it to Tirana. In the meantime, the statue featured as a centrepiece of the Albanian pavilion in *La Mostra del Oltremare* in Naples in 1940. War prevented its return and, unlike three other statues featured in this exhibition, it survived an Allied bombardment. Such was its status that on its return it became the subject of a novel by Teodor Laço, *Korbat mbi mermer* (The rooks on the marble, 1987), as well as a prominent symbol of hotels in Saranda and even of Butrint United – Saranda's football team. Small-scale terracotta copies were made for sale at

Butrint to the first accompanied Western tourists, and commonly are to be found in Albanian homes, such is the affection felt for the statue. But the most surprising detail of all is that the 'goddess' is . . . a god! Most scholars now concur that it is an especially effeminate version of Apollo (sometimes known as the Sorrentine type), a statue associated with the Augustan ensemble that graced the Asclepian sanctuary as Butrint prospered from courtly patronage following the battle of Actium in 31 BC.[15]

Life for Ugolini in such circumstances was both thrilling and exasperating. As early as 1928 the Gendarmerie at nearby Delvina reported that finds were missing. The Ugolini archives in Rome reveal endless diplomatic issues with the distrustful local officials. By 1931 the Albanian government had appointed Hasan Ceka, an Austrian-trained archaeologist (commonly described today as 'the father of Albanian archaeology'), to serve as a representative on the dig in order to ease the burden of local relations.

In July 1929 Ugolini was ill and left the excavations to prepare lectures on his discoveries. No doubt he was mindful of catching malaria as the summer progressed, so he spent part of August at Phoenicê before returning to Butrint in September. Terminating the dig as autumn approached, he began a lecture tour of northern Europe to promote his discoveries. Meanwhile, King Zog had conferred on him the Order of Skanderbeg, Albania's highest award.

Ugolini was a celebrated lecturer. He made the fullest use of his extraordinarily well-staged photographs as glass lantern slides, and on occasions showed clips from the Istituto Luce propaganda films as well. He lectured all over Europe and, perhaps significantly, in many places in Albania. Upstaging the French excavators at Apollonia, he secured more support and encouragement from the Ministry of Foreign Affairs in Rome. The excavations at Butrint were now enlarged. In 1930 Ugolini suffered the August heat at Butrint preparing for the visit of the prestigious *Crociera Virgiliana* (Virgilian cruise), organized to celebrate the bimillenary of the birth of Virgil. Those who came on this mid-September visit would have seen half of the Theatre exposed. Around this time, he took receipt of a light railway line, supplied by the Ferrovie dello Stato (Italian State railways), along which little carts ran, transporting spoil to the edge of the Vivari Channel.

Intensive efforts were made not to destroy structures without good academic justification. When he did so, as in the case of the Medieval church in the so-called Gymnasium area, a careful survey was made first by Ugolini's engineer, Dario Roversi Monaco. A corollary of Ugolini's approach was the proper conservation of buildings. Hence his roster of mission members through the 1930s included mosaic conservators, specifically the Vettraino brothers from Rome. Where he was less scrupulous was in drawing the plans and elevations of the trenches he made. Some drawings do survive, but for the most part Ugolini was not interested in the archaeological strata. Perhaps it was because he himself was a poor draughtsman that he omitted to make such vital records. More frustrating still is Ugolini's grasp of the correspondence between finds such as statues and dateable objects and the well-preserved layers in Butrint. These problems doubtless were compounded by the simple living conditions and the basic team involved in the project.

Nonetheless, the inadequate field documentation is often compensated for by the remarkable water-colour paintings prepared by Igino Epicoco, the fine surveys by Carlo Ceschi (especially of the Theatre) and above all by the extraordinary quality of Ugolini's own quarter- and half-plate photographs. Some 1,700 glass negatives survive, almost all crisp elegantly arranged shots that capture not only the monuments and excavations but also the spirit of Butrint and its setting.

A photograph from 1931 of Ugolini and his team assembled in the Theatre captures the times. The Theatre is half-excavated, but already the lower seating and steps are spotlessly clean. The excavators are no less spick and span, all in white shirts some with high collars. Some, like Ugolini sitting alone on the lowest seat, wear sola topis as protection from the heat. Nearly all have high-laced boots, protection against the perceived menace of vipers. By February 1932 Ugolini was able to report to the Albanian government that the Theatre excavation had been completed and few such monuments were as well preserved. He was especially pleased to report that six marble statues had been placed on four piers between the three arches of the stage

FIGURE 2.5 *Ugolini and his team in the Theatre, c. 1930.*

building, the *scaenae frons*. His report also described the excavations of the Roman sanctuary of Asclepius, where an important votive deposit had been discovered (see Chapter 3). With the discovery of the Theatre of Butrint, somehow myth and reality were brought into alignment. Unfortunately for Ugolini, the Ministry of Foreign Affairs became increasingly parsimonious, and the excavation seasons became shorter. Later seasons were taken up with smaller excavations combined with rebuilding the Medieval tower on the acropolis as a permanent base for the mission. The new castle encouraged many visitors then and subsequently to erroneously think of Ugolini as a count with a personal room graced with a mural depicting the lion of Venice. Ugolini's aim was undoubtedly to help Butrint, creating a site museum of the kind he had seen in Greece and Italy, and with it the prospect of a steady flow of tourists.

All this came to a surprisingly sudden end, paradoxically as Italy's hold over Albania was on the ascendant. Taken ill in the summer of 1936, Ugolini died of kidney failure (aggravated from his war wound) aged forty-one on 4 October 1936, having penned a general account of his research but no significant definitive report. Undoubtedly, because he had tightened 'the spiritual chains between Rome and Butrint', the project outlasted his death. Indeed, in death he was regarded as a shining model Fascist 'New Man', 'a pioneer of Italianness in Albania'. Perhaps he was a malleable instrument of Italy's colonial policy but, then, his heart lay in the past not the present and he deployed his outgoing personality to sustain his odyssey. Notwithstanding the fact that he was a prehistorian by training, he adopted to good effect the historical positivism of Rodolfo Lanciani and Giacomo Boni – the archaeologists who made the huge excavations in Rome at the start of the century. He was an effective organizer who created the Virgilian myth for Butrint, putting the ancient city and its ruins back onto the Mediterranean map. At Butrint, as at Phoenicê, Ugolini's interests extended well beyond the narrow ideological imperative of discovering the earlier phases of the ancient capital. With his background in prehistory, he encouraged innovative work on the Palaeolithic and earlier prehistory of the Albanian littoral by the Florentine scholar, Luigi Cardini, just as he took a keen interest in the archaeology of Butrint's Byzantine phase and its history (left unpublished in the Museo Nazionale della Civiltà Romana).[16]

After his sudden death, the mission continued on a reduced scale under the direction of Pirro Luigi Marconi (who died in an aeroplane crash in 1938) and then Domenico Mustilli. A museum was opened in the acropolis castle in 1939 and outside it a bronze statue of Ugolini was erected. (Sadly, the statue has long since disappeared.) When the Greek army overran the area in the late autumn of 1940, the excavations effectively ceased, having been only partially published. Investigations resumed on a desultory scale after 1941 but ended with Italy's withdrawal from the Axis alliance in 1943. The projected series of five volumes of *Albania Antica* was eventually reduced to three, with the excavations of the Theatre and Baptistery appearing in an abridged form in Ugolini's lyrical, posthumous *Butrinto. Il Mito d'Enea. Gli Scavi* (1937) as well as in earlier reports and essays.

Butrint since 1945

Following the war, Butrint lay abandoned until the late 1950s. Photographs show that much of the site became overgrown and the museum was closed (many of its smaller finds were reputedly looted during the war) despite the presence of a site guard, Qerim Cuka, a disabled ex-partisan from approximately 1948. That year, as it happened, a Centre for Archaeology was established within the newly-formed Academy of Sciences. A triumvirate guided it: Selim Islami, Skënder Anamali and Hasan Ceka. All three had been trained abroad and so, as they planned a new archaeological institution in the service of the nation, it was natural that they looked to obtain specialist training for chosen students in major communist centres. One of the first selected was Dhimosten Budina.[17]

Dhimosten Budina was born in 1930 in Korçë, in south-east Albania. During the Second World War his family joined the partisans, earning the young man a respectable pedigree once hostilities were over. Budina studied history at the higher state college (later the university) of Tirana. In 1952, four years after the creation of the new centre for archaeology, he was selected to go to Moscow to study archaeology. Returning to Albania in 1956, Budina was instructed to study Butrint for his doctoral thesis. Skender Anamali (who had studied in Italy in the inter-war period) was keen to encourage a young archaeologist to take up where Ugolini and the Italian archaeologists had left off. Ugolini's published works were given to him and Butrint and its surroundings became his main area of study for the rest of his career.

Budina was a principal figure behind the invitation to Vladimir Blavatski to lead a Soviet archaeological mission to Albania in 1959–60. The mission coincided with closer ties between the government of Albania and the Soviets under Nikita Khrushchev. So, Budina helped to build the road to Butrint on the occasion of Khrushchev's visit in May 1959 and was no less active in the making of the present cable ferry over the Vivari Channel. Speaking fluent Russian (he was to marry a Russian woman), Budina took part in the resulting programme of excavations and surveys. He assisted in a small excavation of a sanctuary at Apollonia and, following Ugolini, together Budina and Blavatski re-surveyed Çuka e Ajtoit (near Butrint), often called Kestrine after the son of the Trojan exiles Andromache and Helenus.

The growing status of the Centre for Archaeology led to many new initiatives around Albania. Pre-eminent among these projects was the preparation of an Archaeological Map of Albania. Budina played a key role in assembling the map for southern Albania and, following the break with

Moscow in 1960 (when his wife was compelled to return to Russia), he continued the survey in the Drinos Valley and the Delvina basin. Over the next twenty years he excavated and published energetically, working on all the places that had fascinated Ugolini – Butrint, Kalivo, Çuka e Ajtoit, Phoenicê – and one site – Antigonea, high on a promontory overlooking Gjirokastra in the Drinos Valley, that had evaded Ugolini's intervention.

In the 1970s, with the creation of the local offices of archaeology, Dhimosten Budina became head of the Saranda section and the chief archaeologist at Butrint. In this new role he led guided tours for dignitaries and visitors, undertook excavations in the Roman forum, and nurtured a new generation of archaeologists to work on his projects, including Dhimetër Çondi, Kosta Lako and Astrid Nanaj.

In 1992 he returned to Moscow and took Soviet citizenship. He was to remain there for the rest of his life, characteristically getting involved in major excavations in Red Square.

Nikita Khrushchev's Visit to Butrint – May 1959

Enver Hoxha's post-war communist regime in Albania had close ties with Stalin's Soviet Union. Even young Albanian archaeologists were trained in Moscow. But with Stalin's death, Hoxha began to suspect the Soviet leadership of betraying the ideals of Leninism. In May 1959, in an effort to heal the growing rift between the superpower and its Mediterranean ally, Nikita Khrushchev and his defence minister, Marshal Malinovsky, visited Albania. In keeping with Hoxha's obsessive interest in Albanian history, the Soviet leader was taken first to the Greek colony of Apollonia and then by ship down the Albanian coast to Butrint.[18]

The preparations made at Butrint ultimately revealed the motives and fundamental differences between the two leaders. Thanks to Dhimosten Budina, a new road was made from the port of Saranda, where Khrushchev landed, to the archaeological site – a distance of 20 kilometres. At Butrint itself, though, where archaeology and nature are inseparably intertwined, Hoxha feared for the Soviet leader's life and had taken extraordinary steps. The beehives of the site custodian were burnt lest the bees sting the Soviet leader, while the snakes were poisoned with saucers of doctored milk. (No-one recalled the significance of the snakes to the Asclepian sanctuary.) Their bodies filled the ancient Theatre. Ismail Kadare, Albania's renowned novelist, used this episode in *Dimri i vetmise së madhe* (*The Winter of the Great Loneliness*).[19] Khrushchev, however, seems not to have noticed the listless carcasses of Butrint's poisoned reptiles. In *The Khruschevites* (1980), Enver Hoxha described his visitor as a boorish man, insensitive to the wonders of Albania's greatest archaeological site:

FIGURE 2.6 *Nikita Khrushchev and Enver Hoxha at the Lion Gate, May 1959.*

He even criticised our archaeological work as 'dead things'.... He called Malinovsky, at that time Minister of Defence, who was always near at hand: 'Look how marvellous this is!' I heard them whisper. 'An ideal base for our submarines could be built here. These old things should be dug up and thrown into the sea (they were referring to the archaeological finds at Butrint). We can tunnel through the mountain to the other side', and he pointed to [the village of] Ksamil. 'We shall have the most ideal and secure base in the Mediterranean. From here we can paralyse and attack everything'.[20]

Khrushchev's wish to build a submarine base was rejected by Hoxha. To make matters worse between the two leaders, the launch taking them across Lake Butrint, back to Saranda, broke down. The Soviet leader was furious. Six months later Hoxha cut relations, denouncing the Soviets as traitors. Except for a spell in the 1960s and 1970s, when Albania formed an alliance with China, the country entered a period of isolationism. However, the tarmacked road to Butrint made it a viable tourist destination, and within a decade, foreign tour groups were chaperoned not only to see Albania's model tractor factories, but also the marvels of Butrint, where, in Hoxha's opinion, the special link between the Albanians of history and the prehistoric Illyrians was forged.

* * *

Dhimosten Budina's presence at Butrint, combined with the growing value placed on archaeology by Enver Hoxha, led many young academics to re-examine Ugolini's work. The communist regime encouraged the search for the Illyrian origins of Albania (as opposed to Greek/Roman or Venetian), and to reinforce the struggle to defend itself against outside (imperialist) forces. This was the context, for example, for the major studies of Butrint's multi-period fortifications by Neritan Ceka (Hasan Ceka's son) and Gjerak Karaiskaj, challenging Ugolini's interpretations (see Chapter 3). In 1975–6, Kosta Lako undertook a large excavation in a previously unexamined area on the interior of the Hellenistic wall between the Great Basilica and the so-called Gymnasium. In 1982, Selim Islami and Aleksandër Meksi led a high-

FIGURE 2.7 *Dhimosten Budina (centre right) and Kosta Lako (in cap), Butrint*, c. *1970.*

profile summer training excavation which prompted renewed excavations of the Baptistery and Theatre areas, as well as excavations on the acropolis and on the extra-mural cemetery to the west of the city and a survey of the Great Basilica. Lako pursued the Triconch excavations throughout the 1980s while Astrid Nanaj investigated the acropolis, and Dhimetër Çondi and Budina explored the so-called Gymnasium (continuing the earlier unfinished investigations by the Italian mission).[21]

In 1990, with the beginnings of a democratic movement in Albania, the Institute of Archaeology was formed and immediately launched collaborative projects with foreign missions. The first of these was with Pano Doukellis of the Ionian University of Corfu to survey the Roman field systems outside Butrint, and Kati Hadzis of Athens Technical University who excavated on the acropolis at Butrint, exploring the origins of the ancient city. When the Butrint Foundation project began in 1994, it was clear that notwithstanding the rich historiography of Butrint before and after Ugolini, it was his shadow – his ideas – that governed scientific and public understanding of the place. Our aim, therefore, to honour Ugolini and Budina and his colleagues, was to develop a new interpretation that included rather than excluded their contributions.

Large-scale excavations and training digs were supported by the Butrint Foundation from 1994–2012. Many publications arising from these investigations have significantly advanced our understanding of Butrint's history from its foundation until the modern era.[22] The Butrint Foundation also investigated the archaeology of settlement in the hinterland of the port. Excavations were made of the Bronze Age sites at Kalivo, Mursia and Cape Stillo, the Roman bridgehead suburb on the Vrina Plain, the maritime villa at Diaporit, the Venetian Triangular Fortress and the Ottoman Ali Pasha's castle. Together this research has made Butrint and its territory the best studied in Albania and put it on the Mediterranean map. The Butrint Foundation, however, did much more than scientific work. Its cultural heritage strategy was to protect all aspects of the place and transform it into a premier tourist destination. Conservation of the site accompanied training in all aspects of restoration. In addition, information panels throughout Butrint accompanied the refurbishment of the museum and, with it, the stores. As part of this strategy, Butrint was designated a national park in 2000 with its own administrative office. The combination of all these works has seen it become a destination as global tourism has boomed with about 300,000 visitors a year.

Research excavations continue under the auspices of the Institute of Archaeology with the University of Notre Dame's Roman Forum Project,[23] and with the University of Bologna. In 2022, however, a major new direction was taken by the Albanian government, recognizing Butrint's pivotal place in international tourism. To facilitate better management of the UNESCO World Heritage Site, a new foundation has been created composed of directors from the Ministry of Culture and the Albanian American

FIGURE 2.8 *Conservation training on the Vrina Plain excavations.*

Development Foundation (AADF). Called the Butrint Management Foundation (BMF), the Albanian government believes that the foundation will provide Butrint with the governance that Albania's premier tourist destination merits. The BMF will assume full responsibility for all aspects of Butrint in 2024 with the intention of improving all aspects of its maintenance and presentation.

3

Butrint, Corfu and the Trojan Myth

I saw before me Troy in miniature, a slender copy of our massive tower, a dry brooklet named Xanthus. . . . and I pressed my body to a Scaean gate.

VIRGIL, *AENEID* III[1]

Luigi Maria Ugolini first arrived at Butrint by boat towards evening. Little had altered since the visit by Leake more than a century earlier. Vlach

FIGURE 3.1 *Shepherd huts on the acropolis, 1924.*

shepherds were camping in their little igloo-like thatched huts on the north-facing slope of the acropolis. Doubtless one or more of these shepherds in immense woolly fleeces met the Italian archaeologist and conveyed him along the lower flanks to a stretch of well-preserved Hellenistic walling where a tall, narrow gate remained intact. Ugolini's eloquent photograph may be a give-away. Did he immediately settle on this as the Scaean gate of Virgil's elegiac poem? His photograph shows a splayed spill of soil and vegetation streaming through the portal (Figure 3.7). A later one, following excavations, captures Ugolini beside the gate, an exiled Trojan beholding Troy in miniature.[2]

Only a few traces of the Bronze Age have come to light at Butrint in the form of coarse potsherds. Some archaeologists have suggested that the neighbouring hog-backed hill, the Kalivo, is indeed the Troy in miniature and others have favoured the pyramidal mountain known as Çuka e Ajtoit (Eagle Mountain or Mount Aetos). Bronze Age evidence has been found at both sites as well as at the small farmstead on Cape Stillo and a fortified site at Mursia. Judging from the hand-made pottery exchanged between these places, the great hilltop of Kalivo was the hub for all these sites arranged around the edges of a deep embayment.[3]

The best archaeological evidence for this period was found in excavations at Mursia. An encampment dating to the thirteenth century BC overlooked the embayment extending up to Lake Butrint. Here the low sand dune was terraced on its eastern slopes and a large fortification/retaining wall was erected. Considerable labour and organization were required to quarry and transport the massive stones up the hill and construct the wall.

According to the pollen study undertaken by Mario Morellón and his colleagues, the formation of the later lagoon – Lake Butrint – may have been the catalyst for the indigenous colonization of this coastal area.[4] However, the thirteenth century BC also corresponds to the Late Helladic IIIB period that witnessed the expansion of Mycenaean material culture and settlements, some thought to be Mycenaean 'colonies' in southern Italy, southern Epirus, Macedonia and Thessaly.

Mycenaean merchants certainly sailed these waters, en route for southern Italy, so there is genuine expectation that one day archaeological confirmation of Virgil's association with Butrint will come to light. These absences should not worry us. Settlement around Butrint dated back to the Middle Palaeolithic era. Butrint and the edges of the marsh had attracted hunters and fishermen since at least 100,000 BC judging from the Neandertal flint implements found first in Luigi Cardini's survey for the Italian Archaeological Mission and then, the Butrint Foundation's project, using Cardini's notebooks to re-trace his steps. Cardini identified an important collection of lithics from a fossilized beach site (on the former embayment) at Xarra, near Butrint. It is now clear that these belong to a long time-scale, ranging from

FIGURE 3.2 *Upper Palaeolithic flints from Xarra found by Luigi Cardini, 1930s.*

c. 100,000 years ago (mainly Levallois flakes, scrapers and denticulates) to the Mesolithic, or post-glacial period, represented by a single but crucial microlith. The most notable aspect of the assemblage is the small number of tools reminiscent of Aurignacian technology, dated to about 40,000 years ago and indicative of the transition between Neandertals and Modern Humans.[5] A number of small pebble-tools, dating to between 10,000 and 7,000 BC, resemble specialized shellfish toolkits found in Italy.

Sooner or later, given this evidence, traces of the first farmers are certain to come to light in the vicinity of Butrint. Presently, however, it is not clear whether these will be lagoon-side villages built on piles, as in south-east Albania, or on hilltops. The absence of all phases of the Neolithic, as well as the Eneolithic, Early Bronze Age, and Middle Bronze Age, is striking, in particular given their prominence in other parts of Albania.[6] These results do, however, match those from Fier-Mallakastra to the north and from Thesprotia to the south.[7] As for Bronze Age traders of the Mycenaean Age, their remains, apart from the camp at Mursia, small pottery assemblages from the acropolis at Butrint, on Çuka e Ajtoit, Kalivo and the Cape Stillo promontory, show mobile groups favoured these high points above the embayment reaching into Lake Butrint but resisted any thought of making a Mycenae or Troy here.

Colonial Origins or Refuge?

N. G. L. Hammond in his seminal monograph on ancient Epirus paints a picture in which, intermittently, Butrint was on the northernmost frontier of the Hellenic world. Its history is not only caught up in the periodic struggle between Greeks and Illyrians, but also in the breath-taking audacity of Greek adventurers who set out to control the sea route to Italy.

Located today in southern Albania, where in recent decades the Illyrian myth has been adopted as a national myth, it is not surprising that there is no unanimity on the early history of Butrint. Apart from the distinctive Bronze Age sherds, the earliest potsherds found on the acropolis are unprepossessing earthenware fragments that may date back to the eighth to tenth centuries BC. Associated with these are painted fine wares that belong to the age when Corinth colonized Corfu and converted its harbour into an axiomatic hub that would possess trans-Mediterranean status until the Napoleonic era.[8]

The Roman historian Strabo pinpoints the colonization of Corfu to 733 BC. Euboians, he says, from eastern Greece were evicted by the Corinthians. Such epic events cannot have bypassed Butrint, as K. W. Arafat and Catherine Morgan note, following the 1989–94 excavations on the acropolis: 'Interestingly, the earliest non-Corinthian import we have is a Euboian pendent semi-circle skyphos, a form which dates mainly to the ninth or very early eighth century. Yet since these are now appearing at a growing number of Western sites, they should not be taken as evidence of Euboian presence'.[9]

Corfu grew into a great emporium occupying a spindly hill ranging south from Palaiopolis, the little suburb today lying on the south side of Gardiki Bay. Known today as Kanoni, the hill is partly covered by the regency British colonial residence of Mon Repos and its grounds, and partly by smart hotels and villas overlooking Corfu's Kapodistrias airport. By the sixth century BC the city had become a metropolis by the standards of its age, encompassing an area as extensive as 600 hectares. A small tower once part of the east-facing curtain wall stands above the airport; close to it are the remains of the great temple of Artemis. Traces of the paved agora, the city's public square, can still be seen today at Palaiopolis. The public square was accessible from two great harbours: the lagoonal harbour now largely covered by the airport, and a north-facing harbour, partially protected by moles that opened onto Gardiki Bay and the Straits of Corfu.

Butrint owes its origins, it seems, to the quest to connect traders between Greece, Italy and Dalmatia. Its importance doubtless grew as the Greek colonies in the heel of Italy at places like Metaponto and Taranto prospered and sought to encourage commerce with their homelands. Equally, connections with the Corinthian colony at Epidamnos (modern Durrës) as well as Apollonia about 200 kilometres up the coast must have boomed as these towns enjoyed a prosperity to match Corfu's. Cemeteries excavated at both

FIGURE 3.3 *Surveying the cyclopean south wall of the acropolis.*

places have brought to light Greek pottery and personal jewellery as well as Corfiot products and pottery made in southern Italy.

Tucked discreetly at the entrance to Lake Butrint, Butrint's location was its great asset. It was protected from northerly winds that made the Adriatic Sea dangerous, and southerly winds that made traversing the Straits of Corfu impossible. In calm weather the coast of Corfu might be reached in ten minutes, and Corfu Town in an hour. For this pragmatic reason, the histories of Butrint and Corfu have been intertwined since the eighth century BC onwards.

Hammond was the first to identify Butrint's close connection with Corfu, affirmed by several of the ancient sources. He went so far as to speculate that it might have been part of Corfu's domain, the so-called *peraia*.[10] The fourth-century Pseudo-Skylax lists Corfu among the tribes of the Illyrians, the Iron Age peoples occupying much of modern Albania. The Greek historian, Thucydides tells how after the civil war in Corfu of 427 BC, the defeated families occupied Corfiot territory on the mainland as a base from which to launch vengeful attacks. Hammond translated the passage as 'the Corcyraean territory across the channel'.[11] He interprets this to be the adjacent 13-square-kilometre Ksamil peninsula, which terminates in Butrint. Command of this, he proposes, enabled the north entry into the Straits of Corfu to be controlled. If so, the so-called Dema Wall closing the narrow neck running between the Ionian Sea and Lake Butrint immediately north of Ksamil Bay, probably dates to this time. Built of massive blocks quarried from the local stone, the wall is 9.6 metres wide. The same isodomic ashlar masonry was employed in the fortifications of the Kanoni peninsula surrounding the colony of Corfu. Very similar ashlar construction can still be seen today in the tower of the church of Panayia Nerantzicha close to Corfu's Kapodistrias airport.[12]

This Greek origin has caused dismay in some quarters in Albania. A key source is the sixth-century BC geographer Hekataios who, in his book *Europa*, includes Butrint with Apollonia and Oricum (on Vlora Bay) as an Illyrian town, describing it as a '*polis*'. This single reference encouraged the Albanian archaeologist Neritan Ceka to propose that Butrint was first a proto-urban Illyrian town (he described the walled acropolis as Butrint I) before becoming a town in the fifth or fourth centuries.[13] But, did Hekataios, a native of Miletus in Asia Minor, really know Butrint? Inevitably, this has led to a lively debate, first because being a *polis* conjures up the status of a town with its own administrative functions as well as its own territory (or *chora*) as opposed to a refuge and, second, because being Illyrian means, to quote the late Albanian nationalist dictator, Enver Hoxha, 'what is Illyrian is Illyrian and what is Greek must be considered Greek'!

The Italian mission shed light on this enigmatic period in their 1938–9 excavations on the acropolis. At the eastern end of the narrow hill, at its highest point underneath the remains of the early Byzantine Acropolis Basilica (see Chapter 4), a sacred pit or *bothros* was found. A substantial amount of pottery, including proto-Corinthian and Corinthian wares dating from the seventh century BC and Attic pottery of the sixth century BC, were associated with the pit. A graffito on one of the Corinthian vases led the excavators to hypothesize that Athena was worshipped here. Certainly, this commanding location would be an ideal spot for a sanctuary or temple. One tentative possibility is that the sacred pit is somehow connected to the most prominent relic of this period at Butrint – a sculptured architrave depicting a lion in bold relief devouring a bull.[14] This architrave is to be found today, re-used as a lintel in the Lion Gate in the lower town. Parallels with a sculpture from the Temple to Athena at Assos suggest the architrave dates to the sixth century BC.[15]

The Italian excavators also drew attention to the polygonal wall enclosing the acropolis. Four sections of 'Cyclopean' polygonal walling survive around the top of the hill (forming what Ceka later called Butrint I). These appear to be surviving stretches of a hilltop fortification, though it is possible that each section belongs to a separate terraced building. Several phases of construction, renewal and repair have been identified. One section has been interpreted as a modest gate, leading down the steep south face to the Vivari Channel below.

Next, the Greek archaeologist Kati Hadzis's excavations on the acropolis produced a notable array of Corinthian amphorae (types A and B) and painted tablewares, products of potters based in Corfu. Diagnostic potsherds of Ionian and Attic cups were also found, revealing seaborne connections to parts further away. Among them was a cup inscribed ΑΡΜΑΝΟΝΔΑ and the lip of another was inscribed ΑΛΧΜΑ. It appears that the Ionian and Corinthian imports declined in number in the later sixth century, being replaced by distinctive vessels made in Attica.[16]

Recently, the American archaeologist David Hernandez has advanced a major reinterpretation of archaic-period Butrint based upon a new hypothesis regarding the Temple of Athena.[17] In his view this temple was constructed on the acropolis in the late sixth century BC, its architectural design being influenced by the contemporary Kardaki temple on Corfu and by the 'Ionian Sea style' dominant in Doric lands. Its distinctive epistyle blocks suggest that this temple was built without a Doric frieze as well. Hernandez further conjectures that the architrave depicting a lion attacking a bull (from the later Lion Gate) originally came from this temple as the scene is related to the cult of Athena. In Hernandez's opinion, the monumental stone architecture and carved relief rendered with Greek craftsmanship and using Greek iconographic vocabulary signifies the likely presence of a Greek community at Butrint in the sixth century BC.

The Temple dedicated to Athena on the acropolis may also have been part of the reason that Virgil and Ovid claimed that Butrint was modelled on Troy. Built in the *peraia* of Corfu, a temple dedicated to Athena Polias on Butrint's acropolis would have been a tangible link to Athens, the one city that Corfu depended upon in its struggle for autonomy. Tellingly the temple did not face Corfu. Instead, it was positioned to be visible from the landward side, and its immediate hinterland (*chora*) reaching into the hills as far east as Çuka e Ajtoit (Eagle Mountain). This was intended to be a monumental visual message of sovereignty and power on mainland Epirus.

Hernandez's deep excavations in the Roman forum immediately below the acropolis have shed light on other aspects of Butrint's early history. Far beneath the fine pavement of the Roman forum, his excavations revealed an old shoreline that ran up to the base of the acropolis hill. On this shore were deposits containing mixed ceramics dating from the overall period of habitation (*c.* 625–475 BC), starting from the time when Butrint was first permanently settled. These deposits lasted until the town was resettled in the second half of the fourth century BC. The deposits of the late fourth to third century BC are essentially homogeneous with almost no material from the earlier archaic period. On these grounds Hernandez argues that the fortification wall around the acropolis was rebuilt by the Chaonians in the late fourth century BC bringing an end to a period of downslope deposition ending up on the shoreline below.

Hernandez concludes that Butrint began as a small dependent *polis* whose inhabitants exploited and controlled a *chora*. Looking to the wider region, the archaeological evidence for urbanism is limited. Remains from the archaic period at Apollonia, Epidamnos (modern Durrës), Ambrakia, Anaktorion, and Leukas besides Corfu itself are meagre. These mostly comprise poor and often questionable parts of archaic fortifications and temples. On the other hand, Apollonia, Corfu and Epidamnos all had cemeteries rich with objects that reveal the far-reaching mercantilism of this period. Epidamnos, for example, boasts a Corfiot louterion stand with relief panels which comes from the same mould as a vase with a relief representation of the Judgement of Paris found on Corfu. By comparison, Butrint was smaller, both in size and population. Its grave field and possibly its habitation almost certainly lay in places that remain buried by overburden, having eluded a century of archaeological investigation. A solitary fifth-century grave found close to Ksamil Bay gives some idea about the likely riches in Butrint's cemetery. The grave had a triangular cross section made of six large, pan-tiles, of flat Corinthian type, forming a pitched roof. The burial was a cenotaph, containing intact ceramic vessels and no human remains. Among the grave goods were a black-slipped skyphos of Attic type, with torus foot and horseshoe-shaped handles, and a little one-handled bowl. The cenotaph follows Doric customs, like others known from Corfu, possibly a memorial to someone from the *peraia* at Butrint who perished at sea.[18]

The Hellenistic Town

The next episode of Butrint's long history emerges in the aftermath of the Peloponnesian War, when Corfu lost its *peraia* on the mainland. After a period of abandonment (*c.* 475–350 BC) at Butrint, the ceramic evidence shows the re-emergence of the settlement in the second half of the fourth century BC at about the same time as Phoenicê and Çuka e Ajtoit were established as inland tribal urban centres.[19] Trade once again defined this new era as imported and local imitations of Corinthian Type B amphorae occur at Butrint. The context for the town's revival was the growing power of the Epirote tribes. The northern part of the earlier Corfiot *peraia* was annexed by the Chaonian tribe, and the southern part by the Thesprotians. Butrint became a southern centre for Chaonia, a subsidiary to the tribal capital of Phoenicê. The influence of Macedonia (Philip II) and Molossia (Alexander I) spread across Epirus before the end of the century. Five years into the third century and Corfu was bequeathed as a dowry to King Pyrrhus of Molossia in his marriage to Lanassa. Butrint, too, was

FIGURE 3.4 *A reconstruction of the Hellenistic sanctuary and Theatre.*

almost certainly associated with Pyrrhus, in many respects Epirus' most celebrated leader.

Pyrrhus claimed descent from Achilles, but reminded everyone of Alexander the Great, whom, according to the Roman historian Plutarch, he resembled 'in appearance, speed, and movement'. Pyrrhus governed one of the most powerful kingdoms in the Mediterranean at the time, famously coming to the defence of the Greek cities of southern Italy against Rome. He made benefactions throughout Epirus, founded the town of Antigonea near Gjirokastra, and was probably responsible for building the theatre at Dodona. He may well have supported the sanctuary at Butrint although a dedicatory inscription on a seat in its Theatre indicates its construction occurred towards the end of the third century BC. By this time the port controlled an emerging sub-region, the Praesebes *koinon*, comprising some sixty tribes, later described in second- to first-century BC inscriptions found at Butrint. From these inscriptions it is also clear that the *koinon* was administered by a *strategos*, a military leader, aided by a *prostates* (a president), a representative of the Chaonian central authority.[20] Pyrrhus, however, may have left his mark at Butrint on the neighbouring hilltop of Kalivo, formerly an enigmatic Late Bronze Age site.

The Rise of Kalivo

Kalivo is generally overlooked in scholarship owing to its enigmatic role in relation to Butrint.[21] The name of the hill is believed to derive from the Vlach *kaliva*, meaning shepherd's hut and campsite. It is related to the modern Greek word for hut, καλύβα. Transhumant Vlach pastoralists, who occupied the site in the winter months during their seasonal migration from mountain villages, may have given the site its modern name. The hill commands views of the Pavllas River Valley and, to its north, the whole of Lake Butrint. Environmental studies of the lake suggest that before the end of the Hellenistic period the hill was an isthmus of sorts with water on three sides and, in particular, a wide stretch of water on its northern, unfortified flank (much like it is today). Given its proximity to Butrint, in 1924 Luigi Ugolini regarded Kalivo as a 'second acropolis' (*seconda acropolis*), noting that it held a privileged position in the landscape that was higher, better fortified and offered more commanding views of the lagoon and valley than Butrint. As a prehistorian who was devoted to classical scholarship and mined ancient literary sources for topographical information, Ugolini describes coming to a perplexing impasse. He felt confident that Virgil's third book of the *Aeneid* described Butrint as a 'little Troy' (*parva Troia*). However, he could not reconcile this account with the nearly contemporary writings of Dionysius of Halicarnassus, who noted the following: 'The presence of the Trojans at Buthrotum is proved by a hill called Troy, where they encamped at that time [when the town was founded].'

FIGURE 3.5 *View of Kalivo from the air.*

In something of a quandary, the young Ugolini pondered whether it was Butrint or Kalivo that was called Troy in Epirus. Telltale numbers of prehistoric sherds at Kalivo indicate a settlement of some substance in the Late Bronze Age, as we noted above. The precise date of its cyclopean and polygonal walls with their well-made narrow gates, however, have remained a matter of conjecture. This fortification wall possessed at least two principal phases of construction. The earliest masonry is represented by a series of regularly spaced large boulders and smaller stones occupying their intermedial space; this wall was later replaced with one of well-crafted polygonal masonry that featured three gates. The frequency of Bronze Age ceramics at the site points to one possible date. However, studies of wall typology and regional comparisons suggest that these distinctive walls are Hellenistic in date. Significantly, several forts with walls and gates strongly resembling Kalivo were discovered in archaeological surveys in the neighbouring region of Thesprotia. In his study of two Thesprotian fortresses, Mikko Suha found a similar gateway design – involving thresholds – at Ayios Donatos and Elea that resembles the detailing discovered during the Butrint Foundation excavations of the east gate at Kalivo.[22] The similarities are too striking to ignore. Suha proposes that both these Thesprotian fortresses date to the expansionist era of Pyrrhus in the earlier third century BC. In all likelihood this is when Kalivo's second fortification was built.

Kalivo's fortifications enclose an area of c. 23 hectares. This is over fifteen times the size of the fortified acropolis of Butrint (c. 1.5 hectares) in the fifth century BC and almost four times that of the entire fortified headland of Butrint (c. 6 hectares) in the third century BC. It also eclipsed the fortified acropolis of Çuka e Ajtoit (c. 5 hectares). In fact, Kalivo was by far the largest fortified site in the entire region, second only to the Chaonian capital, Phoenicê, where the fortifications enclose an area of c. 50 hectares.[23]

Despite the size and grandeur of its fortifications, archaeological surveys and excavations discovered that Kalivo with its three narrow gates never sustained any major settlement. In their assessments of the hill, Ugolini and later Budina failed to find any internal structures. Surveys by the Butrint Foundation identified several simple structures on the summit, particularly

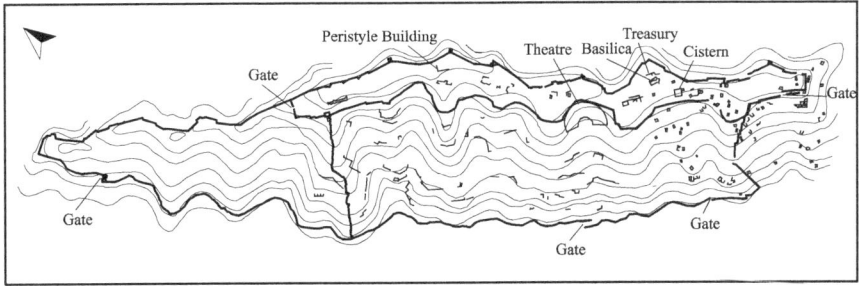

FIGURE 3.6 *Map of Phoenicê.*

within a stone-wall enclosure, which featured remains from small 2 × 2 metre rooms to larger buildings. The intramural structures, however, are perplexing. They do not appear to represent the remains of an urban settlement. Instead, the interrupted building lines and lack of tumbled masonry surrounding the buildings suggest that the original walls were probably very low and/or not constructed entirely of stone. The scale of Kalivo's fortifications, the absence of settlement remains, and the paucity of classical and Hellenistic pottery are puzzling.

Two hypotheses might explain the enigmatic character of Kalivo. First, it is possible that it was a place for the seasonal corralling of large herds of either cattle or sheep. According to the ancient sources, stock-raising had always been a distinctive economic characteristic of Epirus. From the time of the seventh-century author Hesiod, down to the Roman Empire, historical accounts of Epirus repeatedly refer to pastoralism and animal husbandry as the principal source of livelihood in the region. Later, Cicero and Varro describe the *Epirotici* and *Synepirotae* as the collective names of wealthy Romans who controlled large-scale pastoral and cattle ranches (*latifundia*) in Epirus. A principal interest of these Italian stock breeders was the production of quality goods (wool, racehorses, cows) for export to Italy to meet the new consumer demands of the time. Julius Caesar, reflecting on his campaigns in the region, dismissed Epirus as harsh (*aspera*) and mountainous (*montuosa*), but noted that while cereals were scarce, the region produced a plentiful supply of cattle (*pecus*). Evidently, in his war against his rival, Pompey, Caesar's troops survived on meat and a native root called *chara*.

Do Kalivo's encircling walls belong to episodes when livestock was exported from the valley? Certainly, the construction of such a large enclosure for holding animals would seem to be the work of a community with an explicit purpose. Yet the extent and scale of Kalivo's fortifications, larger than the fortified acropolis of Butrint, begs for another explanation.

A second, more compelling hypothesis is that Kalivo functioned as a fortified military camp and defensive refuge for the town's inhabitants during the classical and Hellenistic periods. A reference to these defences appears to have been made by Thucydides, when describing the *stasis* (civil strife) on Corfu in 427 BC that emerged shortly after the start of the Peloponnesian War. In this conflict, the oligarchic faction (*oligoi*), supported by Greek Corinthians and Epirote Chaonians, were in conflict with the island's democratic faction (*demos*) allied to Athens. Thucydides (3.85) reports that 500 Corfiot oligarchs seized the forts (τείχη) on the mainland (*peraia*) and occupied them as a base to attack the revolutionary citizens on the island. The word τείχη used by Thucydides is the plural form of τεῖχος, which means fort or the walls of a Greek military camp. Kalivo was evidently the largest fortified site in Corfu's *peraia*.

The focus of the Butrint Foundation's surveys and excavation within the fortifications was the unique walled enclosure (described above) on the southern summit of the hill, measuring *c.* 70 × 40 metres and built of cut limestone. Numerous close-built structures were identified, which originally would have consisted of a superstructure of either mud-brick or wood built above low stone walls. These buildings could have served as living quarters, shelters, barracks or other installations associated with a fortified military camp. Among the structures surveyed, the most significant was judged to be a rectangular building (c. 8 × 5 metres) on the northern end of the enclosure. It was built of cut stones and boulders that were similar to those comprising the fortification wall. Excavation of the building yielded Hellenistic pottery and numerous floor- and roof-tile fragments. The building commanded views across Lake Butrint and along the Vivari Channel, beyond Butrint, towards the Straits of Corfu.

The rebuilding of Kalivo's defences and reuse of the encampment coincides with the militarization of Epirus under King Pyrrhus, who at the time fielded one of the strongest Hellenistic professional armies in the Mediterranean. Kalivo and its contemporary fortified sites in Chaonia may represent some of the military structures of Pyrrhus' professional armies in Epirus.

The interpretation of Kalivo as a classical and later Hellenistic military encampment and refuge attached to Butrint conforms to the general framework of Greek territorial defences. In this respect, Butrint was no different to a typical *polis*. The acropolis of Butrint, with its sanctuary dedicated to Athena Polias, was simply not large enough to accommodate Butrint's population as a defensive refuge. Kalivo, by contrast, would have served as the nexus of its small territorial forts, particularly at Mursia and Malathrea and, as we shall see below, Çuka e Ajtoit. The northern boundary of this enclave was designated by the elegant Dema Wall, which closed off the Ksamil peninsula at the north end of Lake Butrint.

Only extensive excavations will establish with more certainty the purposes of the large and enigmatic hilltop of Kalivo.[24]

After Pyrrhus

Inevitably Pyrrhus' death led to turmoil and, in 231 BC, to the end of the Epirote alliance. A new republic was created at Phoenicê but, within a year, an Illyrian army led by the formidable Queen Teuta invaded the region and captured Phoenicê. Writing shortly after this, the Arcadian historian Polybius describes the impact on the Greeks of this conquest as follows: 'For seeing the most securely placed and powerful city of Epirus thus unexpectedly reduced to slavery, they one and all began to feel anxious, not merely as in former times for their property in open country, but for the safety of their own persons and cities' (Polybius, *Histories*, 2.6). The Illyrians, though, left Butrint at the centre of its own territory, perhaps profiting from its effective role as an intermediary with Corfu and the Ionian Islands. Soon, though, Queen Teuta's overreaching ambition led her to besiege Corfu, bidding to evict the Greeks from the entire eastern Adriatic. Initially successful, Teuta's aggression attracted a powerful Roman reprisal. On one front Gnaeus Fulvius sailed with 200 ships and took Corfu; on the other front, consul A. Postumius landed at Apollonia. Linking up, the two forces lifted the Illyrian siege of Epidamnos and invaded Teuta's heartlands, compelling her to conclude a treaty with the Romans. In a stroke, the balance of power in the Adriatic region shifted in favour of seaborne communities like Butrint. After a further generation of wars, around 200 BC, Rome replaced Macedonia as the major force in the Balkans. Then, thirty years later in 167 BC, the Romans under Consul Aemilius Paullus conquered Greece, harshly treating the defiant tribes of Epirus.[25]

The Chaonians and Butrint successfully came to terms with the invader. They were largely unaffected by the new order until the western Balkans, and Butrint in particular, became inadvertently ensnared in the civil war between Julius Caesar and Pompey. The history of these centuries is often incomplete and written to inform and entertain sympathetic audiences. Rarely can the changing topography of a place like Butrint be tied to precise moments in time. Only inscriptions and sometimes coin-dated archaeological levels offer the promise of connecting historical events and people with the making of monuments. Nevertheless, Hernandez's extensive excavations around and under Butrint's Imperial Roman forum provide invaluable insight into the broad outlines of the town's transformation in the later Hellenistic age.

Between the third and first centuries BC Butrint evolved to occupy the steep lower flanks of the already fortified acropolis. A circuit of exquisitely cut stone was used to make a powerful enclosure with as many as six gates. Of these only the Scaean Gate, giving access to Lake Butrint, survives intact. Butrint now covered at least 4 hectares in area. At this time many dwellings were almost certainly transposed from the exposed and constricted hilltop to terraces on the north flank overlooking Lake Butrint.

Ugolini was fascinated by the elegance of the fortifications. Unlike the 'Cyclopean' blocks used some centuries before to enclose the acropolis with its temple dedicated to Athena, the new circuit was made of blocks skilfully fitted together without mortar. In places plumblines, the width of a fist, were incised by the engineers. Ugolini admiringly concludes that these were to ensure the correct, straight arrangement of the blocks; the precision of the builders is unswervingly awesome.

The Scaean Gate itself is an architectural gem. Simply made, the high lintel conceals stone architraves supported by console cornices. ('Could this be the gate that Virgil might have seen and tells us about?' asks Ugolini elegiacally.) The same technique was employed at the Lion Gate, where it can be seen encased in a later Late Antique and Medieval construction. Gates on the north and west side, as well as leading to the western end of the acropolis, are less well preserved. Undoubtedly, though, the main entrance to the town lay on its south side, providing access to the sanctuary from the

FIGURE 3.7 *The Scaean Gate before excavation, 1924.*

Vivari Channel. At this ferry-point, in the later third century BC, an imposing entrance (the Tower Gate) made of smaller blocks was inserted into the circuit flanked by a round tower on one side and a rectangular tower on the other. Arrow slits in the forward positions offered guards the opportunity to control access. Wooden gates sealed the front and back of the 7-metre-long passageway between the two towers. The passageway between the towers was a mere 1.6 metres wide, just large enough for a cart.

The walls and their formidable gates were a symbol of the new authority invested here, probably as it assumed the administrative authority for the Praesebes tribe. Immeasurably more significant, though, was the creation of a civic ensemble of monuments that evolved over these centuries.

After entering through the Tower Gate, the first important shrine to be encountered was dedicated to the Zeus Soter. The temple has been located in excavations adjacent to the findspot of the three inscriptions in the foundations of the Roman Stoa and is also close to the so-called 'Tower of Inscriptions', where over a hundred manumission inscriptions were found in excavations in the 1980s. Largely lost beneath the Roman stoa, the excavated remains show that this temple had a *naos* with a mortar floor enclosing a wellhead for a natural spring and basin for ritual use. Astonishingly, this spring still gushes water today.[26]

West of this small temple lay the agora extending westwards along the foot of the steep slope below the acropolis, just inside the wide town wall, to an ensemble of buildings that made up the sanctuary dedicated to Asclepius, the god of medicine. This gave Butrint new meaning as a place. Why the waters of Butrint were deemed to have had healing powers remains a matter of speculation.[27] Later, it seems, there was some possible rivalry between the great oracle at Dodona and this smaller sanctuary at Butrint. Both places, by Imperial Roman times, sought their genesis in the myths of the Trojan exiles.

Such was the attraction of this healing sanctuary that donations by pilgrims afforded the town the means to develop facilities for the visitors. The complex rose up in a series of terraces from a paved area in front of the present Theatre. At the bottom, tucked inside the south-west corner of the defences, lay the council building (*prytaneion*). To one side of the Theatre, as we shall see, lay what Ugolini believed was the celebrated shrine, which has been re-interpreted as the treasury. Above the Theatre on a mid-slope terrace was the stoa, probably a hostelry for pilgrims. Slightly higher still, and palpably visible from the arc of the lower town, was a temple, for many years believed to have been dedicated to Dionysus, but now the likeliest candidate for the celebrated shrine itself.[28]

Let us look at each of these buildings in turn, beginning with the shrine of Asclepius.

Ugolini in his second season at Butrint in 1929 believed he had found the shrine tucked immediately to the west of the Theatre at the bottom of the hillslope. It consisted of a small temple-like building (7 × 5 metres) partially hidden underneath the substructures of the adjacent Theatre and internally divided into two parts, which Ugolini defined as *pronaos* (a small porticoed entrance) and *naos* (the focal room of the building). The façade featured a central door with two symmetrical windows on either side. The central door opened into the *pronaos*, irregularly paved with stone slabs. Beyond, passing over a threshold, was the *naos*, which was also paved, and had a bench on its west side and a small window next to the north-east corner. The upper side of the bench was furnished with a series of square and rectangular fittings, into which inscriptions or votive objects were probably inserted, as is confirmed by the rectangular shapes still visible on the plaster of the western wall. Ugolini realized that the bench itself was made of re-used material, in particular fragments of *stelai* and inscribed blocks, and he decided to dismantle it to recover the objects. Exploring the window on the rear wall led to the most surprising discovery: behind the back wall of the shrine, in a rock-cut compartment closed and roofed by slabs, a rich votive deposit was found, containing 340 objects mostly of Hellenistic date: ceramics, dedicatory objects and inscriptions, many mentioning Asclepius. These were not the only finds. Others were found scattered around the monument. These included fragments of statues, dedicatory inscriptions to Asclepius, the lion-shaped foot of a *trapeza* (Ugolini believed that this had been located by the back wall of the building and used for cult purposes) and what Ugolini described as the 'altar of the priest Philistos'. The altar consisted of two square stone blocks of slightly different dimensions, one set on top of the other, bearing the dedicatory inscription of the *hiereus* Philistos.

Ugolini had no doubts that he had found the main sanctuary at Butrint and quickly published a reconstruction drawing. Moreover, ever attentive, he identified that there had been a smaller, earlier building that he ascribed to the Hellenistic era on the basis of the associated assemblage of objects. Recently, the Italian scholar Milena Melfi has questioned Ugolini's interpretation of this special monument. She contends that it was the treasury of the sanctuary as opposed to the shrine itself, as Ugolini believed.

'Sanctuaries of Asclepius', Melfi writes, 'normally consist of many different buildings, devoted to specific cult practices, ranging from healings to sacrifices and public spectacles. It would then be somewhat unusual to find a single shrine, of particularly small dimensions, dedicated to the cult of the god'.[29] Certainly, Melfi argues it would be unusual if it were, for example, a temple because it is virtually concealed by the adjacent Theatre. This would have made it difficult to hold sacrificial ceremonies in front of it. This is further complicated by the archaeological discoveries. The sculptural and epigraphic materials found in the room belong to the entire lifespan of the cult. Some of these were kept in the building even when it was obviously no longer in use. The number of finds confined to such a small space suggests that the room was, at least in its last phase, cluttered with statues and votive objects and consequently not usable for the day-to-day performance of the cult, even despite the presence of the *trapeza* and the so-called altar of the priest, Philistos. Melfi interprets the altar as a *thesauros* or safe-box for the coin offerings to the god. 'The coins [she writes] could have been easily introduced through the opening in the upper block and eventually collected by the priests using appropriate lifting machines'.[30] Similar safe-boxes have been found in the Asclepian sanctuaries of Corinth, Lebena and Melos.[31]

If Melfi is correct, where was the shrine to Asclepius? Almost certainly it occupied the terrace immediately above the putative treasury where, on the mid-slope, Ugolini excavated a temple. Occupying a natural rock ledge, stoutly reinforced by polygonal walling, the small prostyle temple resembled the treasury building below, as though the latter was modelled upon this one. It had a portico supported by two columns and two pilasters. The main cell was constructed of square blocks, while a mosaic pavement dating to the middle Roman period covered the floor. At the back of the main cell Ugolini found the base of an altar. Located behind the Theatre, it has been interpreted by many archaeologists as a temple to Dionysius, but increasingly it seems likely that, high above the Vivari Channel and also visible from the Theatre, this was the centre of Butrint's celebrated cult.

Running away eastwards along the steep mid slope are more remains of a 30-metre-long, narrow colonnaded building made of fine stonework and including consoles for supporting upper floors. This is evidently one of the major features of the Asclepian sanctuary. Ugolini was the first to identify it as the stoa. Much of it was removed in Roman and Medieval times. Perhaps it served as a hostel for the pilgrims and sick attending the sanctuary. It had its own well cut into the rock face which, because its water was also venerated, was maintained long into the Roman period.[32]

The Theatre is without doubt the most prominent monument at Butrint. When it was built, it would have been one of the many facilities offered to the benefactors and pilgrims visiting the sanctuary. The original Theatre probably dates to the late third century or the earlier second century.[33] Pierre Cabanes and Faik Drini showed that the dedicatory inscription engraved on a seat in the Theatre dates to the Epirote Republican Period (232–168 BC) and argue for a date in the early second century BC.[34] This is also supported by the results of recent excavations at nearby Phoenicê, the capital of Chaonia. Stratified deposits at Phoenicê's theatre related to its original construction date to the late third or second century BC, with one of the construction deposits dated to the second century BC.[35] Butrint's Theatre

FIGURE 3.8 *Excavation of the Hellenistic Theatre, 1931.*

was built within a square structure measuring 100 Epirote feet (28.5 metres) along each side, backing onto the natural rock face of the hill. Perhaps not surprisingly, the engineer modelled the structure upon the imposing theatre beside the oracle at Dodona. Lateral buttresses support the structure, within which are twenty-three rows of seats divided by six staircases into five sections. Up to 2,500 people might have been seated here. Several small details are revealing. A common shape of a Greek as opposed to a Roman auditorium at the base is that of a horseshoe. (The Roman theatre tended to have a semi-circular auditorium.) Butrint's Theatre is a relatively modest horseshoe by the standards of the time, possibly because the space was restricted. The Hellenistic stage was not found (having been subsumed within the later, Roman stage building). Several authors have proposed a simple rectangular building with a row of columns on the front much like the stage buildings at the cities of Apollonia and Byllis in central Albania. The orchestra area was paved with carefully cut slabs (today, with the higher post-classical water table it is almost always under water).

The seats are of three types. Those of the front row have a footrest, profiled edges, footwells, and terminate in lions' feet. The next five rows have footwells. The top six rows are plain rectangular blocks. The lions' feet are particularly interesting. Similar seats are found in theatres in Asia Minor from the mid-second century and then, a little later, in Italy at Pietrabbondante from the end of the second century, and Pompeii from *c.* 75 BC. Another remaining feature can be found in the twelfth row marked by a line of inscribed blocks, some dedicated to Asclepius. This row formed the *diazoma*, a passageway separating the elite from ordinary townsfolk. A further extension up to the rock face probably dates to the early Roman Imperial age when the stage building was added and the entrances either side were considerably aggrandized.[36]

The administration of the growing town would have taken place in the council building, known as the *prytaneion*. This modest town-hall – a palace by any other name – gives us a sense of scale of this heroic age. It was tucked in the far south-west corner of the sanctuary with a paved piazza separating it from the treasury and the Theatre. Here the town's *strategos* as well as its venerable magistrates gave audiences, offered sacrifices and held feasts. The building was extensively remodelled in Roman times but enough survives of the Hellenistic complex to conclude that it lay in its own enclosure, entered from the paved piazza to the east. It had a central courtyard and an Ionic portico provided access to a surrounding suite of rooms.[37]

A gate in the town wall close to the *prytaneion* gave visitors direct access to the sanctuary from the Vivari Channel – without entering the Tower Gate and traversing the length of the agora – by way of the temple of Zeus Soter.

The precise origins of the sanctuary are unknown.[38] Why, to begin with, were the waters here associated with Asclepius, the son of Apollo and Coronis, daughter of King Phlegyas of Thessaly? Legend has it that Apollo removed the boy from Coronis' body because of her infidelity and turned the infant over to the centaur Cheiron to raise. Asclepius learned the art of healing from Cheiron. His arts were so great that he could even raise the dead, prompting the rage of Zeus. The most famed Asclepieion was at Epidauros where Coronis, it was claimed, happened to be as she was about to give birth. Many more sanctuaries were created in the later fifth century BC at places considered to have healthy environments. Animals associated with the god included the snake, and he is often shown with one wrapped around his staff.

How precisely the sanctuary was managed also remains a matter of speculation, but from the mid-second century BC surviving inscriptions indicate that it was subject to the authority of the tribe. The priesthood must have been reserved for prominent persons within the immediate tribal territory, the *koinon* of the Praesebes. Indeed, quite possibly only the richest and most important families served in turn as *strategoi*, *prostates* and priests of Asclepius. As a result, the sanctuary itself was a privileged place for the exhibition of public documents such as the display of epigraphic texts describing the freeing of slaves (manumissions).

Butrint possesses a remarkable group of major inscriptions from this period, numbering 165 in total, and recording the liberation of about 600 slaves. These manumission decrees were first discovered at Butrint by Ugolini. In 1932, he reports finding 'numerosissime inscrizioni' in the Theatre. He enlisted Italian epigrapher Luigi Morricone to study the collection but, due to Ugolini's premature death in 1936, most were left unpublished. Fifty year later, 162 of these were published by the French epigrapher, Pierre Cabanes, with his Albanian colleague, Faik Drini, who ascribe them to the sanctuary's zenith under Roman rule in the second and first centuries BC.[39]

Most of the inscriptions forming the *diazoma* of the Theatre are manumissions by their owners through a procedure that entrusted them to the custody of one of the town's gods. Other inscriptions were inserted into the high front walls of the Theatre (revetting the seat-ends), the so-called *parodos*, prominent to anyone entering the Theatre. Many more came to light curiously used in a tower set in the Hellenistic town wall half-way between the Theatre and the Tower Gate, next to the temple of Zeus Soter. In essence, the manumission records would have originally been located in the fortification wall fronting the two sanctuaries of Asclepius and Zeus Soter, situated at the polar ends of the agora.

A typical inscription reads as follows: 'While Nikostratos was general of the Praesebes and Appoitas was *prostates*, on the seventh day of the month Panamos, Philostratos sets Stilbon free as sacred and dedicates him before Zeus Soter (and declares him) exempt from seizure'.[40]

David Hernandez, in a new study of these inscriptions, believes that the high number of named places suggests that the territory of the *koinon* of the Praesebes was far larger than is presently assumed and included territory to

FIGURE 3.9 *A manumission from the 'Tower of Inscriptions'*.

the south of the present border with Greece. The *koinon* gained sovereignty after Aemilius Paullus' extensive destruction of towns in Molossia and Thesprotia in Epirus in 167 BC. It is possible that the new Roman administration awarded territories to Butrint that had once been Molossian and Thesprotian lands.[41]

The evident esteem in which the sanctuary was held had an impact not only on the changing townscape but on the lagoonal landscape around. Visitors and pilgrims approached Butrint at this time either from the Straits of Corfu by boat up the Vivari Channel or by a road that descended from the high passes to the east through the fertile valley to Çuka e Ajtoit (probably the small town of Kestrine) and along the elevated hills on which are located the modern villages of Mursia (where a small fortified Hellenistic farm replaced the Mycenaean-era encampment described in Chapter 2) and Xarra to arrive at the edge of the marshes. In pre-Roman times the road, as in the 1930s, probably ended in taking a ferry from Xarra to Butrint, following the narrow passage between the low hill of Shën Dimitri and Kalivo, before arriving on the south side of Lake Butrint.

As Butrint prospered, so did its region. Ten kilometres from the lake, Çuka e Ajtoit (probably ancient Kestrine) was transformed into a miniature Butrint with an elegant well-preserved 'palace', the size of Butrint's council building, on its steep, west-facing slope, first surveyed by Ugolini and then again in more detail by an Albanian–Soviet mission in 1959–60.[42] Opposite, prominent on a lower bluff, the compact, fortified Hellenistic farmstead of Malathrea dates to this time too.[43] Another farm was found in Butrint Foundation excavations beneath the Roman maritime villa at Diaporit, on the south-east shore of Lake Butrint. Dating to the second century BC, the evidence suggests that the complex covered an area of at least 60 × 40 metres. These early Hellenistic buildings were constructed in a characteristic technique using large poorly shaped limestone blocks bonded with earth.[44] They indicate a long porticoed structure running close to the shoreline in a broadly north–south alignment. The portico was constructed using a series of cross-shaped pier bases, probably supporting wooden uprights. Thick layers of green clay associated with these structures contained quantities of roof-tile, suggesting that there was a superstructure of rammed clay or mud-brick sufficiently robust to support a heavy tiled roof. The ground behind this shorefront complex appears to have been terraced with a substantial wall built using irregular polygonal masonry. This majestic setting must have been chosen by one of Butrint's prosperous new citizens.[45]

How wealthy was Butrint and, indeed, was it really a town? These questions, like so much about its early history, elude us. The affluence invested in the civic areas was considerable. On the other hand, no more than fragments of town-houses have been excavated in the town, and its cemetery – probably disposed along the spine of the hill running west from the acropolis – has yet to produce the kind of objects and wealth that distinguish Apollonia and, indeed, the nearby Chaonian capital of Phoenicê. In short, everyday life in Hellenistic-period Butrint remains a mystery.

FIGURE 3.10 *The archaic and later Hellenistic fortifications at Çuka e Ajtoit.*

It was almost certainly as a healing centre that Butrint came to Julius Caesar's attention, while the mid-first-century BC correspondence between Titus Pomponius Atticus, a great landowner here, and the literary lion, Cicero, conjures up an impression of a Homeric landscape, both elegiac and beautiful. Cocooned by marshes on three sides and a water table that was dropping remarkably, by as much as a metre since the sixth century BC, the pragmatic, driven Caesar spied the context for a colony. The reclaimed marshlands might serve as generous reward to faithful veterans who had sustained his cause against Pompey. Caesar's cavalier decision attracted Atticus' ire, as we shall see in the next chapter. Institutional, political and social issues aside, his vision effectively altered Butrint's century-old status from a tribal sanctuary to a town.

FIGURE 3.11 *Butrint and the Vrina Plain looking east.*

4

Caesar's Legacy

... there were many places called Troy in that part of the world, and Buthrotum itself was also known as 'Troy'. In this sense, Virgil did not 'invent' a non-existent stage in Aeneas' journey . . .; rather, he was following here a quite precise tradition. Except that, in Virgil's new version, this legendary location already associated with Helenus and with Troy has become a second Troy, identical in each and every way to the Troy that once stood upon the Dardanelles. And this is what makes the episode a magnificent literary invention rather than a tedious reprise of the tradition.

MAURIZIO BETTINI[1]

Strabo, the first-century geographer, associates Butrint's harbour with *Pelodes Limen* or muddy harbour (Strabo, *Geography* 7.7.5). Whether he had actually visited the town is doubtful. More probably he had heard from merchants or pilgrims who recalled disdainfully the murky waters in the Vivari Channel. Epirus has high rainfall, and today even in a heatwave the rivers and streams leaving the mountains are seldom less than full. Storms bring down soil which darkens not only the rivers but also Lake Butrint, leaving great muddy fans exuding from the mouths of the channels into the Straits of Corfu. The mud must have been very apparent to any visitor in the second and first centuries BC. The water table was dropping, leaving a shallow skirt of land running out into the Vivari Channel directly in front of the formidable Hellenistic town walls. Similarly, land on the south side of the Channel was now elevated above the waterline and, except after thunderstorms or prolonged winter rain, must have been exposed and covered in vegetation.

So, when Julius Caesar visited Butrint in 48 BC, he would have discovered the skirt of muddy terrain cocooning the celebrated healing sanctuary. From here, unlike today, he might have gazed directly down the Vivari Channel to see the Straits of Corfu and indeed the eastern flank of Corfu beyond.

The contrast between this rim of salt-stained land with its untidy vegetation and the ordered urban environment inside the formidable gate cannot have left the micro-managing dictator unmoved. One can almost imagine Caesar's rasping conclusion: everything was in Butrint's favour to exploit growing Roman economic dominance of the region and invest in major urban renewal and agricultural expansion.

Three small corroded bronze coins issued at Butrint between 44 and 31 BC, by two (Roman) magistrates of the town (P. Dastidius and L. Cornelius) show that Caesar's intentions were implemented.[2]

Butrint's Imperial Connections

Book three of Caesar's *Bellum Civile* describes (in his inimitable third person) that 'Caesar was at Butrint, opposite Corfu' (3.16). He arrived in 48 BC with part of a legion in search of supplies for his troops, still engaged with his nemesis, Pompey, in a series of battles and skirmishes mostly around Dyrrhachium (Durrës). His presence at Butrint, according to the French historian Elizabeth Deniaux, was neither accidental nor related to its mythic or healing associations. Caesar had come for a purpose. Corfu, the most northerly of the Ionian islands, controlled the sea routes to the East and West. Since its annexation by Rome, Corfu had been a pivotal point in Roman campaigns in the Balkans. Pompey had recognized this and stationed a fleet under M. Calpurnius Bibulus to patrol the Adriatic Sea. After Pompey had been defeated, the survivors retreated to Corfu. To contain any eventual uprising in Corfu, as well as to control the vital straits, it made sense to make full use of Butrint. Besides, Caesar was well aware that the Buthrotans had followed Corfu in favouring Pompey's cause and had failed to pay all their taxes. By way of punishment Caesar opted to create a colony for his veterans here.[3]

We learn more, instead, from the correspondence between Titus Pomponius Atticus, who had an estate here, and his friend, Cicero. At a dinner party Cicero handed Caesar a petition, drawn up by Atticus, which asked him to repeal the designation. Cicero received a most encouraging response. Provided the Buthrotans paid their tax arrears all would be well. Atticus immediately advanced the money from his own resources. In fact, Caesar was somewhat embarrassed by the case and revealed later that he was reluctant to offend the veterans who had been promised *Buthrotum* until they actually left Italy. They were then diverted at the last minute to some other location.

Two thousand years later it is easy to be seduced by Cicero's fulsome correspondence with Atticus. More than 400 letters survive, the earliest dating from copies made in the late fourteenth century.

Titus Pomponius (the cognomen Atticus, 'the Athenian' was a personal acquisition recognizing his love of things Hellenic) was born about November 110 BC, four years before his friend Marcus Tullius Cicero. His family was, like Cicero's, equestrian, but Roman as far back as could be traced. After the death of his father in about 86 BC, Pomponius made his home in Athens. In 65 BC he returned to Rome, though he made long visits to his estate in Epirus, near Butrint. Atticus' life was spent in cultural and antiquarian activities, as well as managing his financial affairs. He was a devotee of the philosophy of Epicurus, attaching great importance to friendship. Perhaps his most enduring achievement was as Cicero's publisher, putting slave copyists to work on Cicero's writings.

Atticus seems to have avoided political involvement and, although a steadfast conservative, tended not to vote at elections. He attempted to retain good relationships with everyone. He was a close friend of Mark Antony's family yet was on excellent terms with Octavian, the future Emperor Augustus. His daughter, Caecilia Attica (probably born in 51 BC), became the first wife of Marcus Vipsanius Agrippa, Octavian's admiral (Agrippa later divorced her to marry Octavian's daughter, Julia), and their daughter (Atticus' grand-daughter), Vipsania, was the first wife of the future emperor Tiberius. She was betrothed to him as early as 32 BC, when only a year old (Tiberius was ten), in a shrewd alliance before the battle of Actium.[4]

Atticus spoke fluent Greek and loved witty conversation. He was intellectually omnivorous – fascinated as much by ancient texts as Butrint's problems. Yet first and foremost Atticus was renowned as a trustworthy man, indefatigable in pursuit of whatever he undertook. Cicero described him thus: 'In the things that really matter – uprightness, integrity, conscientiousness, fidelity to obligation – I put you second neither to myself nor to any other man' (Cicero, *Letters to Atticus* 16.16a–f). Atticus died in 32 BC, the year before the battle of Actium, where, so close to his Epirote home, his son-in-law Agrippa comprehensively defeated Mark Antony and Cleopatra.

Was it Atticus' death that paved the way for the newly elevated Emperor Augustus to re-affirm the Roman status of Butrint and re-found the colony? The change is signalled in the legend of the local coinage from *C(olonia) I(ulia) Buth(rotiensium)* to *C(olonia) A(ugusta)*. Once again, the role of Corfu may have influenced Augustus' decision. The island, it seems, had favoured Mark Antony, only to fall to Octavian/Augustus on the eve of Actium. Afterwards, Corfu, with its harbours now suffering from silting due to the dropping water table, was effectively eclipsed by new investment made on the mainland at Butrint and the Victory City, Nicopolis.

Does Virgil give us a few clues, too, as to the circumstances at Butrint at this time? By choosing to promote Butrint, the poet may have been snubbing an older tradition in Epirus that recalled Helenus' association with the great sanctuary at Dodona, near Ioannina. In the new Roman geography, Butrint was destined to eclipse Dodona. Similarly, we need to note that in Virgil's *Aeneid*, Butrint was the turning point for Aeneas as he stopped holding onto the past, the last time he flirted with building an imitation of his home, Troy. In this the poet was suggesting parallels with the foundation of Nicopolis,

FIGURE 4.1 *Bust of Agrippa found by Ugolini in the Theatre excavations.*

'the Victory City' overlooking Actium Bay especially constructed to commemorate the turning-point in Augustus' life.[5]

More prosaic evidence affirms this fashioning of court poetry to serve a political purpose. As we shall see, it is likely the colony was now afforded state support to aggrandize its infrastructure. A new aqueduct, a long road bridge over the Vivari Channel and a grandiose civic centre were the most conspicuous monuments to the imperial favour now awarded to the port.

We must not underestimate, too, the regional impact of the foundation of Nicopolis, the so-called Victory City (or to Pliny, *civitas libera Nicopolitana* – the free state of Nicopolis). It confirmed Roman control, along with Patras, over western Greece. Moreover, lying between the Ionian Sea and the inland Ambracian Gulf, a location reminiscent of Butrint, it was strategically placed in every way. Its creation, apparently, led to the forced desertion of the earlier Hellenistic towns of Leukas and Kassope.[6]

The key to understanding the next decades in Butrint's history, though, are the collection of statues found by Ugolini in his excavations of the Theatre. As we shall see in some detail below, these are imperial portraits which as a group, according to the American art historian Elizabeth Bartman, should have been erected between 27–12 BC.[7] The most securely dated group is that of Augustus, Livia and Agrippa. To this group can be added a fine head of Apollo – best known as the 'Goddess of Butrint', a name lent to it by Ugolini (see Chapter 2) – as well as a second portrait of Agrippa discovered in the 1980s. A marble portrait of Augustus depicts him with a certain amassing of forehead locks similar to a version from Actium. The Empress Livia (Augustus' wife) is portrayed in a simplified version with the addition of a ribbon or fillet visible in profile hinting at a Hellenized royal portrait.

The emphasis on Butrint as the town of Helenus and on Aeneas' visit chosen by Augustus' court poets, Virgil and Ovid, must be seen in the same context. Their great poems, by adapting long-standing traditions linking Troy and Epirus, underscored a notion of a network of 'Roman' cities in the Ionian region, highlighting the 'founder' status of Augustus himself. As the officers and priests of the Asclepion sanctuary were soon to discover, courtly patronage was heaped on them. Butrint prospered as a gateway into the Balkans at the expense of its erstwhile partner, Corfu.

Butrint's strong imperial connection in the early Augustan age now seems well established. The most convincing evidence comes from a dedication stone to Augustus' grandson, Germanicus, found in the area of the Roman forum. The inscription describes how in 12 BC Germanicus was awarded an honorary magistracy at Butrint; C. Iulius Strabo, acting on his behalf, had the stone carved. As we have seen, the early imperial coinage lends further historical support. Only during the reign of the Emperor Tiberius, Augustus' successor, did a lull exist in imperial dedications but, from the time of Claudius through to Galba (during the middle decades of the first century AD), the imperial image reappears in the local mints.

The familial relationships between those receiving honours at Butrint illustrate two things. First, it is a very particular, largely local group and, second, it consists of those who were close to the Emperor Augustus. Two men with close ties to the Julio-Claudian imperial family received honours at Butrint.

The first of these, Atticus, not surprisingly is honoured in the town with a statue, of which only parts of the inscribed base survive. Members of his family held magistracies in the town and, as we have noted already, his daughter was married to Augustus' successful general, Agrippa. It is tempting to speculate whether the position of Agrippa was partly due to his relationship with Atticus, and if his status in turn influenced the choice by Butrint's magistrates of dedications to his son-in-law (Germanicus), and his great grandson (Nero).

The second, L. Domitius Ahenobarbus, was honoured with a statue erected by the town, on the base of which he is named the patron of the colony.

Likely as not this was stationed at the western end of the new Roman forum, where a monumental pavement inscription in front of an imperial cult building, originally in gilded bronze letters, names Ahenobarbus and Quintus Caecilius Eumanius from the family of Atticus as *Augustales*, members of the civic collegial association linked to the imperial cult.[8] Dated between 27 and 7 BC, the dedication itself is most probably connected to Ahenobarbus' consulship in 16 BC. We should remember, though, that his family may have had a strong client base in the area, since his father, who famously joined the Augustan side in 31 BC, commanded a fleet in the Adriatic between 42–40 BC. This relationship may explain not only how a freedman of the family could rise to prominence in the new colony – paying it seems for the restoration of civic buildings associated with the sanctuary – but also the town's decision to include the Emperor Nero, his grandson, on their coinage. It may also suggest why there are two female portraits from the sanctuary in the court styles, believed to be Agrippina the younger (his daughter-in-law and mother of Nero) and Valeria Messalina (his granddaughter).

From the later first century onwards, Butrint seldom catches imperial attention. Nevertheless, it prospered with the creation of the province of Epirus in the earlier second century, like its peer down the coast at Nicopolis as well as the inland town of Hadrianopolis (near Gjirokastra) in the Drin valley. From this time onwards its episodic history can be pieced together.

Butrint was not only important as a seaport but also appears on two important Roman road maps of the region. The second-century *Itinerarium Maritimum* depicts the main Adriatic Sea coast road passing from Nicopolis to Butrint to Sazan Island off Vlora Bay. This probably served as a source for the better-known fourth-century Peutinger Table (which some scholars think is based upon an Augustan original). This map locates Butrint lying between Phoenicê and Glykys Limen (situated at the mouth of the river Acheron in northern Greece). The road, N. G. L. Hammond deduced, passed 'along the east and south side of the lake [Butrint] to a point across the channel from Buthrotum'.[9] More probably, Butrint, as we have seen in Chapter 2, lay on a spur road, the main Adriatic highway passing from Phoenicê to Çuka e Ajtoit, and from there southwards towards Nicopolis and Patras.

Perhaps the most important later reference is an *enkomion* to St Terinus, who died a martyr's death under the Emperor Decius (AD 249–51) in the Theatre at Butrint. This is thought to have been written by Bishop Arsenios of Corfu (in the late ninth or early tenth century AD). Terinus was thrown to wild animals but, according to Arsenios, the beasts kneeled before the saint in a story reminiscent of Daniel in the lion's den. The story begs many questions, not least that it is hard to imagine this martyrdom being staged in the confined orchestra of the Theatre excavated by Ugolini.

As we shall see, Butrint, being a seaport, was a weathervane of geopolitical and climatic changes. So the town almost certainly prospered as a result of Epirus being divided into two at the beginning of the third century. Epirus Nova encompassed the land from ancient Byllis to Dyrrachium, the northern tract of the old province. South of this, the new administrative province, Epirus Vetus, continued to be a point of interchange between West and East, growing in standing when the empire was divided into two parts by Constantine in AD 330. While closer geographically to Constantinople, for much of the later fourth and fifth centuries, its church looked to Rome. Its religious beliefs may be connected to the historical sequence of earthquakes and other cataclysmic events that Epirus suffered in the later Roman period. Contemporary authors often associated such climatic events to episodes with spiritually wayward emperors or regions. So, we must be cautious when reading Libanius, writing in the fourth century, who describes the cities of Greece being devastated by an earthquake during the reign of Julian the Apostate (AD 361–3). Likewise, Cedrenus, a twelfth-century Byzantine historian, recalls a sea-wave that overwhelmed Epirus during the reign of Gratian (AD 373–83). Nevertheless, powerful seismic events at Butrint figure prominently as we shall see later in this chapter.[10]

The Archaeology of Late Republican and Early Imperial Butrint

Ugolini was surprisingly uninterested in the nature of Roman Butrint. In his posthumous book, *Butrinto. Il mito di Enea* (1937), where burnishing the might and glory of Rome may have been expected, Ugolini instead takes the reader through a familiar story derived from the ancient sources. The status of Butrint as a Roman colony is barely touched upon. Archaeologists from the Albanian Institute of Archaeology between 1960 and 1990 showed similar diffidence: the nationalist tendency in Albanian archaeology dismissed the role of the Romans as imperialists in Albania.

Relatively little is known about Republican Butrint prior to the arrival of the colonists. Two inscriptions record the presence of *magistri*. These officers controlled sectors of the town, indicating that the town was divided into *vici* in imitation of Rome. One of these inscriptions was dedicated to Stata Mater, whose cult (associated with protection against fire) is seldom found outside Italy. As we have already seen, the origin of the colonists themselves is not known. If indeed any actually came, it has been suggested that, rather than being veterans themselves, they may have been civilians displaced by veteran settlement in Italy.

What did these newcomers find? We have to envisage a town that first and foremost was a healing centre. Next, we must imagine that the line of the Hellenistic wall (see Chapter 2) originally marked the edge of a much wider Vivari Channel. With the drop in the level of the water table, a skirt of land would have been exposed running from approximately the Tower Gate beside the sanctuary area to the far, western corner of the ancient town. This sheath of marshy, salt-stained ground gave the architects of the

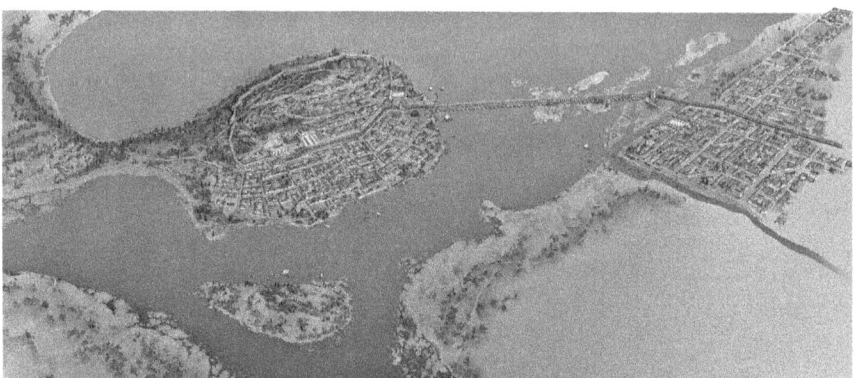

FIGURE 4.2 *Reconstruction of Roman Butrint, c. AD 100.*

new colony the opportunity to expand beyond the line of the Hellenistic fortifications. A late Republican tomb is the earliest monument on this exposed marshland. Today tucked within the so-called Gymnasium area, it would have been situated just outside a postern gate close to the east end of the agora. More importantly, exposed on the skirt of land, it was visible when sailing up the Vivari Channel from the Straits of Corfu.

The first major episodes in the make-over of colonial Butrint were the construction of three major enterprises: a new road-bridge over the Vivari Channel, alongside which was run a new aqueduct reaching back to a sweet-water spring at Xarra, and the creation of the Roman forum, involving the aggrandizement of the civic and sanctuary areas. There is as yet no evidence of new housing quarters being designated in Butrint, whereas, as we shall see, a new planned suburb, possibly with port facilities, was created at the bridgehead on the Vrina Plain. Let us examine each of these new elements in Butrint's townscape.

Traces of the bridge amount to a large masonry block located on the town side of the Vivari Channel, though divers have reportedly seen the remains of piers in the channel itself.[11] Reconstructing it, the bridge was 400 metres long and had about 45 arches. It almost certainly carried wheeled traffic, as well as the aqueduct. The location of the bridge close to the Tower Gate perhaps reflected an earlier crossing point, by ferry, that Hammond took to reach Butrint in 1930. Crossing the Vivari Channel, the new bridge closed access to Lake Butrint for sea-going vessels. The new port of Butrint therefore must have been located on the seaward side of the aqueduct, possibly necessitating the creation of the Vrina Plain suburb (see below). One further possibility is that the bridge and/or aqueduct is the arcade depicted on bronze coins issued by the colony during the reigns of Augustus and Nero. If so, we must imagine a low bridge encompassing many arches rather like the 64-arch bridge over the River Guadiana at Mérida, Spain.

FIGURE 4.3 *A section of the Roman bridge.*

The source of the aqueduct was probably a spring 12 kilometres away in the vicinity of Çuka e Ajtoit. Its line can be traced to a point slightly to the south-east of Xarra and then, thanks to the stumps of brick-built piers, across the Vrina Plain.[12] A feeder tank close to the south-east shore of the Vivari Channel marks where the aqueduct traversed the channel beside the road-bridge. From here, its line took it close to the Tower Gate. A large cistern (or *castellum divisorium*) lay next to the gate (an area now occupied by the Great Basilica), where a section of the Hellenistic wall-circuit was removed. The aqueduct ran westwards alongside the Roman forum off from which were branch lead pipes (one of which was found in excavations at the east end of the forum).

Excavations by David Hernandez and a University of Notre Dame team have discovered the Roman forum and charted its complex architectural history.[13] Hernandez has shown that the designation of the colony entailed a large-scale demolition and rebuilding of the Hellenistic civic centre and the massive procurement of new materials to make an Augustan monumental centre. This involved not only the importation and installation of hundreds of large limestone slabs to pave the urban centre but also the construction of many new forum buildings. These buildings included the imperial cult buildings (the so-called Tripartite Building), the two-storey building – a possible temple, a curia, a basilica, a stoa and a bath complex. The paved

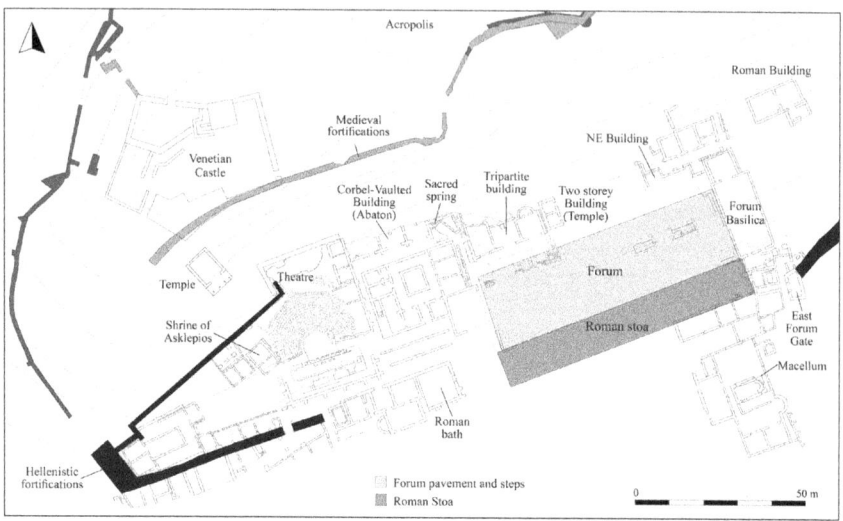

FIGURE 4.4 *A plan of the Roman forum excavated by the University of Notre Dame.*

area of the forum covered a long wide stretch about 20 × 72 metres, replacing the earlier agora and Hellenistic fortification. The focus of the forum was a basilica at its eastern end, which featured granite columns imported from Egypt. The head of a lost statue of Agrippa (described above) was found in this area now identified as the basilica. The inscription dedicated to Germanicus Caesar dating to AD 12–13 was also discovered near the basilica.

Adjacent to the Asclepieion, the Tripartite Building featured a central shrine built and dedicated to Minerva Augusta by a freedman of the early colony, Manius Otacilius Mystes, on public land granted by the town council. A colossal statue, probably of Augustus, was unearthed in front of the building.[14] To its west, a narrow alleyway separated it from the sanctuary. This led to a spring set into the face of the hill, where the wear of bucket ropes has left deep incisions in the low limestone orthostat closing the wellhead. Immediately east of the Tripartite Building, a small temple (the two-storey building) elevated 7 metres above the forum floor was fronted by a flight of twenty-two steps. The function of the north-east building remains unknown; a monumental inscription found nearby states that its upper floors (*cenacula*) were built by two named *duovir*s. A stoa with sandstone columns ran along the length of the south side of the Roman forum. The original architectural intention was probably that the forum looked out to the Vivari Channel, most probably with no other buildings obstructing the view between it and the water (as the Hellenistic fortification wall along this stretch had been demolished). From a reverse point-of-view, with the removal of this section of town wall, merchants, pilgrims and visitors

FIGURE 4.5 *View of the buildings in the north-east corner of the Roman forum in 2013 (courtesy of David Hernandez).*

arriving by boat would have seen the monumental heart of the town with its celebrated sanctuary rising in tiers up the side of the acropolis.

Early in the second century AD, probably under the Emperor Hadrian, the forum was refurbished and extensively rebuilt. This entailed the aggrandizement of the basilica and all the buildings on the northern side of the civic complex, as well as the reconstruction of the Theatre, now including a *scaenae frons* (a stage building).

Somewhat greater munificence is suggested by the statues associated with the sanctuary described above. Most of these statues were found by Ugolini in a line in the muddy excavation of the orchestra of the Theatre. They appeared to have been toppled from the niches in the second-century stage building. Ugolini's engineer-draughtsman, Carlo Ceschi, depicts the statues standing in the niches, a reconstruction that has stimulated a good deal of academic speculation.[15] A more probable explanation, though, is that the statues were assembled in the orchestra in the later fourth or fifth centuries AD in anticipation of being re-worked as the town switched its allegiance to Christianity. A similar group of toppled statues was found recently in a temple at the Roman colony of Narona in Croatia and is thought to have been desecrated following an edict by the Emperor Theodosius in the late fourth century AD sanctioning the destruction of pagan shrines.[16]

The dedications and honours heaped on the new political leaders at Rome following the battle of Actium in 31 BC clearly paid off. Butrint's civic centre was re-envisioned and now readily connected by a major road bridge

FIGURE 4.6 *View of the Theatre and its stage building, the* scaenae frons.

FIGURE 4.7 *Igino Epicoco's reconstruction (for Ugolini) of the Roman Theatre's* scaenae frons *from Carlo Ceschi's plan.*

to the reclaimed land on the far side of the Vivari Channel. The investment may have been intended to reward the Buthrotans for their support at a crucial time, but it led to the very development that, only a few years before, Atticus had lobbied Caesar to prevent.

Pan and His Shrine in the Forum at Butrint

During construction of an anti-aircraft installation close to Fshati i Vjetër, 'The Old Village' high on Mount Mile, overlooking Butrint and the Straits of Corfu, an exquisite bronze statuette of the god, Pan, came to light in 1981.[17] Reportedly, as the gun battery was made, ruins of some ancient building and pottery were also found. These suggest, in view of the pastoral setting, that a sanctuary of Pan had stood there in antiquity. Now this chance find has more meaning as research shows another sanctuary dedicated to Pan existed in Butrint itself.

The Mount Mile statuette was immediately exhibited in the National Museum in Tirana. Shortly afterwards, it graced an Albanian postage stamp. Above all it is a striking but small work of art, standing to a height of 17 centimetres. Broken just below the knee, the statuette is otherwise well preserved. Pan is depicted as a mature bearded man with slightly coarsened features, a strong, muscular body, rough hair, pointed animal ears, and dewlaps hanging from either side of his chin. His eyes are wide and staring and his mouth slightly open. His face is shown with human features; the horns are discreetly rendered and the ears small.

From the waist up he is essentially human. From the waist down he has the characteristic goat-legs, which would have ended in cloven hooves had they been preserved. He is shown naked, ithyphallic, and wearing the pelt of a wild cat (identified as a lynx in the Homeric Hymn that describes him), knotted at his right shoulder and slung over his left arm. His torso is twisted slightly, with his left leg in front of his right, giving the figure movement and grace, and the smooth musculature of his upper body is complemented and contrasted by the swirls on his goat-legs and on his lynx pelt, both of which possess the same patterning.

The statuette is cleverly modelled, with a noble expression and harmonious proportions and movements. In his left arm Pan is carrying a *lagabolon*, a shepherd's crook and throwing stick. Pan, the *lagabolon* tells us, was simultaneously a shepherd (and hence a protector of animals) and a hunter. His right arm is raised and, in his hand, he holds an *alabastron*, from which he is pouring oil onto his erect phallus, a pose far more commonly adopted by another fertility god, Priapos, with whom Pan is sometimes depicted. As a god of nature, Pan was always associated with orgiastic rituals and as a hedonistic participant in the feasts associated with the Dionysian mysteries, serving to ensure the fertility of the herds and the harvest.

FIGURE 4.8 *The Hellenistic figurine of Pan found on Mount Mile.*

On the basis of style, the statuette appears to be an early Hellenistic original, probably of the third century BC, although the possibility that it was an early Roman copy cannot be ruled out.

Pan has an especially colourful story. He is the only Greek god to die. Worship of Pan was thought to have originated in the mountainous lands of Arcadia in the Peloponnese, in a pastoral landscape similar to that of Epirus. His name comes from the Arcadian Doric Πάων, deriving from an early Greek (Mycenaean) word for shepherd. Above all, Pan was a god who lived in beautiful and wild countryside, who inhabited the shadows of woods and forests and haunted the pastures and the uplands of hills and mountains.

Gods did not die, so Pan's death has had an enduring fascination. News of a divine revelation – the death of Great Pan – spread to Rome during the reign of the Emperor Tiberius (AD 14–37). The matter was taken seriously. The emperor convened scholars, summoned witnesses, and ordered an investigation. The announcement of this unprecedented death of a god was said to have occurred at Butrint. Plutarch soon after described the affair (*Moralia. De Defectu Oraculorum* 17). The ominous event reportedly began near the Echinades Islands (known today as the Ionian Islands). One of the major islands in this group is Ithaca, the legendary home of Odysseus and Penelope. As noted by Tiberius' scholars, Penelope was considered to be the mother of Pan, and the god was thought to have been born on Ithaca, an opinion held by Herodotus among others. The ship's captain Thamus and the passengers on board heard the mysterious voice as the ship drifted to Paxi (Paxos), which is the smallest of the Ionian Islands, located immediately south of Corfu, opposite Epirus. It is in this context that in describing the coastline of Epirus in his *Geography*, Strabo, a contemporary of Tiberius, remarks that the seaport of *Buthrotum* was known to sailors as *Pelodes*, the 'muddy harbour'. These geographical markers represent the typical route sailors took from Greece before crossing the Straits of Otranto to Italy. Plutarch's later account suggests that the pronouncement of Pan's death was directed to what must have been a well-known sanctuary to the god at Butrint, where his devotees lamented his fate. Now, as a result of detective work by David Hernandez in the archives of Albania's Institute of Archaeology, a seaport counterpoint to the Mount Mile sanctuary has come to light.

In 1964–6 excavations in the Roman forum of Butrint, under the direction of Dhimosten Budina, unearthed an intact stone base, bearing a Greek inscription. Dating to the first century BC, the inscription records a dedication to Pan by a Roman named Cassianus (Cassius), who is described as the head priest of the cult dedicated to the god. This dedication served as a rough boundary stone in a sanctuary to Pan. This was not the first evidence of Pan to be found in Butrint. In the late 1920s, Ugolini unearthed a small stone pedestal that bore the following Greek inscription, Πάσαι | Κασιαινός. The inscription is a dedication to Pasa, the female consort of Pan, made by the same Cassianus. The pedestal originally would have supported a statue of Pasa and represents another offering by the head priest of the mystery cult.

The findspot of the boundary stone dedicated by Cassianus indicates that the sanctuary of Pan was situated somewhere in the west courtyard of the Roman forum. The courtyard's most prominent building was dedicated to the imperial cult (west building). This featured, in front of its doors, a monumental three-line inscription in gilded bronze letters (*litterae auratae*) on the pavement of the courtyard. Dating between 27–7 BC, the inscription names two freedman (*liberti*), Quintus Caecilius Eumanius and Gnaeus

Domitius Eros, from Butrint's leading families in the Augustan colony. These grandees held the title *Augustales* (priests of Augustus), members of the wealthy associations that emerged in Rome's western provinces in the time of Augustus. The two benefactors paid for the pavement and probably the imperial cult building as their honorary gift to gain admission into the association of the *Augustales*.

The courtyard was a sacred space beside the sanctuary of Asclepios. The worship of Pan may have centred around a small building in the courtyard that functioned as a *Compitum*, a crossroads shrine built on the western side of the sanctuary at the intersection where the street through the Asclepieion Gate met a colonnaded walkway to the Roman forum. The *Compitum* consists of two symmetrical *cellae* or shrines, which were approached by two steps. A limestone column *in situ* and circular attachment holes for others show that a single *pronaos* (porch) fronted the two *cellae*. An elevated platform on the western side of the shrines provided side access to the *pronaos*. Two dedicatory monuments, forming part of the *Compitum*, remain *in situ*; both are integrated into the southern wall of the platform facing the courtyard.

On the western side is a large marble drum bearing a Latin inscription: *A(ulus) Granius/ mag(ister) vici/ Lar(ibus) Vic(inalibus) sacr(um)*. It is an altar dedicated by the *magister vici*, Aulus Granius, to the *Lares Compitales*, which were the old ancestral neighbourhood deities from Republican Rome. *Magistri vici* oversaw the cult of the Compital Lares.

The second monument, on the eastern side, is a rectangular pedestal bearing a Latin inscription: [*A(ulus) Gr*]*anius/ mag(ister) vici/ Statae Matri/ Sacr(um)*. The same *magister vici*, Aulus Granius, dedicated the pedestal, together with a statue, to the titular deity of *Stata Mater*, who served 'to put a stop' (*stata*) to urban fires. The pedestal would have supported a statue of the goddess. (A similar pedestal was found in the forum in Rome.) A semi-circular limestone base *in situ* is located in front of Granius' two monuments. This was the base of an honorific bench where the *magister vici* presided annually over the *Compitalia*, in which sacrifices were made to the *Lares Compitales* at the crossroads. A brick water basin lies between this bench and the steps leading up to the shrines. The basin, built onto the two steps, has the form of a small *aedicula* with a rear niche. All these structures form part of the Compital shrine.

Piecing this evidence together it is now clear that the epigraphic evidence and architecture resemble the *Compitum* in the Piazza dei Lari at Ostia. Ostia's *Compitum* consists of a round marble altar adjacent to a basin and a building with two shrines (*cellae*). This altar in Ostia is of Julio-Claudian date and was dedicated by the *magister vici* from his own money to the *Lares Compitales* at the crossroads. In similar fashion, the *Compitum* of *Buthrotum* was probably dedicated to Hercules and Pan as well, in this case close to the Theatre.

Plutarch's story is all the more intriguing because Tiberius is also known to have received the news of the death of another god, Christ in Judea. The parallelism between Pan and Christ in this account did not go unnoticed by early Christians, who thought that Pan's name was a metaphor for *all* pagan gods. Bishop Eusebius of Caesarea (AD 265–339), who recorded Constantine's account of his Christian vision before the battle of the Milvian Bridge, interpreted the death of Pan as the death of *all* pagan gods at the hands of Christ upon his death and salvation of the world. In time, Pan became the prototype for the devil.

The Archaeology of the Suburb on the Vrina Plain

When Julius Caesar arrived at Butrint he doubtless observed the plain east and south of the town where, since later Hellenistic times, the water table had been dropping leaving a number of topographical highpoints. The drained alluvial soils dissected by water channels were ideal for cultivation. Here, we may imagine, Caesar envisaged settling his veterans. Today the plain is divided into large sub-rectangular fields by a grid-like network of drainage and irrigation channels as a result of engineering works in the late 1950s, causing dramatic topographical and hydro-morphological changes. However, making use of earlier maps as well as aerial photographs from the Second World War, the Butrint Foundation project began a variety of interventions: geophysical survey, field survey, trenching and extensive excavations. The results shed new light on the Roman colony at Butrint and the afterlife of this bridgehead community. Most importantly, 8 hectares of Roman building lying within a gridded arrangement have been identified, forming a southern suburb of Butrint, close to the bridge across the Vivari Channel.[18]

Using this mixture of archaeological techniques, the layout of the earliest colonial phase of the settlement was discovered. It took as its axial starting-point the line of a road that appears to have run from Çuka e Ajtoit to Butrint. This appears to have been a short spur road off the Adriatic highway described in Chapter 2. The actual alignment ran from Çuka along the spine of the hills from Mursia to Xarra, and with the land now drained, passed down onto the Vrina Plain heading to a point on the Vivari Channel slightly to the east of Butrint. If our calculations are correct, the Roman road engineers were using the summit of Mt. Sotirës behind Butrint and fixing their line on the prominent settlement on Çuka e Ajtoit. The geometric simplicity, ignoring the marshy obstacles and jumble of local topography, appears to conceal a brilliant design. Only one pre-existing building follows this alignment: the temple of Asclepius. Were the engineers fusing the sacred and natural in their choice of routeway?

The new aqueduct followed the alignment as it crossed the Vrina Plain. At a point now lost, the road and aqueduct almost certainly joined as they angled sharply into the town to arrive close to the Tower Gate.

The baseline was to serve as the alignment from which all subsequent axial measurements for buildings, *insulae* and centuriation were set out. This in turn fixed the land allotments as well as, in the case of the southern suburb of Butrint, its street plan. Within the suburb, individual *insulae* within the street grid would have been either of a single *actus* or consist of larger units, such as the 1 × 2 *actus* (or 1 *iugerum*) *insulae* discovered by David Gilman Romano at Corinth.[19] Normally these were a square of 35.80 metres (120 Roman feet), though this might often vary.

In fact, the resulting grid is not entirely regular, and it is possible that *insulae* were not of exactly uniform size. As the suburb evolved over time, irregularities in the overall form of the street plan are likely to have developed. Some well-defined structures clearly extend across several squares. This is likely to be evidence of later phases of the town, as their plans were remodelled.

We must imagine a landscape that was effectively ordered for many square kilometres. Probable traces of centuriated field boundaries have been identified beside the late Medieval triangular fortress, as well as far up the

FIGURE 4.9 *A reconstruction of the centuriation on the Vrina Plain south of Butrint.*

valley towards the modern village of Xarra. The fields themselves were parcelled within a 20 by 20 *actus* grid – a comparatively common formula in Greece at this time. The environmental archaeologist, David Bescoby, however, has speculated that traces of another set of land divisions following the same alignment, but conforming to units divisible by 12 and 16 *actus*, also was detected. He proposed that this could relate to an earlier system of division. Unfortunately, no archaeological dating exists for either system. Ground-truthing and associated excavations of farmhouses within the centuriated landscape is now needed to definitively ascertain its form and chronology. Both systems, however, appear to belong to mid-first- to late second-century AD management of the Vrina Plain by a multitude of property owners pre-dating the construction of a major property on this east side of the channel around AD 200.[20]

By contrast, the main outlines of the early topography of the suburb are now known. Geophysical survey shows a linear feature, probably a river channel, delineating the south-western limits of the occupation area. A similar channel defines its northern extent. Close to the water's edge on the western limit lay a slightly raised area, today covered by Roman ruins standing particularly high. Here, the excavations revealed a long sequence probably beginning in at least the later first century AD and continuing, with interruptions, until the thirteenth century. It is tempting to speculate that the major walls on the side facing the channel (and thus looking directly towards Butrint) are the remains of a wharf or harbour works. Was this raised hillock a point of disembarkation for ships coming up the Vivari Channel, and now unable to enter Lake Butrint because the channel was blocked by the aqueduct and bridge?

Between the two channels, remains of several gravel-surfaced roads were found in the excavations, including one where wheel-ruts were still visible. Within the grid of roads, we have identified the changing character of the bridgehead community. The high water table prevented any detailed excavation of the earliest period of occupation by a simple one- or two-room farmhouse, presumably colonists. In the mid-first century AD, the Flavian period, the area was reorganized. A number of large well-appointed houses were constructed, several of which incorporated shops fronting the roads. In the following century the size of the community expanded, and a new public bathhouse was built, along with its own large cistern. This extra-mural settlement was completely altered in the third century AD when a single individual erected a large double peristyle suburban villa here. In the earlier fourth century AD, the villa was aggrandized still further, notably when an octagonal tower was added to its western bathhouse. The villa prospered until it was struck by a massive earthquake in the second half of the fourth century AD.

A little east of this residential area lay a sequence of small monuments, elegantly constructed close to the shoreline and intended to be viewed by all passing along the road to and from the bridge. The later of the two has a well-preserved stepped base within which were found the remains of a free-standing column. Much like the columns in a painting of a great palatial villa at Stabiae in Italy, the monument would have provided a focal point on the plain. The present second-century AD structure is interpreted as honorific in function, though equally the column might have constituted an aniconic depiction of Apollo. Representations of the god in this form appear on the plaques decorating the Augustan temple of Apollo on the Palatine in Rome, where they were used as allusions to the battle of Actium – an interpretation of particular significance for Butrint being so close to Nicopolis, the Victory City. Certainly, it would have been eminently apposite here, celebrating Apollo Agyieus, the protector of roads and crossroads.[21]

The paved area in front of the monument was occupied by a porticoed building, perhaps for visitors or priests, which looked southwards out onto an open area. To one side of this open area lay the remains of what appears to be a temple raised on a podium, its brick-built walls still standing over 1 metre high. Associated with it are dressed blocks and hundreds of fragments of marble from sculptures and decorative revetment. The building is twice as long as it is wide, corresponding to the Vitruvian formula for laying out a temple. The rectangular chamber would form the *cella* with a wide door giving onto a limestone paved atrium, the *pronaos*, beyond which lay a set of steps.[22]

Like Ostia Antica, the great port of Rome, and ports nearer to Butrint like Corinth and Piraeus, this was not a quarter identified by a common factor such as a single commercial activity or housing for those of a particular trade or social class, but an extra-mural armature encompassing most urban activities. In many ways, it was an extension of the settlement along the north side of the Vivari Channel that grew up in the second century AD on the skirt of reclaimed land that once was separated from the sanctuary by the former Hellenistic wall. Conceived perhaps in the early years of the Augustan colony, this bridgehead extension only really took shape in the Flavian period. Following this, it grew by stages over the following two centuries to become eventually a mirror image of the large channel-side dwellings on the north side of the Vivari Channel. None of this should really surprise us. A similar new development at the (north-facing) base of the Phoenicê was found by Ugolini and has been recently mapped by the University of Bologna team. Like the Vrina Plain settlement, the lower settlement at Phoenicê was laid out in the later first century AD and occupied until at least the third century AD. In this case the steep north flank of the Phoenicê separated the two parts of the ancient town as opposed to the Vivari Channel. Certainly, what this shows is that the occupation area of Butrint grew in the mid-first century AD from 6 hectares (the town) to as much as 18 hectares. Further afield, it is exactly at this time too that the Greek colonies of Nicopolis, Patras and Corinth appear to have developed intensive new farming regimes for their associated territories. This new initiative at Butrint, then, belonged to a larger Roman programme to invest in, and of course tax, Greece.[23]

Of all the finds from this area, the so-called Nike relief, purchased by Ugolini in 1930, is without doubt the most outstanding. Probably found by fishermen, its date and iconographic interpretation continue to cause debate. Most probably, though, the relief belongs to a public building in the suburb. The relief depicts a winged Nike, the Greek goddess of victory, in front of a trophy of armour. The marble slab measures approximately 80 × 50 centimetres and would have been topped by a moulded cornice. The classicizing figure of Nike is shown in a slight three-quarter pose, with her left hand resting on a cuirass placed on a stylized rock. Her wings are articulated only along their upper edge and further detail may have been added in paint. Along the right edge of the relief the outline of wings from a second Nike figure can be discerned suggesting a linear, processional arrangement of figures. On the right-hand side, it is possible to imagine a motif repeating that in the extant relief, but on the left, the blank space behind the Nike figure precludes this – a third Nike could conceivably have held a less voluminous piece of equipment, like a spear or a sword. The rear of the relief is flat, but the sculpted front has a slight curvature leading Ugolini to propose that it could have been intended for a circular monument. Certainly, the size of the relief suggests that it would have adorned a public monument and the style – with its compositional links to the round monument at Nicopolis as well as the celebrated Corinth *puteal* (wellhead) inspired by this – that it should be understood in the light of the Actium victory. Certainly, given the great changes at Butrint as it became a colony, it is very tempting to associate this exquisite example of Julio-Claudian sculpture with the Augustan victory. Using this visual language would have found imperial approval and would have shown Butrint to be a Roman town worthy of imperial attention.[24]

The Cemeteries

In this densely occupied Roman landscape, as was customary in the Graeco-Roman world, the dead lined the routes into and around Butrint.[25]

The main cemetery extends from the line of the westernmost Hellenistic fortifications on the headland and covers the shoreline of both the northern bay (up to the Lion Gate) and the north side of the Vivari Channel. Ugolini excavated a large Late Roman mausoleum in this area and a similar building was discovered in trial excavations by the Butrint Foundation to the west. More masonry tombs can still be seen along the isthmus connecting the headland to the main peninsula and on the south- and east-facing slopes of Mount Sotirës up to a height of 50 metres above sea level. Ugolini excavated fifty-six burials in this cemetery and dated the burials to between the fourth century BC and the third century AD, a date range confirmed by subsequent excavations.

One tomb features in a palpably Romantic drawing entitled 'The Robber's Castle' by the mid-nineteenth-century artist, Henry Cook. Closer inspection and survey in 2004 showed it to be a two-phase structure built right at the water's edge. It must have constituted a prominent landmark, clearly visible from the town, as well as from the Roman new town on the Vrina Plain. Two distinct phases are evident. The first was a shallow barrel-vaulted building, 3.70 metres wide and 2.40 metres deep. The vault survived until a boulder hit it, probably when the new Saranda-Butrint road was being constructed for Khrushchev's visit in 1959. A stylobate with a central threshold marks the front of this building, but there is no sign that it ever had a substantial front wall; the interior originally may have been open to the gaze of passers-by on the water. Critical for the dating of the original building and the first phase of painted decoration is the presence of fragments of ceramic vessels in the north, rear wall. Here they had been used to fill fissures in the natural rock face to create a level surface for applying the earliest layer of plaster to the wall. The ceramic archaeologist, Paul Reynolds has identified rim- and body sherds from one or more cooking pots with a characteristic grooved rim, of local manufacture. These can be dated securely to the late second/early third century AD.[26]

The decorative scheme of this initial phase is best preserved on the east wall, although even here the surface is extremely worn and faded, and the design is preserved only in disjointed and often indistinct fragments. The pattern consisted of a rectangular grid drawn out in red and sometimes yellow, describing squares. The intersections of the grid were marked by red discs, apparently contoured in green or girt by green accents. A red exploded star was set at the centre of each square. Later, the tomb was re-used, re-painted and modified as a chapel, possibly the chapel identified as St Demetrios on Lechevalier's 1802 map of Butrint (see Chapter 5).

Ugolini identified a second cemetery area on the opposite bank of the Vivari Channel, 'to the east of a Venetian fortress'. More recently a second- to third-century AD cemetery of single tombs has been found in the Butrint Foundation prospection of the Vrina Plain. Several mausolea were dotted along the shoreline. Others, though, were sited on the west-facing flank of Kalivo and the west-facing slope of Shën Dimitri designed to overlook the Roman road leading from Butrint to Çuka e Ajtoit.

Beyond Butrint

The flush of new activity in Butrint cast its spell far and wide. *Onchesmos* (Saranda) and Phoenicê, the two nearest towns, both prospered. At Phoenicê, rather mirroring Butrint, an extra-mural settlement was created at the south-facing base of the saddle-backed hill. Beyond this, extensive traces of centuriated fields have been identified. Closer to Butrint, though, did Çuka e Ajtoit (ancient Kestrine; the southeasternmost point of the pre-Roman *koinin* of the Praesebes) survive or did its citizens move to Butrint, mirroring the many later Hellenistic towns deserted when the colony of Nicopolis was founded? As yet it is unclear.

Nevertheless, beyond Butrint a managed landscape evolved in which its wealthier citizens built villas. Indeed, a villa on the north entrance to the Vivari Channel (where the modern Customs House stands) would have been the first sign of the town.[27] Constructed on a terrace on the foreshore, this seamark had unequalled views of the straits to Corfu and beyond. An even grander complex occupied the south-eastern foreshore of Lake Butrint at Diaporit. First explored by Ugolini, the Butrint Foundation has exposed large parts of this complex villa.

At Diaporit the grand lakeside Hellenistic house determined the terraced arrangement of the subsequent earlier Roman house.[28] During the first century BC and the early first century AD, the alignment of the early buildings was retained as the complex became increasingly elaborate. A substantial waterfront complex existed here using the architectural vocabulary of the Italian maritime villa, exemplified in the oft-cited painting from the house of M. Lucretius Fronto in Pompeii. This included terracing and substructures

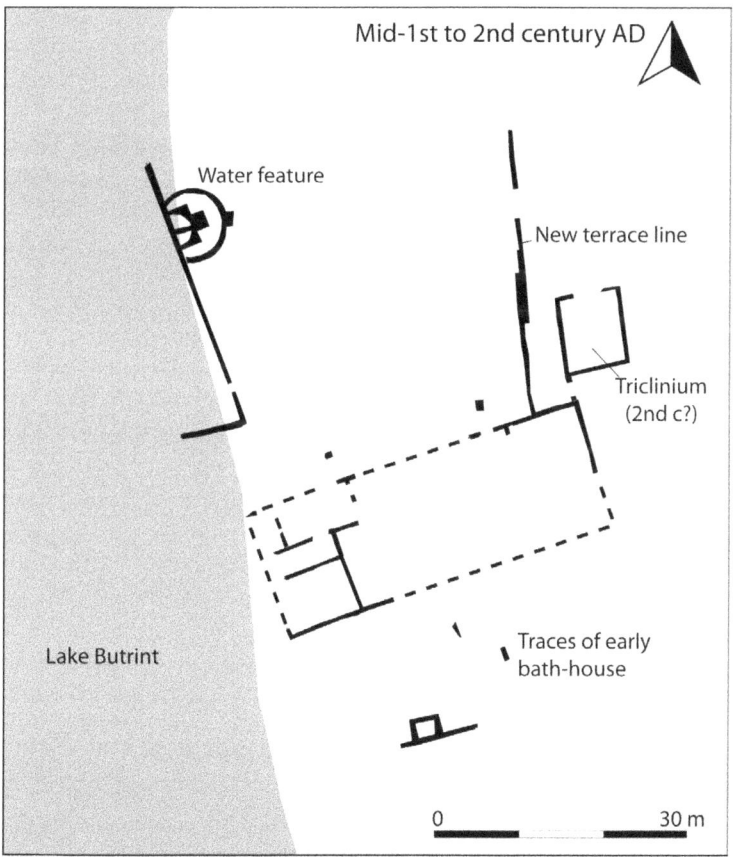

FIGURE 4.10 *A plan of the mid-first- to second-century maritime villa at Diaporit.*

to accentuate the visual impression of the complex as it was approached from the lake: long ranges of buildings with porticoes running parallel to the waterfront and almost certainly extending into the lake itself to create the direct contact between structures and water that was so emblematic of the *villa maritima*.

Whether Diaporit can be associated with Atticus' celebrated villa is doubtful although the site was at least occupied in the mid-first century BC when Atticus was active in Butrint. A more concrete link to the potential proprietor is provided by a tile stamp reading GRA[E], found in probable first- to second-century AD levels on the eastern terrace of the later villa. This may well refer to P. Pomponius Graecinus, *duovir* and *quinquennial* at Butrint. Graecinus was a major public figure in Augustan Butrint and is known from an inscription and on coins issued by the colony during the reign of Augustus. A second, partial tile stamp possibly referring to Graecinus was found in the Roman forum excavations. The Diaporit tile plausibly represents the ownership of a Latin-speaking patron and someone who was, moreover, a major figure in the Augustan town.

It is possible but unlikely that Pomponius Graecinus had either a family relationship with Atticus or a relationship as a client taking the name of his patron. Pomponius, as it happens, is a relatively common name in the period and Atticus' freedmen known from Butrint took the name Quintus Caecilius, after Atticus adopted his uncle's name in 58 BC. A Gaius Pomponius Graecinus is also named as a suffect consul in AD 16. This Pomponius Graecinus was apparently a *homo novus*, elevated to the senate by Augustus between 18 BC and AD 3, and it is interesting to consider the relationship between him and the Butrint Pomponius Graecinus, given the close involvement of the Julio-Claudian family in the affairs of the town.

Diaporit is one of a relatively small number of early villas to the east of the Adriatic. In Greece, the concept of luxurious rural residences tended to develop rather later and never to the same extent that it did in Italy. Similarly, the colossal villas of Istria and the Dalmatian coast seem to develop in the first century AD, although the spectacular maritime villa at Verige Bay on the island of Brijuni has its origins in the mid-first century BC. Like these villas, Diaporit has direct parallels in Italian contexts. Indeed, the early establishment of a *villa maritima* at Diaporit suggests a patron of Italian origin or one thoroughly familiar with the *mores* of the elite living in the Italian peninsula. In this respect it seems reasonable to associate the site with one of Varro's *synepeirotae* (Var., *Res Rust.*, 2.5.1) and view its early phases as a clear manifestation of a direct Italian influence on the Epirote coast.

This connection may explain the next phase in Diaporit's history. Around the mid-first century AD, the villa underwent a transformation involving the demolition of much of the earlier complex and the construction of a new villa on an entirely different alignment. This new villa faced south-west towards Butrint, involving a shift in orientation of around 45 degrees. The reasons for this change are obscure, although it must in part relate to a desire to create a more impressive façade to greet those arriving across the lake by boat from Butrint.

Little is known of the west wing of the villa, which seems to have extended out into the lake. The excavation in this area mainly removed overlying beach gravel along the edge of the lake and no stratified deposits were uncovered. The main structure revealed was an ornamental water feature. This enigmatic structure seems most likely to be some kind of fountain or *nymphaeum* that was intended to be viewed from the west, perhaps from within the building represented by the long wall or alternatively from the lake itself as one approached the villa.

The south wing also seems to be newly laid out at 90 degrees to the new lakefront structures. Relatively little excavation was carried out on this part of the building, but some clearance allowed the outline plan to be discerned. The exposed walls indicate a southern range of at least 40 × 15 metres, fronted to the north by a portico, suggesting the presence of a large courtyard or garden on the lower terrace. Beyond, to the south of this wing, was the earliest phase of the villa bath suite. This early bath complex was entirely buried beneath later phases, but an early wall and hypocaust were located and could be dated to post-AD 40–80.

The most complete element of this phase was the eastern wing. Here a new terrace around 35 metres long was laid out. The upper level of the terrace was fronted by a corridor or portico *c.* 4.7 metres wide. Behind this corridor was a large *triclinium*, measuring 8.25 × 6.60 metres, with its function denoted by a mosaic pavement, with plain plaster denoting the areas that would have been obscured by dining couches. The focus of the pavement was a central *emblema* formed of slabs of *africano* marble, of which two survived *in situ*, albeit heavily burned. This was surrounded by a black and white border with a swastika interlace interspersed with motifs of dolphins and kraters. The room, somewhat obscured beneath later structures, was not quite rectangular in shape, requiring the mosaicists to compensate slightly by gradually staggering the placement of the three geometric panels, which were of unequal size. This rather awkward arrangement could suggest that the pavement was later than the construction of the room or that the shape of the room was forced on the builders by the presence of pre-existing structures.

The scale of the *triclinium* is indicative of a date no earlier than the second century AD. Its orientation is curious, as it might be expected to have been positioned to allow the reclining diners a view out across the lake towards Butrint. Instead, it faces northwards along the terrace, suggesting the presence of a further courtyard or garden on the upper terrace, and a more sheltered dining experience, perhaps a response to the stiff breeze that habitually blows across the lake from the northwest. The slightly awkward fit of the pavement to the space could also suggest that the creation of a large *triclinium* represents the alteration of an existing space to accommodate the changing social *mores* of the second century AD.

During the second century AD, the villa was subject to almost continual aggrandizement and redevelopment. The most spectacular of these additions was a large bathhouse laid out on both the upper and lower terrace, presumably replacing the baths associated with the previous phase. This presumably had the effect of emphasizing the height of the buildings as one approached from the lake. The excavated remains of the bathhouse on the upper terrace comprise a suite of architecturally adventurous rooms. A suite of heated rooms lay to the west along the present lake front. These perhaps were used prior to a final immersion in the cold plunge. In total across both terraces, the bath suite must have comprised at least twenty rooms.

In the late second century AD, the *triclinium* on the upper terrace was demolished and partly buried beneath a much larger room (15 × 9 metres). No floor levels were found associated with this huge new room, but it was re-used in Late Antiquity. Was the villa abandoned in either the late second or early third century AD before this *triclinium*, or it is possible that it was never completed?

The villa at Diaporit was undoubtedly one of several, probably owned by absentee landlords in the hinterland of Butrint. Similar villas were situated to exploit maritime vistas like the comparable villas from Benitses and Roda on Corfu.

The Mid-Roman Town

By the second century, Butrint was evidently booming. By now it was perhaps the *Buthrotum Municipium* mentioned on an inscription found by Ugolini dedicated to Q. Trebonius, one of the town's decurions. Constant rebuilding occurred in the forum as earlier public monuments were refurbished or altered. But this was a period of accelerating private wealth, displayed in townhouses, chiefly along the reclaimed skirt of land beside the Vivari Channel.

In the sanctuary, a new mosaic floor was laid in the temple dedicated to Asclepius, while the stage building of the Theatre was rebuilt on an imposing scale in the early second century. From the council building, the *prytaneon*, comes a marble bust of a private portrait imitating the Emperor Hadrian's young favourite, Antinous – evidence that this too was remodelled at this time.[29] Elsewhere, civic munificence was strong, though seemingly no longer so attached to the imperial court. The wellhead beside the Lion Gate, for example, was aggrandized and dedicated by a local woman. Her name is recalled in Greek on the orthostat slabs closing off the deep shaft that plunges into the rock-face here. The inscription reads: 'Junia Rufina, friend of nymphs'. Presumably, the well was associated with a cult dedicated to the nymphs, as protectors of the spring and perhaps its associated healing properties.

FIGURE 4.11 *A sculpture discarded in a third-century drain in the Roman forum.*

At probably the same time, a monumental fountain with statues of Dionysus and Apollo in two of its three niches was constructed on the street frontage outside the Tower Gate and opposite the proposed *castellum divisorium*, where the aqueduct entered the town. A second fountain stood on the opposite side of the street, creating a monumental entrance into this part of the town from the bridging-point. A similar arrangement can be seen at the west entrance in Nicopolis, where the aqueduct enters the town. At Butrint, the fountain was supplied from a cistern at its rear, fed by a branch of the aqueduct, which then continued into the town. Not long afterwards the channel was raised (perhaps during the later second or third century) to feed a cistern above the fountain. The reasons for raising the channel are unclear, although the intention was perhaps to deliver a higher pressure of water elsewhere in the town.

The growth in the population is best illustrated by the construction of private housing. By the second century large properties were spreading out within the grid of radial alleyways across the exposed land to the Vivari Channel. Deep drains followed the lines of the alleys, ridding the terrain of high water in winter. One sample transect illustrates this best. Extending out from the old town wall, south of the Roman forum, a large complex was built around the monumental fountain known as the Gymnasium at this time. Rather than a Gymnasium it is likely that this area began life as a *macellum*, a market-place close to the forum, much like the well-known *macellum* at Pompeii. Beyond it, overlooking the Vivari Channel, townhouses occupied plots in the area later dominated in the fifth century by the Triconch Palace (see Chapter 5).

The Late Roman residence known as the Triconch Palace, situated on the north bank of the Vivari Channel, was a focus of archaeological research by the Butrint Foundation between 1994–2003.[30] Ten years of excavations revealed a complex archaeological sequence encompassing some 1,400 years or more of an urban quarter next to the water. The earliest channel-side houses here probably date to the second or third centuries. At the Triconch Palace two major phases of a townhouse or *domus* pre-date the construction of the short-lived fifth-century palace (*c*. AD 400–420) (see Chapter 5). In its earliest phase we can discern clear elements of a plan that dates to the fourth century. The public focus of this building, incorporating earlier elements, lay on its south side. The visitor to the building entered through a door in the southeast corner of the complex and was immediately in a small but highly elaborate space. Painted architectural vistas graced the walls, while the floor was paved with mosaics featuring theatrical masks. From here a visitor could proceed into the corridor or gallery, with its carpet of mosaic pavement stretching into the distance and subsequently into the reception room beyond. At the same time access to the remainder of the house was restricted, although our understanding of the form of the rest of the house in this period is limited.

The arrangement whereby the main audience chamber is relatively accessible from the street, without visitors needing to enter the remainder of the house, is quite common (although by no means universal), oft-cited examples being that of the Palace of the Dux at Apollonia and the Bishop's Palace at Aphrodisias. In the case of this townhouse, its long gallery parallel to the Vivari Channel fulfilled the function of leading the visitor to the audience hall, while at the same time allowing a view over the water. There may have been a small garden between the gallery and the channel, or alternatively the channel may have almost lapped against the southern wall of the gallery.

A particularly noteworthy feature in this house at Butrint is the significant alteration that took place with the addition of the apse, perhaps in the fourth century. The conversion of rectangular reception rooms to apsidal spaces is not uncommon in Late Antiquity. This is an illustration of the increasing importance placed on the use of apsidal spaces in reception rooms. Apsidal spaces in aristocratic houses are thought in part to mirror the growing importance of patron–client relationships within Roman society, forming a space in which the owner of the house or patron could be seated to meet his clients (a feature that seems to originate in the throne room of Domitian's palace in Rome). The increasing use of apses in triclinia also reflects changes in dining habits as the semi-circular dining couch (*stibadium*) seemingly replaced the traditional arrangement of three rectangular couches from the third century onwards.

The audience hall could be used for the *salutatio* or 'morning greetings' and the triclinium used for grand dining. Alternatively, the audience hall would be used for pre-dinner drinks and entertainment. However, after excavation here it emerged that the two rooms may not have functioned together in this way. It appears likely instead that the gallery and reception room served as the principal public wing of the building in the fourth century. The gallery allowed easy access to the reception room that served as an audience chamber, this function being augmented by the subsequent addition of an apse. This embellishment reflects the owner's desire to greet his clients in an environment suitable for the purpose. The layout at Butrint is common to many fine townhouses from the Middle Roman period and parallels those examples in which a public room is located close to the street and could be accessed without visitors being allowed into the rest of the house.

The flourishing construction alongside the channel only tells half the Mid-Roman story. Buildings on the acropolis almost certainly associated with the temple of Athena were abandoned at this time. By the third century a drain in front of the Tripartite Building in the Roman forum was blocked with a statue, suggesting wholesale changes. The abandonment of the villa at Diaporit, as well as the consolidation of the bridgehead suburb into one sprawling villa, also reflect an era of change. Nevertheless, Butrint continued to flourish as a port and residential centre as the archaeology of the *domus* found at the Triconch Palace clearly shows.[31]

Change eventually came in the violent form of a massive earthquake.[32] It is most evident in the Roman forum but left its mark on the extra-mural suburb as well. During the excavation of the southern sections of the forum, the impact of an earth-shaking event was revealed in the apparent subsidence of the pavement, which was declined *c*. 2 degrees to the south. The southern section of the pavement, extending away from the bedrock of the acropolis, is constructed over unconsolidated sediments and so a degree of subsidence might be expected. However, the pavement was also found to be overlain by a 0.20-metre-thick deposit of alluvially derived silts, suggestive of a more sudden downward movement of the pavement, the changing levels leading to an inundation of water. The northern sections of the pavement, constructed over a dipping apron of limestone bedrock, effectively allowed the southern portion to hinge downwards as the sediment below gave way. The forum pavement and silts were sealed by destruction layer deposits that represent the widespread spoliation of surrounding buildings, within which the latest ceramics date to the fourth century AD. From exactly this time, part of the sprawling villa at the bridgehead suburb collapsed and a store containing amphorae was sealed with rubble until it was discovered in the Butrint Foundation excavations.[33] As mentioned at the beginning of this chapter, there are textual references to severe earthquakes in the region in the later

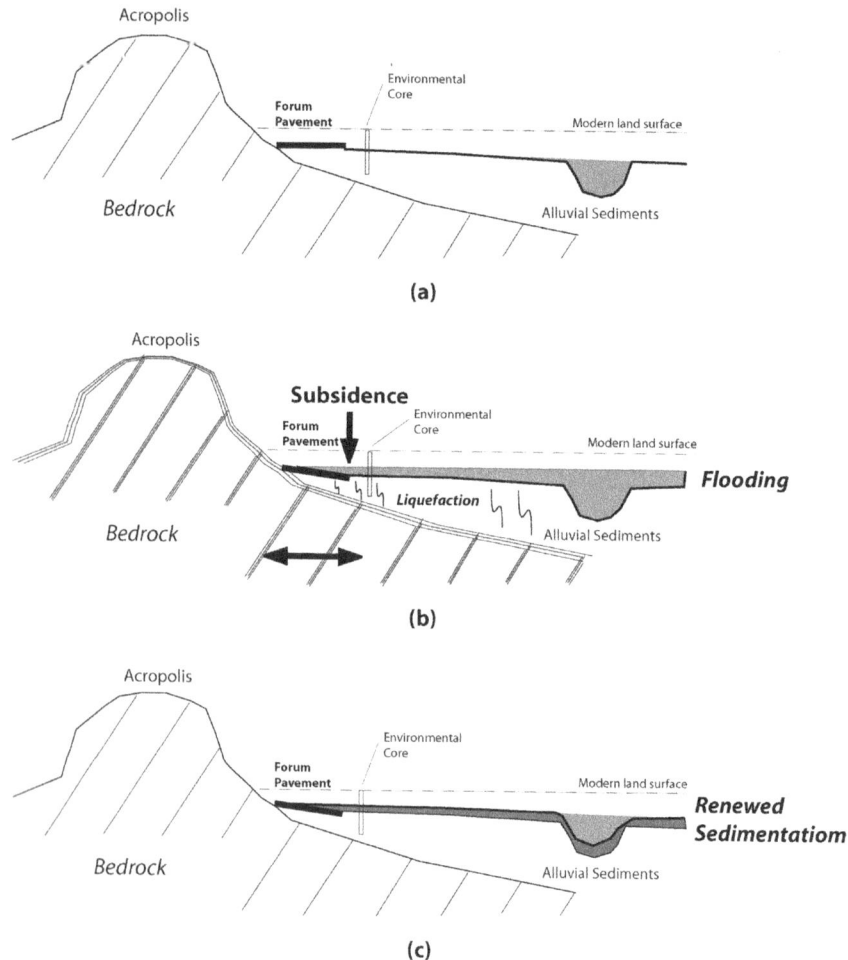

FIGURE 4.12 *A diagram showing the impact of the fourth-century earthquake on the lower town at Butrint.*

fourth century. What is less evident is how these escalated changes, already underway at Butrint, set the scene for Butrint's Christian apogee.

* * *

Butrint became a true town in Roman times. Caesar's moneyers chose the bull as a symbol for the town, appropriating an earlier Greek past to engineer a new future.[34] This presumably was the bull sacrificed by Helenus in honour of Aeneas, a legend now appropriated by Butrint as it promoted its establishment Roman status. Under Augustus, thanks especially to Virgil, it metaphorically became Troy in miniature – a point on Aeneas' odyssey to

FIGURE 4.13 *Ugolini on the acropolis, spring 1928.*

found Rome. Ugolini, with a reference to Gabriele d'Annunzio's protagonist in the *Città Morta* (1899) – an archaeologist who finds the golden mask of Agamemnon and is changed forever – dreamed as he sat on the acropolis of Mycenae in 1925 of bringing Virgil's legend to life. This was to be an illusion. Instead, as we have seen, Ugolini's excavations gave rise to an entirely different image of Roman authority and ambition. Butrint was neither a Troy nor a modest reflection of Rome itself. Rather, we may now safely conclude, the new civic authorities skilfully took advantage of Butrint's strategic importance just as Nicopolis, the so-called Victory City, did. As such it flourished at the centre of the Mediterranean, experiencing intermittently the economic benefits and travails of the Pax Romana.

5

Early Christian Butrint

If European civilization is built on that of Rome, it now appears obvious that the Rome involved was not that of Augustus, Cicero, the Institutes of Gaius and classical urbanism, but that of Constantine, Augustine, the Justinianic Code, and the Church.

MARK WHITTOW[1]

By the third century AD, this corner of Epirus had been under formal (let alone informal) Roman control for almost 400 years, some centuries longer than the North American colonies survived under British dominion, and far longer than the entire lifespan of the Aztec empire. Empires are dynamic, with continual internal shifts and readjustments inevitably calling forth change within all their constituent elements. A social revolution was underway that soon became inseparable from the new monothetic religion, Christianity. Power lay not simply in monetized exchange, but in social opportunity, wherein began a cycle that resulted in large-scale consumption of commodities and secondary-product production. Both were monetized and market-based. Regionalism was both state catalysed and home-grown. This brand of social opportunism may have been tied to increasing imperial presence and intensified taxation. Change in the political circumstances had an inevitable impact upon the townscape of Butrint. So, for example, while closer geographically to Constantinople after the seismic division of the Roman Empire under the Emperor Constantine, for much of the later fourth and fifth centuries its church looked to Rome. Only slowly did its spiritual axis shift eastwards.

This regionalism and, with it, shifting associations are reflected in the few textual mentions of the town. In the inventory of provinces and cities, drawn up in all probability by Hierocles in AD 527/528, which provides an approximate account of the situation under the Emperor Theodosius II (408–450), *Buthrotos* appears in seventh position of the towns lying in the province of *Palaia Epeiros* (Old Epirus), then subordinated to the metropolis of Nicopolis. The identity of *Zenobius Bostroensis*, whose name occurs in AD 451 in the list of bishops of Epirus, remains disputed. Nevertheless, Butrint was undoubtedly a bishopric of the metropolis of Nicopolis after AD

458. So, at the end of a letter that the metropolitan Bishop Eugenius addressed to the Emperor Leo I, the name of *Stephanus episcopus Buthroti* is the last of the eight bishops mentioned. A little later, in AD 516, Bishop Matthew of Butrint describes the election of John to the position of metropolitan Bishop of Nicopolis. The Emperor Justinian's chronicler, Procopius, makes no mention of its fortification, unlike Phoenicê where, apparently, the walls were refurbished in the sixth century. Nor does Butrint feature in any account associated with the Slavic attacks in the western Balkans in AD 586–7.[2]

Butrint in Late Antiquity is a fascinating paradox. Clearly the town suffered from the rising water table, making occupation of much of the skirt of land beyond the old Hellenistic fortifications uncomfortable in wintertime. Much of the bridgehead suburb too would have been intermittently waterlogged. Nevertheless, the archaeology is spectacularly rich, culminating in what might been seen as an economic apogee of sorts in the early sixth century when, a generation or more after Vandal attacks on the Epirote coastline in *c.* AD 475, new fortifications were erected here and in neighbouring Adriatic Sea cities.

A similar paradox exists in the extraordinary architectural contrasts within the town where a redirection of public patronage is evident. The great monumental buildings of the Hellenistic and early Imperial ages were mostly abandoned, though the bathhouse beside the forum possibly remained in use. In their place, the fifth century was an age of great houses while sixth-century Butrint was, like many towns, to become filled with churches. In place of a forum, it boasted a Great Basilica and an exceptional Baptistery as well as a basilica on the highest point of the acropolis and equally impressive churches on the Vrina Plain and at Diaporit. Around these, a mixture of townhouses was constructed, many being less prepossessing timber dwellings that had more in common with the traditional peasant houses of the lagoon. Surplus wealth, in short, was no longer invested in the sanctuary dedicated to Asclepius and its associated shrines, but to a Christian God. One further contrast needs to be borne in mind too. Butrint became overtly a maritime port, judging from the results of our excavations. Specifically, Butrint fostered active commerce with, first, central and west Mediterranean merchants, then from the first half of the sixth century, with the east Mediterranean. Following this, over one or two generations in the later sixth and early seventh century, after an existence spanning a millennium, the town all but disappeared.

Let us take in a few snapshots of this town over these two extraordinary centuries.

Fifth-century Grand Houses

Butrint in the fifth century was essentially a town of fine houses. Churches and other monuments belong to the following century. The most extensive

FIGURE 5.1 *Reconstruction of the Roman houses and later Triconch Palace.*

remains of a townhouse exist at the Triconch Palace.³ But standing parts of other houses intermixed with poorly made dwellings are dotted around the lower part of the town and probably existed on the acropolis too. Between the Tower Gate and the former forum area, several houses have been identified. The Baptistery occupies part of the bathhouse of a large residence. Close to it, the *nymphaeum* of a major townhouse still stands well-preserved. Next to this, the so-called Gymnasium, a *macellum* in earlier times, was possibly transformed at this time into a townhouse, with mosaic pavements in its rear rooms. Closer to the Vivari Channel lie a line of major dwellings, commencing with a well-preserved bathhouse near the present entrance to Butrint and traces of a townhouse beneath the western defences. Indeed, the remains of several buildings can be seen incorporated into the sixth-century fortifications, culminating at the point where the wall dog-legs out into the channel, circumventing the so-called Merchant's House and the Triconch Palace. Later Roman Butrint, in short, was packed with buildings, within which were islands of ruins belonging to an earlier age. These houses were an expression of the conspicuous consumption to be found from the later fourth century AD throughout the Empire. As Kim Bowes colourfully writes, 'Like houses from Elvis' Graceland to Tony Soprano's suburban mansion, late Roman houses were tiny pieces of science fiction, calling into being an alternate reality for their owners. Such houses did not mirror shared social experience – they sought to change it'.⁴

The Triconch Palace and the Vrina Plain

Around AD 400 the orientation of the *domus* was radically altered by the addition of the western entrance and peristyle, with a large drain from the peristyle cutting across the mosaic of the grand channel-side corridor.⁵ The new entrance vestibule with its colonnaded screens was intended as the principal public entrance into the building, giving access to the new peristyle with its mosaic paved portico. It may have been the destruction caused by a major earthquake that persuaded the owner of the building to radically rethink the design of the house. The deliberate raising of the floor in the western entrance must have been the result of necessity. The new entrance is quite unusual in the degree of elaboration employed within it. A mosaic inscription immediately in front of the eastern tribelon was clearly intended to be read as one approached from the west, announcing the name of the house owner to visitors. The inscription, although very fragmentary, has been transcribed as [. . .]ΑΜΑΡΙωΙωΛΑΝ[.] [.]ΟΙΜ[. . .] and is interpreted as a name or title ending in]*arius* and the rank *to lamprotato* (*clarissimus*), someone of senatorial rank, thereby announcing the owner's name and status to a visitor.⁶

The interior of the *domus* beyond the western entrance is difficult to reconstruct. The peristyle itself was relatively modest in scale, its dimensions

FIGURE 5.2 *A view of the Triconch Palace under excavation, 2002.*

presumably restricted by the size of the actual property and the size of the courtyard that preceded it. It measured slightly over 15 metres across from the outer walls of the porticoes, and is comparable in scale to numerous other examples of peristyles from medium-sized houses across the empire. While its porticos were paved with quite elaborate geometric mosaics, the courtyard itself was paved with simple and irregularly cut limestone slabs. A drain now truncated the mosaic in the long gallery, a clear indication that the gallery was redundant as a public space by this time. A new bathhouse was erected between the house and the Vivari Channel, an example perhaps of the owner of the *domus* being able to expand his property onto adjacent land.

Very shortly after the peristyle and the western entrance were created, they were superseded by the colossal expansion to create the Triconch Palace.[7] This saw the peristyle tripled in size and the whole structure extended to the east with the addition of the triconch triclinium. In addition, the location of the principal entrance was changed again with the blocking of the western entrance and the creation of new entrances to the north and south, which gave access to the eastern portico of the expanded peristyle. The building was also extended to the north with the construction of a whole new northern wing, made necessary by the construction of the north portico of the enlarged peristyle on the footprint of the earlier north wing. The time period that elapsed between the construction of the smaller peristyle and western entrance and their replacement is difficult to establish but was probably not more than twenty years and may have been considerably less.

The most striking feature of the new building is its sheer scale. The addition of the new eastern wing, co-opting adjacent land, seems to have become an increasingly common phenomenon in the Late Antique town.

The triconch triclinium and its north and south entrances are significantly different from the rest of the complex in that they are all of one unified construction, and do not incorporate any sections of earlier buildings. It is clear that this new eastern wing and the enlarged peristyle were conceived as a single project. The new peristyle was almost three times the size of the peristyle of the previous phase with internal measurements of 23 × 13 metres excluding the porticoes. The southern, eastern and western stylobates of the peristyle were built using substantial faced limestone blocks, which were presumably *spolia*, deriving possibly from a disused public building almost certainly in the (now disused) forum. That the owner of the *domus* was able to expand the building dramatically, and at the same time was able to utilize materials from monumental structures elsewhere, sheds light on the fundamental changes taking place in this period.

The reorganization of the entrances to the complex signalled new intentions. The recently made western entrance with its inscription announcing the owner's name became redundant and was blocked. This was presumably possible because the blocking of the street to the east of the building made it feasible to create a grand approach to the house from the centre of the town to the north. New northern and southern entrances also allowed the triconch triclinium to function in the same way as the earlier apsidal reception room had done in the earlier phase, in that it could be easily reached by visitors who would be granted a view across the peristyle without being able to venture further into the house. This could suggest that the triconch served as an audience chamber as well as a triclinium, or indeed suggests that the triconch can be seen as an example of a grand dining room. Such dining rooms were often easily accessed from the street and formed the backdrop for very public dining in which wealth could be demonstrated to clients and peers.

The entrance to the south was a particularly impressive double-apsed structure of a type well known from Late Antique palaces and houses, notably the Palace of Lausos in Constantinople and the Palace of Galerius in Thessalonika. Those passing through it would enter directly into the peristyle, and in many cases would presumably proceed directly to the triclinium. This entrance was reached via one or two small courtyards to the south, which are structurally later than the apsidal vestibule, but which were probably part of the same overall design. It is likely that one of these courtyards led to a small jetty or quay on the Vivari Channel, enabling visitors (and the owners) to arrive directly by boat, although the relationship between the courtyards and the channel was to be obscured by the subsequent construction of the (sixth-century) town wall. This close relationship with the waterfront recalls that of earlier *villae maritimae*.

The focal point of the new building was the triconch triclinium. Triconch reception rooms became increasingly common in the later empire, reflecting the need for rooms suitable for hosting the elaborate dinner parties that formed an important element within the patronage networks of the age. Certain fittings speak to the new era of upwardly mobile affluence and a prominent display of the new religion, Christianity. Most obviously the Chi-rho monograms set into the carved stone lunettes of the windows of the triconch triclinium elegantly display an overt spiritual affiliation.

Triclinia of the early empire were rectangular rooms (as we saw at Diaporit in Chapter 4), with dining couches placed along three walls, an arrangement that is often reflected in the mosaic pavements of these rooms where the areas for the couches are left blank, resulting in the decorative panels forming a characteristic T-shape. Dining habits changed quite significantly, however, with the adoption of a semi-circular arrangement of dining couches, or *stibadia*, on which the diners would lie in a radiating pattern with their heads towards the centre. Depictions of this process invariably (as might be expected) show diners supporting themselves on their left arms, leaving their right hands free for eating and drinking. Food would be placed on a small semi-circular central table or sigma. The most important guest would be positioned at the front left (to the viewer facing the apse) as can be seen in Late Antique representations of the Last Supper that show Christ in this position.

The size of the Triconch Palace apses suggests that seven diners could have been accommodated with reasonable comfort in each, giving a hypothetical total of twenty-one dinner guests. The scale of the Butrint triconch is on a par with the great triconch dining rooms. Its apses are slightly smaller than those of the Palace of Theoderic at Ravenna where the apses are around 7.5 metres in width. They are comparable in width to those of the triconch at Piazza Armerina (Sicily), although the apses at the latter are significantly deeper than those at Butrint.

A mirror image of the Triconch Palace was erected in the bridgehead suburb.[8] The third- to fourth-century *domus* here had suffered badly in an earthquake, but its owners were nothing if not resilient. The main entrance of this Vrina Plain villa, as far as we can tell, faced the deep inlet that flows from the Vivari Channel, indicating that its architectural presence aimed above all to impress water-borne visitors rather than those approaching the town by the inland road. The elements of the house exposed in the excavations certainly conveyed the alternative reality of its owners. By the later fourth century, the main entrance from the deep inlet was almost certainly aggrandized by two octagonal towers (only one of which was excavated), either side of a wide main door, which must have been visible from the Straits

FIGURE 5.3 *A window frame from the Triconch Palace.*

of Corfu. Almost immediate accessibility to the main audience chamber – presumably the triclinium – was essential. This large apsidal triclinium lay parallel to the channel (on an east–west axis), creating a similar sense of grandiosity, comparable with the entrance. The first courtyard dominated by a large fountain was a further element of architectural display, intended to re-state the social aspirations of its owner. Beyond this, the arrangement of the complex, being almost certainly a coalescing of earlier structures, is less clear. As a property, though, at its zenith it may have extended as far east along the shore as the terminus of the road at the bridge.

Such was the ambition of those who outlived the earthquake of the later fourth century. In the case of the Triconch Palace it was to be short-lived. In this instance, unlike the Vrina Plain villa, construction of the triconch and the refurbishment of the earlier complex were apparently abandoned when they were close to completion about AD 420. Although the palatial buildings were roofed, there is no evidence of wall decoration or paving, apart from rough mortar floors lain over the mosaics of the earlier phase. Rough beaten earth surfaces were also found where the earlier mosaics had been removed, while the flagstone courtyard of the earlier *domus* remained as a rather incongruous island in the new and much larger courtyard, which was otherwise unpaved.

What brought about this calamitous decision to cease building operations and give the area over to a collection of smaller, less impressive dwellings? The likeliest answer is that the rising water table caught the owner and his architects off guard. There is no doubt that the aim was to raise the floors of the new palace well above the levels of those of the *domus*. It was to no avail, as a labyrinth of well-appointed drains illustrate.

Immediately following the abandonment of the grandiose construction scheme, the shell of the building was used for other purposes, both domestic and industrial. Most of the new buildings were combinations of timber and drystone or clay-bonded walling. None lasted more than a generation before being reconstructed. Were these seasonal occupants, or simply town-dwellers who coped with Butrint's rising water? The answer unfortunately eluded us in the excavations.

From a fifth-century deposit associated with these changing circumstances comes a small, lathe-turned ivory, probably an elaborate finial from a deluxe domestic article. Initially, it was interpreted as a piece of a chess set. This interpretation now seems unlikely. Chess did not reach the West until the ninth or tenth centuries. Nonetheless, two spirally-fluted bone gaming pieces were found in a late fifth-/early sixth-century layer in the westernmost of the little rooms off the southern gallery, testifying to the games played by probably seasonal occupants in the final phases of use of the abandoned house.

During the fifth and sixth centuries, before and, tellingly, after the town wall was built alongside the Vivari Channel, many small buildings occupied the footprint of the Triconch Palace. These appear to have been fishermen's and metalworkers' dwellings. Their archaeology, though, is intriguing. We might be forgiven for assuming from the simple dwellings that a crushing poverty had overtaken Butrint. The huge quantities of finds well dated by numerous coins leads us to conclude otherwise. Large amounts of imported amphorae and fine tableware distinguish the assemblage of finds, complemented by quality glassware. The *mentalité* of these people is tangentially reflected in this rubbish and the living conditions. Christian imagery had been an intricate element of the opulent house from the later fourth century onwards. Passive movables also had Christian imagery.

FIGURE 5.4 *A copper tag (obverse and reverse views) with an apotropaic motif from the Triconch Palace.*

Ceramic lamps decorated with Christian symbols are the most obvious examples of the new era. Other minor objects are equally intriguing. The art historian, John Mitchell, has drawn attention to a small arsenal of apotropaic devices employed by the owners of successive post-built artisanal dwellings to protect them, their households and their property. Included in this arsenal were amulets in the form of rings, pendants and buckles. The figures on these small objects made references to a sub-lunar world abounding with gods, spirits, good and bad, and with angels and demons, which mediated between the earth and the superior spheres likely to intervene in everyday lives. By the sixth century these items materially expressed the new ethos of the age. Will Bowden, in his report on the Triconch Palace faunal assemblages, stresses the presence of cockerels – birds that appear prominently as talismanic creatures in the Baptistery mosaic pavement but otherwise had limited value as food (see below).[9]

An Age of Managerial Bishops

Ugolini was fascinated by Butrint's palaeochristian monuments. In an illuminating essay he showed how the Church sustained strong connections with Rome, even though it lay within the eastern Roman Empire and should have subsumed itself to Constantinople.[10] The list of churches and shrines of this era found by the Italian Archaeological Mission is significant. Perhaps encouraged by the excavation of the Baptistery, Ugolini studied the Great Basilica, excavated the acropolis basilica, examined the small church erected within the remains of the second-century *nymphaeum* in the so-called 'Gymnasium' complex as well as the Christianization of the fountain of Junia Rufina by the Lion Gate. Indeed, Butrint has all the characteristics of a sanctuary town – a place now thoroughly dominated by the Church as opposed to a cult prizing the healing powers of the spring water. Yet, in amongst the sacred places are significant secular buildings. The most important of these is a massive sixth-century building, about 12 × 12 metres,

FIGURE 5.5 *A view of the Great Basilica and Lake Butrint beyond.*

occupying the north-east corner of the old Roman forum. Set within its own walled enclosure, it appears to date to the earlier sixth century. The building was completely overhauled in the last quarter of the sixth century, when it was raised on great timbers presumably to gain a more conspicuous profile. This enigmatic building looks to be a praetorium, a governor's palace that privileged defence above display.[11] It is strange, however, that this midslope location was selected as opposed to, for example, the acropolis. Its position was intended to be seen, when approaching from the east, above the Baptistery and on the same level as the Great Basilica. No other major secular building survives from sixth-century Butrint. The two-storey house in the dog-leg of the town wall next to the Triconch Palace was a one-up, one-down dwelling made with rubble walls. A similar, architecturally underwhelming building was the small house beside the Baptistery with walls made of puddled clay and rubble. Display in architecture was now the remit of the Church.

The Sixth-century Defences

Butrint had not been fortified with walls since the late Hellenistic period. The architects of the Roman colony in the Augustan age removed most of the channel-side defences. Five hundred years later fortifications were once more deemed necessary. The Late Roman defences re-defined Butrint. Just as the Hellenistic fortifications created a configuration for the town, so the new walls reaffirmed the authority of Romanitas for its citizens. The Butrint Foundation excavations in the Triconch Palace area indicate that the wall was erected in the early sixth century, probably under the Emperor Anastasius (491–518), or very soon afterwards.[12] The new circuit added a formidable towered western line down to the Vivari Channel. In front of it was located a low outer wall, a *proteichisma*, modelled upon the multiple walls at Constantinople and similar to one recorded on the landward side at *Onchesmos* (Saranda). The *proteichisma* was almost certainly an act of display designed to impress those approaching from the Straits of Corfu or from the landward side down the Ksamil peninsula.

The new town wall was, nevertheless, makeshift in appearance, constructed in sections, probably reflecting work-gangs and working periods, and incorporated existing buildings. In many places reused Hellenistic blocks are conspicuous in its fabric. The gates are intriguing. A new gate – the first iteration of the Water Gate – was made by the road bridge, close to the Great Basilica. Other gates within the older wall-circuit (West Gate, North Gate, Lion Gate and Lake Gate) were also refurbished, as they were to be in Medieval times. Compared to other Late Antique circuits, such as at the great cities of Nicopolis and Dyrrhachium (Durrës), the walls of Butrint are plainly the work of expedience, rather than of architects.

The Great Basilica

The principal Late Antique church is the so-called Great Basilica adjacent to the Tower Gate.[13] The church was erected on the site of an earlier Roman cistern, the *castellum divisorum* of the aqueduct. The most thorough study of the building is by the Albanian architectural historian, Aleksandër Meksi, who cleared the aisles and nave revealing the flagstone pavement and sections of an early sixth-century mosaic.

The Late Antique church was a three-aisled basilica with a tripartite transept and a pentagonal apse, which was hemispherical on its interior face. From the outer face of the façade wall to the exterior of the apse it measures 31.70 metres, with the transept measuring 23.70 metres across. The nave and aisles have a combined width of 18.20 metres. To the east, in the confined space in front of the Hellenistic town wall, lay a small atrium. The floor levels of the church are around 2 metres above the level of the second-century and earlier road to the south, suggesting that the ground level had risen considerably by the sixth century, when the basilica was built.

The apse, transept, part of the façade and the side walls survive from the original Early Christian building while the clerestory level, slab pavement, and the piers that divide the aisles date from a later reconstruction (see Chapter 6). In their original form, the aisles were probably divided from the nave by colonnades mounted on stylobates together with the closure screens that were characteristic of Epirote and Greek basilicas. The bays of the transept were divided from one another with masonry piers, creating the classic tripartite transept. Little evidence of the colonnades survives, with the exception of the column bases that divide the lateral aisles from the bays of the transept. A number of Corinthian capitals have been found in the vicinity, together with further capitals embedded in the later floor and a possible capital re-used within one of the later piers. The columns were surmounted by arches constructed using a double thickness of tiles. The later Medieval arcades only used single tiles as voussoirs and consequently the join between the two phases is clearly visible. Also of interest is a foundation of mortared limestone rubble within the centre of the nave, which may represent the remains of an axially positioned ambo.

The apse was pentagonal with the axial wall probably dominated by a five-lobed window that extended onto the angled walls on either side. The apse was semi-circular on the interior with the sanctuary slightly raised above the floor level of the church.

Areas of the walls were decorated with the incised circles and interlocking triangles characteristic of masonry of this period. Within the church there are fragmentary remains of a mosaic pavement featuring the trailing ivy tendrils and scrolling *guilloche* also found in the Baptistery (see below) – a characteristic of Nicopolis mosaicists. The Great Basilica, then, is broadly contemporary with the Baptistery, approximately dated to the second quarter of the sixth century through comparison with the pavement of Basilica A at Nicopolis.

The Baptistery

The Baptistery lay on the south-east side of the lower town, some distance from the Great Basilica. To its north-west lies a small Medieval church with an associated belltower (see Chapter 6). Beyond it is a partially excavated bathhouse. The Baptistery remains more or less in the condition in which Ugolini found it, although his team re-erected the granite columns and repaired the mosaic.

Excavation of the Baptistery began in Ugolini's first season at Butrint in May 1928. The building lay in dense undergrowth, only the north-east wall visible above ground level. Ugolini's team almost immediately found the font. Then, at a depth of *c.* 1.20 metres the mosaic was discovered, whereupon '*nella gioia della scoperta*', a further trench was excavated, following the circular wall. After the excavation, the mosaic was covered in sand. Problems were soon encountered, and the mosaic was damaged by both visitors and the winter of 1928–9, prior to restoration in 1930 by the Vettraino brothers of Rome.

In 1974 and again in 1982 the Albanian Institute of Archaeology excavated around the building to make sense of its complex history. The Butrint Foundation also launched its archaeological programme here, discovering the monument's long, complex history. The Baptistery itself was built within the pre-existing bathhouse of a major townhouse. This townhouse, like the sequence at the nearby Triconch Palace, almost certainly pre-dates the fourth century and was frequently re-built.[14]

In the early sixth century, the bathhouse was re-shaped as a circular Baptistery with a square façade surmounted by a circular cupola. Its size places it firmly in the range of western baptisteries such as those of Milan and Ravenna, and in particular the southern Italian baptisteries, at S. Maria Maggiore at Nocera near Salerno, S. Giovanni a Canosa, and S. Giusto (both in Apulia). The shape of the Butrint Baptistery is less obviously paralleled by the Italian baptisteries, many of which use an octagonal plan, although circular baptisteries are known, as well as circular tombs and mausolea such as S. Costanza in Rome. At Butrint, the circular design was visible only from the interior.

The external aspect of the Baptistery belonged to the tradition of funerary architecture, which is closely associated with the architecture of baptism, and the square external plan and façade at Butrint should be seen as a deliberate concept as well as an architectural expedient. The iconography of baptism is closely identified with that of death and resurrection, the baptismal ceremony itself taking place on the eve of the resurrection. This is further emphasized by the persistent appearance of the number eight (for example, the two rings of eight columns at Butrint). Early Christian representations of the Holy Sepulchre indicate that the tomb of Christ was often shown as a square structure surmounted by a cupola. This image is reflected in the external appearance of the Baptistery, using an architectural form which, in the eastern Empire, remained in common for both funerary and baptismal architecture. The quatrefoil font here is also typical of Syria and Palestine, while circular or octagonal forms were more generally adopted in the West.

The apparently autonomous position of the Baptistery in relation to the Great Basilica is not unusual. Parallels occur in Italy in particular, at Rome, Milan, and Ravenna, where baptisteries were large, centralized structures, independent of both the cathedral church and the bishop's quarters. The situation of the Baptistery at Butrint recalls that of the baptisteries of Italy rather than that of its other neighbours, for example in Dalmatia and Greece, where baptisteries were usually smaller structures attached directly to the basilica, often to the north.

The materials used in the Baptistery reflect changes elsewhere in the town. Sixteen granite columns and bases taken from the (Augustan) Roman forum were deployed to support the Baptistery roof. Like his neighbour, Bishop Jovianus of Kerkyra, it seems that the Bishop of Butrint was able to demolish the 'temples of the Greeks' for church construction.

The Christian associations of the Baptistery continued into the Middle Ages, although it appears not to have been used after the early seventh century. Hence, by the eleventh century, the Baptistery area was the focus for a small cemetery. Graves were inserted into the ruins of the building which continued to be recognized as a cult structure. Recognizing its earlier significance, a small thirteenth-century church with a later belltower was erected close by (see Chapter 6).[15]

The Baptistery Mosaic

The great baptisteries of the Mediterranean are among the most splendid ecclesiastical structures from Late Antiquity. The vault and wall mosaics in the two baptisteries in Ravenna show that their interiors could be sumptuously ornate. Some of these must have had correspondingly magnificent pavements; one that survives is the fine marble floor in black-and-white *opus sectile* in St. Ambrose's baptistery in Milan. Butrint is remarkable as it has a complete pavement in polychrome mosaic, preserved almost in its entirety, and executed in one campaign, in the second quarter of the sixth century.

The overall design of the floor consists of seven circling bands, which revolve around an elegant marble-revetted cruciform font at the centre. The first and fifth bands carry a continuous ivy scroll, the second and the fourth chains of interlocked medallions inhabited with all manner of creatures,

FIGURE 5.6 *The Baptistery with its sixth-century mosaic pavement.*

terrestrial quadrupeds, birds and fish, and plants with bright red blossoms, the third and the sixth have bold fascias of ring-interlace, and the seventh, innermost, ring, framing the font, consists of a circling carpet of interlocking medallions containing kaleidoscopic chequerboard lozenges. The bands are interrupted by two emphatic emblematic compositions lying on the main axis between the entrance and the font. Here the attention of the visitor crossing the threshold of the main entrance is held by two large peacocks in a vine which issues from a great vase and two deer drinking from a fountain.

The design is composed of elements widely deployed by mosaicists active in the western Balkans in the fifth and sixth centuries, carefully selected and combined to create a coherent and complex scheme. On the one hand, it is concerned with the water of baptism; on the other, it visually defines and articulates the various parts of the building in terms of their function and use.

There is no internal evidence for determining an accurate date for the Baptistery and its pavement. A similar repertory of motifs can be seen in the pavements surviving in the basilica of Palaiopolis on Corfu. Most scholars favour that it was the work of craftsmen from Nicopolis, where several fine closely related mosaics from this period can still be seen in the city's basilicas.

A second mosaic surface covers the floor of the adjoining trapezoidal hall to the north-west. In this case the floor is framed by a running ivy scroll. This is a geometrical design except for the south-east panel, which is framed by a sequence of pairs of peacocks flanking vases. Aleksandër Meksi proposed that this pavement was later than the one in the adjacent baptistery.

The Iconography of the Pavement

The principal themes of the mosaic are water: the water of baptism, and the water of life and the salvation that it brings to the faithful. The linked subjects of water and salvation are further associated with the sacramental blood of Christ and with the wine of the Eucharist.[16]

The theme of awakening to the dawn of a new life is announced to anyone entering, or rather leaving, by the main south-west door. Looking down, just over the threshold, the baptizand would see in the second circling band two affronted cocks, birds that proclaim the coming of day and symbolize rebirth and resurrection.

The first panel is dominated by a great vase, a *kantharos*, a large two-handled vessel for wine, from which issue two vine stems bearing large clusters of grapes. Two large peacocks and two smaller birds flank the vessel and seem intent on devouring the fruit. The vine – which in Scripture represents God's people, Israel (Psalm 80.8) – can refer to Christ, and to his followers, and by extension the Church (John 15.1–7). The eucharistic associations of the vessel and the grape-laden vine are unmistakeable. The accompanying peacocks establish a clear paradisiacal setting and context, with implications of rebirth and everlasting life. The association of the water of baptism with the blood of Christ and the wine of the Eucharist was commonplace. The eucharistic reference inherent in compositions of this kind, in which peacocks, deer and other creatures flank a vase with a vine, is also apparent in a number of other pavements of the period, for example, at Heraklea Lynkestis in North Macedonia.

Next lies the cruciform font; beyond this in the wall of the building is the arched front of a fountain which, together with the font, constitutes the principal focus of the Baptistery. This is difficult to interpret, but it may have been constructed over an earlier fountain, set into the apse of an earlier building that stood on the site. Perhaps, like the Asclepieion, it was an ancient source of water with healing powers, subsequently transformed in a new Christian context. A similar fountain is associated with the baptistery of the Lechaion Basilica at Corinth.

The remainder of the pavement is not so easy to interpret. Most striking are the beasts, birds and fish in the two medallion-chains. Animals of all kinds became one of the most common subjects on mosaic pavements in the later fifth and sixth centuries throughout the central and eastern

Mediterranean. The birds and the fish in the medallions are more obviously associated with the themes surrounding baptism than are the motley menagerie of terrestrial quadrupeds. The vast majority of the birds are either associated with Paradise (peacocks and other ornamental fowl with brilliant plumage), or with water (aquatic birds, like ducks, geese, ibises, herons and swans, occasionally surrounded by their young). As we have seen, cockerels are also present. In general terms, in early Christian texts and imagery, birds can embody ideas of moral and spiritual ascent, representing apostles, martyrs, saints, the disembodied souls of the faithful. Waders and webbed-footed water-birds together with fish are often deployed to represent the ocean that surrounds the earth; and the waters of the ocean were commonly associated by early Christian writers with the regenerating power of baptism. The fish on the pavement are strangely few in number and are curiously concentrated in one area. The figure of the fish was identified with Christ as early as the second century and it was associated with baptism at least since the late second century when Tertullian in his treatise on baptism writes 'we little fish, in accordance with our *ichthys* Jesus Christ, are born in water, and are not saved in any other manner than by remaining in the water' (ch. 1). Salvation through water may also be expressed in the numerous plants with brilliant red blossoms. These may be water-plants, perhaps with paradisiacal associations.

The hierarchical ordering of space within the Baptistery is not clear. The strongest sacramental and doctrinal references occur in the two brilliant panels with the peacocks flanking the *kantharos* and the deer at the fountain lying between the main entrance and the font. This would have met the eyes of neophytes as they entered. It is in this sector, too, that the creatures with the strongest baptismal associations, the birds and the fish, are grouped, while in the inner medallion-chain the terrestrial quadrupeds are largely confined to the area beyond the font. The brilliantly coloured sequence of exotic beasts in the inner chain in this far quadrant also catch our eye. These might signify the ignorant, yet to be converted, while the birds and fish together with the lonely deer and ass flanking the south-western axial panel may represent the faithful who, like the processing baptizands, follow the will of God.

The design of the pavement in seven circling bands around the central font invites a symbolic reading. Eight is the number of the final age of Christian history, the number of salvation and everlasting life. St Ambrose, in a famous passage referring to the octagonal baptistery in Milan, says: 'The eight-niched temple rose up for sacred use, the octagonal font is appropriate for that rite. It was fitting that the baptismal hall should stand to the number eight, by which true salvation returned to mankind'. At Butrint, the artist may have had a similar conceit in mind: seven circles culminating in the font, the gateway to everlasting life, which will dawn after the Final Judgement on the eighth great day.

The Pavement and Ritual Space

Grand in conception, the Baptistery pavement was intended to be the principal scheme of imagery in the building. It is unlikely that the walls would have carried elaborate programmes of figural imagery. The interior was not an open unitary space like those of the two surviving baptisteries at Ravenna. The two concentric rings of columns would have created complex screens effectively fragmenting any view of the outer wall-surfaces. Nothing of the painted embellishment of the building survives, although detached fragments of painted plaster were found in Ugolini's excavations. We shall never know how the walls of the building were decorated, but it is likely that they were painted below in imitation of a complex revetment in polished polychrome marble, and above possibly with a purely ornamental scheme. The mosaic pavement must have struck the citizens of Butrint as it strikes the modern visitor, as a colourful composition of wonderful variety and curious complexity – the principal visual focus of one of the most impressive interior spaces in the region.

The mosaic was designed not only to provide an appropriate setting for the rite of baptism, but also to articulate the liturgical functioning of the space. The two compositions immediately in front of the main door establish the principal axis within the building, a line that centres on the font and culminates in the fountain built into the north-east perimeter wall. However, other axes, routes and areas within the building are defined by similar means.

Polychrome glass tesserae are employed in certain animals in the medallion-chains. These tend to lie on or close to the cardinal axes. The densest cluster of brilliantly coloured birds and beasts is to be found in the north-eastern sector, close to the fountain. These effectively draw the eye of the visitor to this focus. Similarly, a brightly coloured peacock is placed close to the north-western axis, in front of the door which leads into the large adjoining room on this side, with its complex mosaic pavement. This room may have been either the *consignatorium*, the room in which, following the Roman rite, neophytes were anointed and confirmed by the bishop immediately after their baptism, or the *catachumeneum*, the hall in which the bishop instructed candidates before baptism. However, a problem with either interpretation is that one of the two entrances in the hall leads into the Baptistery, from which neophytes were excluded before baptism.

Another strikingly coloured bird, an ibis with brilliant turquoise plumage, lies on the south–east axis, to the right of the font at Butrint. Here, the space defined by the four south-east axial columns in the inner and outer colonnades is marked out by ornamental motifs in the outer medallion chain, which are found in no other part of the pavement. These are two variations on a kaleidoscopic chequerboard lozenge with concave sides. The three medallions in the inner ring in this same southern sector are framed by spandrels that all contain triangular chequerboard cusps of the same design. The central medallion of these three, lying directly on the southern axis, contains a magnificent water-plant with three red blossoms. The bay between the two rings of columns defined by these motifs presumably was designated for some particular function. It may have been the place where the bishop stood during the ceremony, or if confirmation was administered in the Baptistery itself, rather than in the adjoining hall, this may have marked the bishop's throne.

Emphasis is also laid on the north axis, which ran from the font through a now-blocked door into a little ancillary corner room. Possibly here candidates for baptism divested themselves of their garments, before entering the water and then putting on pure white robes – the equivalent of one of the fifth-century lateral chapels at the Lateran Baptistery in Rome, known as *ad S. Johannem ad Vestem*.

The pavement was designed and laid with great care. One of its chief purposes was to define and subtly articulate the interior space of the Baptistery as a theatre in which considerable numbers of participants, the bishop, the clergy, the baptizands and their relatives and sponsors, all had parts to play in an elaborate ceremonial.

The Acropolis Basilica

In his investigations of the high east end of the acropolis, Ugolini discovered a church built into the archaic Greek Temple of Athena. This looked out over the road bridge and Butrint's hinterland to the east. Ugolini dated the basilica to the fourth century on the basis of its mosaic pavement, which includes an arcade with land and marine creatures between the columns. Being similar to the Baptistery and Great Basilica pavements, a date early in the sixth century now seems more likely for this mosaic.[17]

The basilica is composed of nave, aisles, and a narthex that opened into both nave and aisles. It was slightly over 17 metres in length, while the combined width of the nave and aisles is 16.70 metres. A further room, 4.5 metres wide, was attached to the southern lateral wall. This was also accessed from the narthex and may have functioned as a *diaconicon*. A large limestone impost decorated with a Latin cross lies in the nave, while a number of other architectural elements (imposts and a probable Corinthian capital) were built into the later phases of the structure. The masonry of the church is mainly composed of large irregular limestone blocks, which has led to speculation that the building sits on an earlier temple (see Chapter 3).

The relationship between the sixth-century pavement and the surviving structural elements is unknown. Indeed, the building as it stands bears little resemblance to an early Christian church, perhaps because it was modified in the early Middle Ages (see Chapter 6). Instead, the plan indicates that it was intended to be a vaulted structure, with a dome supported by four large piers.

Ugolini's excavations within the building also recovered quantities of architectonic sculpture, of a quality that is inconsistent with the other remains of the building. These include fine lattice-work chancel screens of Proconnesian marble, probably dating to the first half of the sixth century, as well as crutch capitals and window colonnettes. It is likely that these elements (which differ from those found in the Great Basilica) originate from an otherwise unknown church elsewhere within Butrint, and were re-used here.

The Vrina Plain Basilica or Monastery

At some point in the last quarter of the fifth century the sprawling channel-side *domus* on the Vrina Plain was transformed.[18] An aisled church that measured 19.7 metres in length and 16.2 metres wide, with two narthexes, was inserted at right-angles to that of the earlier apsed triclinium on an approximate north–south orientation. Whereas the earlier villa had been entered from the deep inlet to the west, the location of the inner and outer narthex of the church as well as the attached bathhouse on the east side of the church strongly suggests that the complex was now approached from the Vivari Channel instead. Indeed, although the bridge may well have been out of use, the presence of a small, apsed chapel at the shoreline terminus of

FIGURE 5.7 *A detail of the mosaic from the fifth-century Vrina Plain Basilica.*

the road suggests that this was close to the landing point. From here, a visitor approached the ecclesiastical complex, first engaging in the necessary ablutions before entering the church through the narthex. The basilica itself was floored with a polychrome mosaic, while the narthexes were paved with slabs taken from an earlier Roman monumental building. Around the basilica, the many rooms of the *domus* were repurposed, almost certainly to accommodate a small monastic household. With the construction of the new sixth-century defences, this became an extra-mural community.

A fine mosaic pavement was laid in the nave, stretching from the main door to the sanctuary screen. The long rectangular central scheme is framed by three borders: the outermost consists of complex panel designs; the middle border carries a six-stranded *guilloche*; and the inner one a garland of laurel leaves, with fruits and flowers and an entwined ribbon. The central field enclosed by these borders consists of a grid of irregular octagons, forming medallions. The octagons are filled with a variety of motifs including sea creatures, birds, terrestrial beasts, fruits, flowers, trees and abstract motifs. In general terms, the creatures of the earth represented in such contexts can be interpreted as the animals that God created on the fifth and sixth days and then typologically, with the faithful of the new creation, reborn in grace after the incarnation, the birth of Christ.

Superimposed on this scheme are two large tablets carrying inscriptions in Greek. The first of the two inscribed panels, *tabulae ansatae*, was by the wide door leading into the nave. It is an anonymous ex-voto dedicatory inscription of a type that appears in various forms in Christian buildings in the western Balkan provinces in Late Antiquity. The benefactors conceal their names and identities, both as a public demonstration of their humility in accordance with Christ's own injunctions not to flaunt one's person (John 7.18), and presumably in acknowledgement of God's omniscience, which obviates any need of spelling out the names. The unnamed benefactors may well have been the occupants of the similarly anonymous large axial tomb situated in the narthex of the church, opposite the inscription, just outside the doorway.

The second inscribed panel at the mid-point of the nave was clearly the principal dedicatory inscription on the floor, considerably longer, more complex and doubtless more revealing than the brief anonymous ex-voto by the entrance. Like the first inscription, it follows a common formula, in this case attested frequently on silver plates of the period from the eastern Mediterranean, invoking the memory and repose of the donor. The subject of the inscription is a female, the donor of the pavement and probably a principal patron of the basilica. This individual person was in all likelihood a member of the laity, a lady of considerable substance, presumably a representative of one of the most prominent families at Butrint – and perhaps the owner of the *domus* – in the decades around AD 500.

Remains of the foundations of an altar were found directly in front of the apse. The apse itself was entered via a step. Unlike the nave, the apse had a flag-stoned floor. A large robber-cut in the centre indicated that originally something of importance had been placed here, possibly a *confessio* or relic-deposit of some kind, subsequently removed.

It is noticeable that only the nave of the excavated areas of the church was paved with mosaic. This pavement terminated at the inner sides of the flanking piers. The spaces between the piers are laid with sheets of limestone. The narthex has a floor of large, re-used limestone slabs, with carefully laid rectangular slabs laid in the central section, which corresponds to the nave, and smaller irregularly set fragments of stone in the two wings, corresponding to the aisles. The aisles appear to have been surfaced with broken limestone and tiles. The differential use of materials for the floors of the various spaces may indicate that the nave and sanctuary with their mosaic pavement were reserved for the enactment of the liturgy and were principally used by the clergy, while the aisles were for the congregation. In the narthex there is a similar distinction between the regular rectangular slabs of limestone paving laid in the central section in front the central nave door, and the small irregularly set fragments of stone that make up the flanking areas outside the doors, which lead into the two side-aisles.

Nothing survives of the superstructure of the church, but its grand entrance and the opulence of the mosaic pavement plainly suggest that it served a moderately affluent lay congregation. Dating of the Vrina mosaic has been fixed by the discovery of two later fifth-century copper *nummi* found in the fill of a post-hole perforating the pavement in the sanctuary. By the mid- to later sixth century – three generations or so later – the church was abandoned, ending over 600 years of continuous inhabitation of this waterfront close to the bridge.

Beyond Butrint at Diaporit

At Diaporit on the south-east shore of Lake Butrint, the sprawling Roman villa occupied from Hellenistic times until the late second century, was re-occupied in the late fifth century as a pilgrimage centre, perhaps supporting and being maintained by a small monastic community.[19] Quite what lent Diaporit its new status remains a mystery. Was it in any way associated with the healing powers of the water, by now a half-millennium old tradition?

The builders gutted most of the earlier buildings of their materials and then set to constructing a large, three-aisled basilica on a terrace well back from the shore. A rare coin, ironically of the Vandal king Thrasamund, dating to the year AD 493, was found in the floor of the church. Around this, a small community was created. Large tile kilns provided the roofing for the church while the main dwelling was a substantial house with a first floor as well as an associated tower, bathhouse and a small chapel with an apse. The principal feature of this complex was undoubtedly the three tombs in the apse of the main basilica, robbed, judging from a coin left behind, in

FIGURE 5.8 *A reconstruction of the sixth-century pilgrimage centre at Diaporit.*

the thirteenth century. The complex lasted no longer than *c.* AD 550, when, with the downturn in Butrint itself, this pilgrimage centre seems to have been forsaken.

The End of Butrint

The Butrint Foundation's excavations have enabled us to write a new history of the end of the Roman port. Several conclusions can now be stated with confidence. First, notwithstanding the political upheavals and Vandal raids on the Balkans in the fifth century, the town prospered. Its early sixth-century defences betray Butrint's ambitions to maintain control over a much larger surface than, say, was thought possible in the Hellenistic age. Huge amounts of imported wares, principally transport amphorae, tablewares and glasses (as well as perishables that we cannot now recover) affirm this maritime boom. It was still enjoying great wealth in the second quarter of the sixth century – the age of Justinian's reconquests of much of North Africa and Italy – when the Great Basilica and Baptistery, for example were constructed. But no sooner had these great Christian monuments been erected than the savage backlash of the era of the Emperor Justinian was felt. Justinian's ambitious efforts to re-unite the Roman Empire in fact led to a spiral of increased taxation, more civil unrest, diminished trading and, of course, barbarian intervention. This coincided with the so-called dust cloud in AD 536, described by Procopius amongst others, that is believed to have brought devastation to European agriculture and then, more perniciously, the so-called Justinianic Plague after *c.* AD 541.[20] This combination of events inevitably stifled the Mediterranean economy, subjecting a maritime centre like Butrint and its dependencies to inevitable recession or worse. The community at Diaporit felt it first. Then, swiftly within a generation the lower town was falling into disrepair and a previously unheard-of thing was occurring as graves were interred around dwellings. Palaeo-pathological study of the skeletal remains shows that these people had many genetic disorders; the stresses and strains of living had impacted upon their physical well-being. Urban life, it seems, was now taking a new character, in some respects rural, before disappearing altogether here. What is perhaps remarkable is that many of those citizens who had witnessed the erection of the new defences, the Great Basilica and the Baptistery as Butrint

FIGURE 5.9 *A mid-sixth-century infant's grave from the Triconch Palace.*

became a prominent sanctuary town, also witnessed its extraordinary desuetude.[21]

As the menace of the Slavs, perhaps perceived rather than real, struck the region in the 580s, so the community seems to have disappeared.[22] The novelist Lawrence Durrell, mindful of the demise of Roman Corfu, colourfully likened this to an Ice Age settling upon the Roman Empire.[23] By the early seventh century, Butrint amounted to little more than a fishing village close to the sea. Its erstwhile citizens had either left or – through startlingly low fertility rates – declined, more or less mirroring the collapse of trade in ceramics, ending in the mid-century. In the course of 200 years Butrint, with its emphasis upon Christian salvation, witnessed both the zenith and demise of Caesar's legacy.

6

Byzantine and 'Despotic' Butrint

L'histoire de l'Albanie entre le XIe et le XIVe siècle est donc celle d'un échec, d'autant plus irritant que tous les documents dont nous disposons pouvent l'évidence qu'il s'agissait d'un pays riche, bien mieux pourvu en resources naturelles que la Dalmatia ou la Grèce. Mais cette richesse naturelle n'a jamais pu en faire un pays prospère, car c'est toujours l'étranger qui a bénéficié de ces resources.

ALAIN DUCELLIER[1]

The Mediterranean coastline is dotted with deserted ancient ports. Relatively few Roman ports survived into the Middle Ages. The proportion of survivors in the Adriatic Sea, though, is a little higher than, for example, the Peloponnese and Asia Minor. Venice, Ravenna, Otranto, Zadar, Ragusa, Dyrrhachium (modern Durrës), and Corfu, like Butrint, were never completely abandoned. As we shall see, these continued not just as ports, but as metaphorical bridges between East and West – between Byzantium and Latin Christendom. This said, archaeological research over the past twenty-five years has conclusively demonstrated that the scale of the social and economic collapse in the later sixth and seventh centuries created a rupture with the past which should not be underestimated. Knowing this, the revival of the Mediterranean as a medium of commerce in the later ninth and tenth centuries, providing a foundation for a mighty transformation of its regions in the eleventh and twelfth centuries, is all the more remarkable. As of the 1080s, the avaricious ambitions of the Normans and the crusaders belong to this revival. After the fall of Constantinople to the crusaders in 1204, the Balkan port was transformed as a window on the Adriatic by the Epirote Despotate, a secessionist sub-Byzantine state. In the turbulent thirteenth and fourteenth centuries, under the Despots then the Angevins, the town prospered. Increasingly its allegiance lay with far-off courts, rather than either the emergent Albanian or Ottoman communities. When Constantinople fell to the Turks in 1453, Butrint's fate lay in the hands of Venice, which by the later fifteenth century was locked in a seemingly interminable struggle with the Ottomans for the mastery of the Mediterranean.

A Short History

Was Butrint overrun by Slavs, as they spread out southwards from central Europe? A broken radiate brooch and a few sherds of the distinctive, coarse wavy-lined pots from the Butrint Foundation excavations, and type fossils associated with the migrants, provide no real answer. It seems very unlikely. Down the coast at *Euroia* (Glyky), though, the sixth-century bishop apparently fled the Slavs and sought refuge at Kassiope, close to Butrint in north Corfu.[2]

Nevertheless, Slavic influence can be detected hereabouts. Butrint lies in the region known in the thirteenth century as *Bagenetia* or *Vagenetia*, a term that can be traced back to the Slavic tribe known as the Baiunetai. The names *Vagenetia*, *Viyanite*, and *Viyantije* survived until the Turkish period, when in the sixteenth century the name Delvina (now the small town between Saranda and Gjirokastra) became commonly used instead. The so-called *Partitio Romaniae*, the document of 1204 describing the division of the Byzantine Empire, compiled on the basis of Byzantine tax registers, records the *Chartularaton de Bagenetia*. Another term used for Epirus in relation to Corfu was *Starea*, 'the mainland' and *Albania*.

A miscellany of casual references over the following centuries illustrate that other geo-political factors impacted upon the region. Butrint owed its primary allegiance to Byzantium. As ever, though, it was a Balkan springboard to Italy. In the so-called *Notitia of the Iconoclasts*, compiled after AD 754, Butrint is listed as the fourth and penultimate city of Old Epirus, subject to the metropolitan see of Nicopolis. The transmitted form of *Bythipotu* can presumably be attributed to a mistaken reading of the original Latin document. In the late ninth century (880–4), St Elias the Younger and his pupil and companion Daniel were accused of being *Hagarenes* (foreigners) and spies and imprisoned at Butrint (*polis epineios*) by a man whose 'rank is lower than that of the *stratelates*'. In 904 the relics of St Elias, who had died in Thessalonika, were brought to Butrint via *Thessalia*, *Hellas* and *Thesprotia*, to be taken from there by ship to Calabria (*Saline*).

The inventories of bishoprics from the tenth to twelfth centuries identify the Bishop of Butrint as a suffragan of the metropolitan bishopric of Naupaktos, the ecclesiastical province which took the name of the old provincial capital of Nicopolis in southern Epirus. Having subjugated the Bulgarian empire of Samuel in 1014, the Byzantine Emperor Basil II transformed the patriarchate of Ohrid (now in western Macedonia) into an independent archbishopric (*archiepiskopos Achridon kai pases Boulgarias*). In 1020, after a request by the Archbishop John, the newly founded archbishopric took over the areas of the metropolises of Naupaktos, Dyrrhachium (Durrës), Thessalonika and Larisa, which had previously belonged to Samuel's empire. Hence, Butrint, together with Himara, Adrianopolis, Bela, Ioannina, Kozyle and Rogoi, now became part of the archbishopric of Ohrid, leaving only the areas to the south of the Ambracian Gulf remaining with the metropolitan bishopric of Naupaktos. The bishops of Butrint and Himara, though, were only permitted twelve clerics and twelve *paroikoi*, indicating their comparative insignificance.

Late in the eleventh century, Butrint suddenly found itself at the centre of a major political storm between the Normans who had captured much of southern Italy and the renascent Byzantine Empire under the Emperor Alexius I. In May 1081 the Normans under Robert Guiscard conquered the town and secured it together with Corfu as a base against the Byzantine Empire. No mention is made of either a siege or of a battle. Guiscard had come by ship from *Aulon* (modern Vlora) to *Bothrenton*, where he met up with his equally formidable son, Bohemund. The Norman chronicler William of Apulia describes how, upon his disembarkation, Guiscard faced a mixed contingent of troops of diverse provinces under Basileios Mesopotamites. Perhaps these were local troops unknown to the most celebrated chronicler of this conflict, Anna Comnena, Alexius I's daughter. In either March 1083 or the spring of 1084, the two Normans returned to Italy. In 1084 Guiscard renewed the campaign against Byzantium and, once again, Butrint was occupied. The following year, though, the Byzantines, now allied to the Venetians, defeated Guiscard in a celebrated sea battle close to Butrint. Shortly afterwards in July 1085, with the sudden death of Guiscard on Kefalonia, the Normans lost all their possessions in the region.

An intriguing appendix to the turbulent Norman saga connects Butrint to the crusaders. The town is mentioned in the twelfth-century epic, the *Song of Roland*, where the town of Podandos in the Cappadocian–Cilician borderland is rendered, apparently under the influence of Butrint, as *Butentrot, Butintros* (*Butrentot, Butrintos, Boteroz, Butancor, Bonne terre, Val-Potenrot, Botzeroit*). Could it be a confused reference made by Bohemond's son Tancred who, while participating in the First Crusade in 1097, came to Cilicia through the *vallis de Botrenthrot*?

As the ebb and flow of crusading armies and the corresponding numbers of pilgrims bound for the Holy Land became more constant, so the town is mentioned more frequently. In the mid-twelfth century, the Arab geographer al-Idrisi describes *Butrinto* as a small and well-populated town with a market. The Arab account contrasts with the laconic mention in the chronicle of Benedict of Peterborough (actually written by Roger of Howden). Benedict claims the passing crusaders were interested in the legend that the abandoned castle of *Butentrost* or *Butrinto* was the birthplace of Judas Iscariot. As we shall see, whether the market was flourishing at the same time that the castle was deserted following the departure of the Normans, is now a puzzling problem.

Butrint felt the aftershock of the Fourth Crusade, which resulted in the Frankish conquest of Constantinople. Two and a half centuries of intense unrest were unleashed on the Balkans as a result, culminating in the Ottoman conquest of the region after the fall of Constantinople in 1453. First, the region was allotted to Venice, co-conspirators, in the division of the Byzantine empire. The Venetian *podestà* in Constantinople decreed in 1205 that the coastal provinces from Glyky (the site of ancient *Eurioa*, inland from Parga in southern Epirus) to Dyrrhachium (Durrës), specifically mentioning the *provincia Vagenecie*, should be subordinated directly to Venice. The Venetians, however, had no interest in the Epirote mainland, and permitted Michael Comnenos Doukas, a prince of the Byzantine House of Angelos Comneni, to become the self-appointed leader of an independent sub-Byzantine state. Michael I titled himself as 'Despot' and ruled as a Venetian vassal. From this moment began the era of the Epirote Despots, as they are known, a colourful and ambitious dynasty that sought to exploit the seismic shift in Mediterranean geo-political relations.

The Despots quickly sought to take advantage of their situation. So, tellingly, in a treaty of 1210, the Venetians required guarantees of protection and safety, free trade with these settlements and the right to have churches specifically for Venetians and Dyrrhachians. Butrint plainly prospered and became a pawn in short-term alliances with the Angevins before it was finally sold along with Corfu to the Venetians on 11 June 1386. An era of vacillation between different masters came to an end.

The Archaeology of the Medieval Town

Few Medieval towns in the Mediterranean have benefited from as much study as Butrint. Most surviving towns are still occupied today, making it exceptionally difficult to decipher their evolving Medieval topography. Even so, we have some sense of the exaggerated rhythms of this era from recent research. Venice is a classic example. Tiny trenches and drilled auger holes have been used to reconstruct its early shape.[3] The original Late Roman emporium evolved around the quarter known as Castello, with a grid of waterways that were entirely re-shaped in the ninth century as the nucleus at Rialto became more important. Constantinople, likewise, appears to have been reduced to a constellation of nuclei around churches in monasteries until its revival under the later ninth-century Macedonian emperors as a coherent urban fabric.[4] Unfortunately, modern excavators have largely foresworn the opportunity to understand the fluctuating fortunes of the city after its zenith under the sixth-century Emperor Justinian. Little detail is known of the High Byzantine capital, except that its walls were sustained through countless sieges. By contrast, in Rome a new generation of archaeologists has discovered a pattern resembling that conjectured for Constantinople.[5] Here, beyond doubt, the Late Antique city was reduced by the eighth century to islands that formed around churches and monasteries. Revival in each of these centres by the later tenth century meant that the dismembered parts became fused, taking a form familiar to our modern eyes.

Butrint was no Constantinople, Rome or Venice. Like most modest ancient cities, it was reduced to little more than a castle, known in the Byzantine world as a *kastron*. Administered by a *stratelates* or someone of similar rank, in many ways the *kastron* sustained the concept of the ancient *polis*, giving its markedly reduced citizenry a sense of belonging to a world that looked for identity to the one remaining city, Constantinople.

Corfu followed the same pattern. The ancient town at Palaiopolis was apparently deserted after being sacked by the Goths in the sixth century in favour of the prominent 'twin peaks' – Corypho (from the Greek 'corphe', summit) that today form part of the immense Venetian castle (*Palaio Frourio*

FIGURE 6.1 *A view of the excavations in the western defences Tower 1 showing the red layer of ninth-century burning and destruction.*

– the Old Fortress). Nothing of the Byzantine period remains on these plugs of rock, whereas at Butrint, the *kastron* appears to have been located in the towers in the western defences. Tower 1, the largest of the three towers built in the sixth century, had at least two floors. Excavations showed that it burnt down in a calamity that dates to the early ninth century. The ground floor had been used as a storage area beneath a residential floor above it that had collapsed. Trapped in the debris were a range of ceramic vessels one side of the ground floor door, and a crate of glass waste on the other side. The ceramics included Otranto transport amphorae, other amphorae from the Aegean region, a Constantinople white ware dish, and a range of local coarse wares including chafing dishes –portable ovens – of a so-called Avaro-Slavic type. The glass waste comprised Late Antique lamp and cup fragments, a distinctive Egyptian lamp fragment, cullet and coloured window glass

FIGURE 6.2 *Local ninth-century pots from Tower 1 in the western defences.*

fragments. Plainly this was an assemblage belonging to an exceptional individual who had commercial relations with the Aegean and around the Ionian Sea region reaching to the Salento peninsula and Sicily. Tower 2 was not as rich but contained all the accoutrements of drinking ceremonies: a Sicilian amphora, a tableware jug from southern Italy and strangely, eleven two- or three-spouted coarse ware pots. Importantly, a bronze *follis* of Basil I and Constantine (869–79), was found associated with the amphora. This shows that Tower 2 remained in use a little later than its near neighbour and was abandoned around the later ninth century.[6]

Similar pottery has not been found in any quantity elsewhere in Butrint in either the excavations of the Triconch Palace or Roman forum. The towers appear to have been an island in a ruinous ancient townscape, possibly complementing settlement on the acropolis (where the later castle destroyed any likely site of earlier Mid-Byzantine settlement).

Following the fire in the western defences, later ninth-century Butrint occupied a new place. Excavations in the Roman suburb on the Vrina Plain, to the south of the walled town, brought to light a new short-lived Butrint.[7] Here, in the ruins of the sixth-century, the central-place – a manor-house or *oikos* – of Butrint's ninth-century commander was discovered. Post-holes found within the (re-used) paved narthex of the sixth-century basilica show that its upper floor was reinforced to take a new residence covering 7.10 × 5.80 metres. With the post-holes fire-blasted through the paving stones, the primitive architecture of the house was striking.

The black earth deposit also extended into the south aisle of the earlier church, while the north aisle, judging from hearths discovered here, was deployed as a workshop. A small Late Antique mausoleum off the north aisle now housed a single-flue pottery kiln. The nave of the basilica was made into an inhumation cemetery from the mid-ninth century AD, graves rudely puncturing the earlier mosaic pavement. A grave with a fine copper-alloy openwork ornamental buckle, closely paralleled by a buckle found at Paleokastritsa on Corfu, which has been dated to the late eighth century,

FIGURE 6.3 *A selection of glass waste (lamps) found in Tower 1 in the western defences.*

accompanied one adult. A secondary cemetery lay beyond the apse of the church and included a disturbed adult possibly associated with whom was a silver-plated horse bit. One adult placed directly outside the apse appeared to have been interred with a Byzantine *follis* in his pocket. The ceramics, like the prolific Byzantine bronze coins, appear to distinguish the culture of this household from that found in the tower at Butrint. Amphorae of a distinctive Otranto type make up about 50 per cent of the pottery, while local kitchen wares almost certainly made at the site itself amount to most of the rest. Perhaps the most important discoveries, indicating the status of the new place, were five lead imperial seals. These would suggest that this was an administrative centre, the new Butrint, clearly recognized by Byzantine imperial authorities.

Apart from the seals, coins and fine metalwork, two dagger-like spikes with knob terminals were found of the kind driven into the boards of codices to take the rings of fore-edge fastenings. In other words, these spikes suggest that a book or books were kept here. Another indication of the standing of this place is illustrated by the presence of remains of eight bears. Bear remains are rare at Butrint and in these cases may have been kept as high-status pets or curios or hunted for their meat and skins. Alternatively, they may not have been local to the area and their presence could indicate traded

FIGURE 6.4 *An aerial view of the post-built ninth-century dwelling made in the Vrina Plain aristocratic settlement.*

FIGURE 6.5 *Four lead seals from the aristocratic house.*

furs. As in the Roman assemblage traded furs may be responsible for some bear remains, as four of the eight Medieval specimens were metapodials, elements of the extremities that frequently remain attached to traded skins. However, the other four elements were long bones (three tibiae and a humerus), providing strong evidence that live animals were present in the local area. One noteworthy feature on a distal bear tibia was osteophyte development on the lateral margin of the distal epiphysis. This reactive bone growth, though not pronounced, is a skeletal abnormality relating to osteoarthritis. It suggests that this particular bear lived to an old age.

The first-floor dwelling with the associated high-status burials, occupying the Late Antique church, judging from the coins and seals, dates to the mid-ninth to mid-tenth centuries. The material culture shows trade in transport amphorae, presumably containing wine, with the heel of Italy while the ornamental metal fittings and jewellery show connections to points in the south-west Balkans. Certainly, the material culture and art distinguish the household from anything yet found in the large excavations inside Butrint, including the tower described above. Was this the household at Butrint in which, according to the *Vita Eliae iunioris*, St Elias the Younger and his companion, Daniel, were held prisoner at Butrint in 881–2, suspected of being Arab spies on their return from the Peloponnese?

Within the ruins of the ancient town, there is no evidence to suggest the Great Basilica was restored to use at this time, though we cannot doubt that its memory was well recognized. However, no evidence of dwellings was found in the Triconch Palace area beside the Vivari Channel though some ninth-century ceramics were discovered in the excavations.[8] Were the channel-side areas within the walls of Butrint temporarily used as a marketplace at this time? Was it an *emboropanegyri*, an emporium for fish? Might we envisage exchange beside the Vivari Channel where traders from Corfu and even the Salento peninsula of south Italy camped while doing business? The coins testify to some simple taxation being in force, as the Byzantine commandant – presumably an *archon* or *stratelates* of *Vagenetia* – oversaw the regional revival of Ionian trade. Bishop Arsenios of Corfu (876–953), who apparently visited Epirus to plead with Slav pirates to desist their raids, recorded that Butrint was rich in fish and oysters, with a fertile hinterland.

The extensive excavations show that the Vrina Plain settlement was abandoned in the mid- to later tenth century. Interestingly, a new study of the geomorphology at Butrint and on the Vrina Plain shows clearly that the environmental conditions changed inexorably and significantly after the sixth century. The continued silting of the estuary meant that the waters became shallower (and probably less accessible to deep draft boats). Effectively this meant that the commander's dwelling on the Vrina Plain by the tenth century was situated in an increasingly marshy and inaccessible location, which may have contributed to its eventual abandonment.

In the later tenth century Butrint once more shifted the locus of administration: in an act of significant urban development worthy of late Republican times, the ruined ancient city was now re-purposed.[9] The first stage is easily characterized as a preparation for the second, more substantive revival of the town. Numerous later tenth- to early eleventh-century bronze coins found in the walled town of Butrint have long since indicated that some significant change occurred at this time. New fortifications were erected around the acropolis, which presumably contained the new administrative centre, as well as around the lower city. Distinctive in making use of *spolia* taken largely from Hellenistic buildings (termed Medieval 1 masonry at Butrint), this was a major investment in reinvention of the town, quite unlike the makeshift earlier Mid-Byzantine phases. At the same time, there is evidence of intensive new activity at Butrint, involving the creation of substantial new terracing on the slopes of the acropolis and a series of

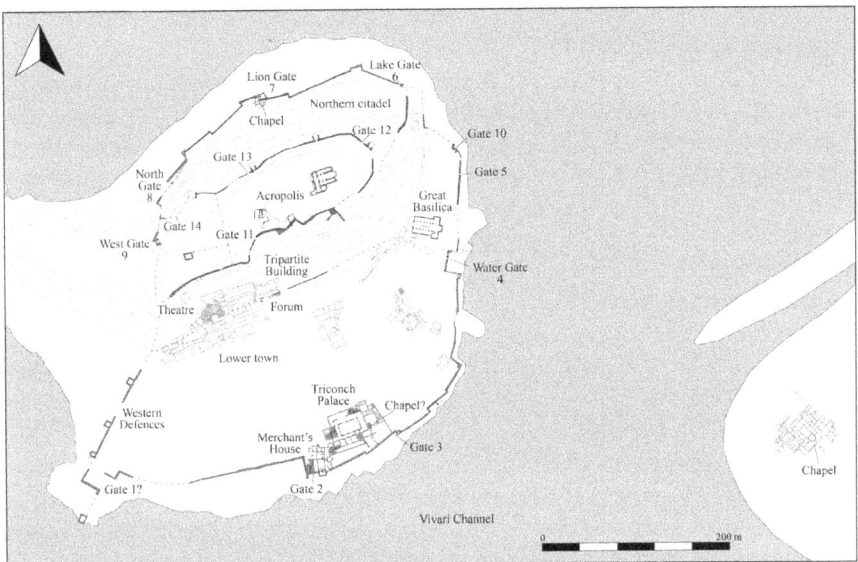

FIGURE 6.6 *A map of the new eleventh-century town of Butrint.*

FIGURE 6.7 *A post-built eleventh-century dwelling found in the Triconch Palace excavations.*

large walls that may represent property divisions in that they are not associated with any building.

The scale of these activities suggests a planned intervention by a single authority. They included the creation of a massive new terrace above the conspicuous levels of fine silty alluvium that overlay Late Antique levels directly on top of the Roman forum pavement. Running east–west over this terrace was an orthostat wall made of roughly reworked Hellenistic blocks, which had two anonymous *folles* (c. 976–1025) embedded in the fabric. Two other tracts of similar walling were discovered either side of the Great Basilica, part of an enclosure. One short tract appears to run from the Hellenistic fortifications eastwards to form part of an enclosure around the Great Basilica. Associated with this was an anonymous *follis* (c. 976–1025). The second tract of orthostat walling, standing a metre high, runs across the top of the Roman bridge. The cathedral – the Great Basilica – was refurbished at this time, just as small chapels were erected in other parts of the town. Extra-mural chapels were also built outside the west, seaward gate and, at the gate on the opposite side of the town, close to the second-century AD sacred well of Junia Rufina. In the Triconch Palace area a tract of new gravel road was found as well as traces of small chapel, stone and timber dwellings. The excavations also produced a rare gold *nomisma* of Basil II (976–1025) in glistening mint condition. Further upslope, at the back of the old Roman forum, a line of stone buildings was erected inside earlier Mid-Roman shells. Timber buildings with stone footings were constructed on the acropolis that belong to this urban revival and pre-date the making of a castle here in the twelfth century. Meanwhile, in the western defences Towers 1 and 2 were overhauled. In each, the ground floor level was raised first with demolition

FIGURE 6.8 *A gold nomisma of Basil II (976–1025) found in the Triconch Palace excavations (obverse and reverse views).*

material and then a thick layer of crushed mussel shells. The intention was evidently to make a rudimentary pavement above the water table.

Huge quantities of ceramics show a similar picture to that noted at the Vrina Plain *oikos*, with southern Italian amphorae forming the bulk of the imported material in comparison with table wares, which were very limited. The emphasis on bulk transport vessels from a single region could suggest supply to a primarily military settlement, although this remains a matter of speculation. The most likely occasion for this investment occurred after 1014 when the Emperor Basil II had subjugated the Bulgarian empire of Samuel. As at neighbouring Epirote towns like Himara and Rogoi, and conceivably for Durrës and points to the north and south, there was renewed and focused Imperial Byzantine intervention in the southern Adriatic Sea. In the case of Butrint this appears to have included the creation of an enclave reaching north to the refurbished Greek wall at Dema, at the north end of Lake Butrint, and east to the refurbished Hellenistic hilltop town of Çuka e Ajtoit, now with east-facing towers, overlooking the north–south road down the western Balkans.

At present, we can interpret the two apparently conflicting twelfth-century descriptions of al-Idrisi and Benedict of Peterborough (actually Roger of Howden) as follows. Al-Idrisi was probably accurate in describing Butrint as a small, well-populated market town.[10] The population on the acropolis and its south flank, if it was terraced, together with seasonal fishermen, may have numbered hundreds or more. Yet again, the *castellum desertum* described by Benedict in 1191, as likely as not, tells us that – after the Normans expelled the Byzantines in the 1080s, and then for long periods controlled the Ionian islands – no Byzantine authority occupied and maintained the castle.

One more piece of evidence needs to be considered. A hoard of ninety-four Byzantine bronze coins concealed in a simple pot was found in a deposit in the Triconch Palace excavations, close to a narrow gate leading out to the Vivari Channel.[11] Three of these coins were issues of the Emperor Manuel Comnenus I (1143–81) and ninety-one of the Emperor Isaac II (1185–95). No coins of either the Emperors Andronius I (1183–5) or Alexius III (1195–1203) were present. It is tempting to associate these with the brief revival of fortune for Byzantium in the Ionian region, after the Normans had been finally expelled in 1191. The deposit itself, though, possibly relates to the Fourth Crusade, lead by the Marquis Boniface de Montferrat, the doge of Venice, Enrico Dandolo and Prince Alexios, son of the deposed Emperor Isaac II. Perhaps, we may speculate, on seeing the crusading armada in the Straits in May 1203, one of the Byzantine officers of Butrint concealed this small sum before fleeing.

The New Town

The Medieval town occupied much the same footprint as the Late Antique one. It is difficult today to get any sense of it, yet a visitor must imagine a

FIGURE 6.9 *A Byzantine hoard dating to c. 1204 from the Triconch Palace.*

smaller version of the well-preserved town of Mistras in the Peloponnese with a powerful castle on the acropolis, and several rings of high fortifications within which were many churches, including the refurbished Great Basilica, and many dwellings, some built in stone, and some in a mixture of materials. The rich array of imported ceramics from Italy, the Peloponnese and further east, possibly Constantinople, point to an urban revival in the thirteenth and fourteenth centuries, under the Despots and Angevins.

The Military Architecture

The dominant feature of the new Butrint would have been its castle. As of the eleventh century, on albeit minimal evidence, the Byzantine *stratelates* almost certainly occupied a small castle at the elevated west end of the acropolis.[12] This was succeeded by a new Despotic castle, commanding as it still does today a clear view of the Straits of Corfu and the Vivari Channel. Even though it was a small castle, tucked within the rounded end of the acropolis defences, it almost certainly necessitated demolishing pre-existing dwellings. Little remains. Ugolini re-built the castle entirely and only small original sections survive. These, together with the photographs he took, provide some scope for interpreting the history of Butrint's premier Medieval building. Our interpretation is that the castle began as a fortified enclosure with projecting towers and an inner keep with at least two floors. The ruined keep appears in Edward Lear's drawings made in 1857 and in Ugolini's first photographs of the acropolis. If, as we have surmised, it belongs to the thirteenth century, it was modest, resembling, for example, Gardiki and perhaps Kassiope on Corfu, rather than the major castle of the Despots at their capital, Arta and Rogoi in south Epirus. The castle enclosure was entered from the acropolis, reached by way of the old Hellenistic gate leading onto the acropolis.

The castle was evidently strengthened, either when it was acquired by the Angevins in the later thirteenth century or more probably after earthquake damage at this time. A second tower was added within the enclosure (this is only apparent in a series of Ugolini's photographs), similar to the ruined castellan's residence at Agirokastro on a high cliff in western Corfu. A lower, subsidiary enclosure was added to the western side. This looked out over the southern skirt below the acropolis. Possibly a road led up to it across the terraces now occupying the ground below which lay the sanctuary and Theatre. At the same time the main gate into the acropolis fortress was formidably strengthened with an enclosed outer gate channelling visitors onto the hilltop in a manner reminiscent of the crusader military architecture of the era.

On at least two occasions the fortifications were refurbished and strengthened, making the castle the hub of at least three different sectors: the lower city, the northern citadel, overlooking the sheltered bay off Lake Butrint, and the acropolis.[13] As in the case of the castle, the walls were probably first repaired in the earlier thirteenth century (when distinctive round put-log holes bonded the poor masonry together (Medieval 2 masonry)), then improved again by the Angevins.

In the lower city this construction phase included the general refurbishment of the Late Antique wall, with a rampart walk in many places. Towers were rebuilt or, in the case of one excavated in the Triconch Palace area, added. Both Towers 1 and 2 in the western defences were rebuilt after a major earthquake in the thirteenth century. The collapsed rubble was used to in-fill the ground floor, while the walls themselves were patched. At this time, too, the Late Roman *proteichisma* in the western defences was refurbished in an act of display.

FIGURE 6.10 *A photogrammetric record of the Medieval and Venetian defences at the Water Gate.*

New gates were constructed. The most prominent of these was the Water Gate at the crossing point of the Vivari Channel. A tower on the seaward side of this gate offered lateral protection from attack. The position of the Water Gate superseded the Hellenistic Tower Gate which had been a principal entrance since the third century BC. The Roman bridge, it seems probable, had long since collapsed. Instead, from the Water Gate, we must imagine, ferries crossed the Vivari Channel and, equally, connected the town to the ferry-head at Xarra visited by N. G. L. Hammond in 1930. Postern gates occur at regular intervals within the lower circuit, suggesting free but defended access from the Vivari Channel to the lower city.

The northern citadel was created by the re-fortification of the earlier lower city wall (north side) and the construction of a new wall between the lower circuit (close to the Lake (Scaean) Gate) and a new acropolis circuit. The fortifications were much more substantial than the lower city area, the walls reaching a height of c. 8 metres. Access into the northern citadel was restricted to four entrances: the North Gate, Lion Gate and Lake Gate, and a new gate in the new stretch of wall.

The old circuit wall encircling the acropolis was extensively repaired. Six gateways provided access, four of which were connected with the northern citadel. A fifth gate provided access to a road that must have descended across the terraces, south to the lower city and the Tower Gate.

A sketch by Edward Lear, viewing Butrint from the slope of Mount Sotirës in January 1857, conveys the powerful form of the fortress and its adjoining northern citadel. Strengthened to confront any landward assault, the ensemble is dominated by the high donjon in the fortress. From here, not only could Butrint's commandant survey the Straits of Corfu, but the arc of the lagoonal landscape reaching deep up into the valley to Çuka e Ajtoit.

The Ecclesiastical Archaeology

Control of the castle passed between many different hands until it was finally abandoned by the Venetians in 1572. By then, the town fortifications were apparently beyond repair. The Church, though, represented a more constant factor in the life of the Medieval town. The Great Basilica, erected in the sixth century, was effectively Butrint's cathedral. Between the seventh and later tenth centuries we cannot be certain that a bishop or his representative was always present, but it is likely. From then until the sixteenth century, when the bishop moved to Glyky, close to Arta in south Epirus (representing both places), he would have been a stable force in the community and the Great Basilica the physical manifestation of his authority.

At some point in the high Middle Ages the church was extensively rebuilt.[14] The colonnades in the nave were replaced with masonry piers and at least part of the façade was renewed. The new arcades were rather clumsily joined to the existing transept piers with a clear difference in height visible on the south side. A new floor of large limestone slabs was laid in the nave, aisles and transept, overlying the earlier sixth-century mosaic pavement. The apse was substantially altered too. Although the width of the axial window was retained, the upper sections of the apse were rebuilt in a semi-circular form with new window arches springing in a slightly incongruous fashion from the remains of the earlier pentagonal structure. Of particular interest is the presence on the southern side of the apse of a series of small decorative brick arches arranged in a fish-scale pattern, the only means of dating the reconstruction.

The date of the new church is a matter of debate. Aleksandër Meksi attributed it to the later ninth century. He associated the reconstruction with the re-establishment of a bishopric, mentioned in the *Nea Taktika* or *Notitia*, a list of dioceses. In support of this date, he cited the absence of *cloisonné* masonry, a highly decorative technique in which squared limestone blocks are enclosed with horizontal and vertical tiles, first used in the Balkans around the mid-tenth century.

We have favoured a much later date in the thirteenth century when, as we have seen, the Medieval town was taking shape under the Despots. This date is also supported by the presence of the decorative brick arches found in several churches of the Despotate. Parallels include the church of Saint Jason and Sosipater on Corfu, with its alternate bands of pale honey-coloured sandstone and bricks set in different patterns, and the churches at Mastron and Megali Chora in Aetolia. These churches maintain a basilica plan in conjunction with arcades supported by masonry piers. Their apses are often constructed with a step just below the roof-line enabling the construction of a semi-dome (although the apse of the Great Basilica does not survive to a sufficient height to establish whether this occurred at Butrint).

Subsequent modifications to the Great Basilica are also evident. A smaller trilobal window surmounted by a single central window replaced the large axial window in the apse. This may have been contemporary with the blocking of some of the nave arcade, presumably as the community began to diminish in number. Further alterations included the insertion of a poorly made small apse that blocked access between the southern aisle and southern transept. A drawing of the south transept, made in 1934, shows that the large bifora window there was also blocked.

Contemporary Corfiot and Epirote basilicas had a severe exterior but inside they were richly decorated with murals, many hanging lamps and, as often as not, an iconostasis screen separating the altar from the congregation that was ebulliently carved and covered in gold leaf. It is commonly agreed that often here might be found an artistic amalgam of the mature High Byzantine styles with the first steps towards the naturalistic rendering mastered by Giotto. The archaeology of the Great Basilica, like the other churches, does scant justice to the iconographic richness that these must have addressed to Butrint's citizens and visitors.

At least six other churches are known to have been erected as the town took off in the thirteenth century. More chapels probably remain to be discovered.[15] Let us briefly tour each in turn, beginning with the decorated church, left suspended on a ledge after Ugolini's excavations above the Theatre.

Ugolini demolished the main body of this church, leaving only the painted wall against the south-facing rock face of the acropolis. Drawings by the Italian mission show a small apse at its east end, standing to a height of c. 1 metre for a small building little more than 4.75 metres long. Today protected by a makeshift roof, traces of wall-paintings show a line of five or six over-lifesize frontal figures of standing saints. Each is set in a rectangular panel framed by red bands contoured in white. Being so close to the Theatre, did the paintings in the church relate the story of the martyrdom of St Terinus at Butrint in the third century? Certainly, the story was well-known by the later Middle Ages, although only the enigmatic upper part of the stage building of the Theatre would have been identifiable.

Two churches, at least, occupied the low skirt beyond the base of the acropolis hill: the Gymnasium church and the Baptistery church. A church almost certainly existed in the ruins of the Triconch Palace, though unequivocal evidence of this has eluded us.

The large fountain in the centre of the so-called 'Gymnasium' complex formed the core of a church dismantled by the Italians. In the Late Antique period the three niches on the eastern apsidal end of the building were decorated with mosaics, one bearing the Christian motif of a *kantharos* flanked by birds. Seven centuries later a small church was built here, again based around the *nymphaeum*. Although this building was subsequently demolished in order to reveal the Roman structure beneath, the Italian plans and photographs of the church provide detailed information as to its form and appearance. The church was rectangular in plan (following the outline of the *nymphaeum*, which measured 9.8 × 5.2 metres) and had two small entrances in its lateral walls. A bell tower, strengthened through the use of two antique columns, abutted the church on its north side. This bell tower was decorated with curving lines of bricks that projected from the masonry. It formed the west wall of a small northern room, 4.3 metres wide, the roof of which was supported by a series of piers that projected up from the exterior wall. An annex of equal size also abutted the original *nymphaeum* structure to the south. The lower parts of the apse were covered with geometric paintings, while several layers of plaster overlay the earlier mosaics within the niches of the apse.

Remains of the accompanying cemetery of stone-lined graves have been found to the north of the Gymnasium, extending into what had been the forum area that was taken over by the Late Antique praetorium.

The Butrint Foundation excavated the second of the churches in the lower city, beside the Baptistery. Here a later church is conspicuously on top of an earlier one, with the earlier apse protruding beyond the east end. It was probably a single nave church, as there is little room for lateral aisles. Rather oddly, it seems that the surviving iconostasis may have been part of this earlier building. A piece of blue and white glazed pottery was visible at one stage in the masonry of this iconostasis, confirming its later Medieval date. Around it was a large cemetery, similar to the one at the nearby Gymnasium church. During the fourteenth or fifteenth centuries, the church was rebuilt on a smaller scale, apparently retaining only the iconostasis of the earlier building. The new church was a single nave structure with a single apse and a door to the south-west. There was a further entrance on the north-west side from which a flight of small steps led into the church. By the time this second church was constructed, the ground level above the earlier trapezoidal annex of the Baptistery had risen by $c.$ 0.6–0.7 metres.

This church underwent still more modifications including the addition of a small atrium and a bell tower like the one at the Gymnasium. The atrium and the floor of the church were floored with rough paving slabs. These additions may date to the sixteenth century or even later, judging from the associated North Italian pottery.

Four more small churches were clearly situated at key points in the town, perhaps on sacred circuits within its bounds.

The best preserved of these lies beyond the Great Basilica close to the Scaean Gate, directly against the Medieval wall that links the lower wall circuit with the acropolis wall. Its presence perhaps signalled a path leading up to the hilltop. It is a single-celled structure, 6.95 metres long and 4.6 metres wide, built of limestone blocks, with a small central apse pierced by a single narrow window and flanked by two niches. As its west wall was formed by the unbroken old city wall, the church was entered via lateral doorways to the north and south. Inside remains of decayed passages of painted plaster can be seen.

As we have seen already (see Chapter 5), the second-century AD well of Junia Rufina, situated just inside the Lion Gate, was an early cult focus within the city with a small chapel and graveyard close by.[16] In the Roman period it was restructured and dedicated to the nymphs by Junia Rufina. In the sixth century the water source was given a new Christian identity and reference, strikingly reminiscent of the mosaic in the Baptistery. During the eleventh century, a new extra-mural chapel was erected to the west of the well. In addition, a wall blocked the opening to the well itself at the lower level and a shaft was cut through the Roman vault above, enabling water to be drawn from a higher level. This wall was subsequently demolished by the Italian Archaeological Mission as was part of a further structure that divided the steps down to the well from the steps down to the Lion Gate. A narrow staircase led down to the area of the well, possibly focused on the small niche to the left of the well described above. The area in front of the well was roofed with a vault of which traces can still be seen.

Another chapel sited at a gateway can be seen beside the Hellenistic Gate leading into the acropolis. Only a painted wall survives, set above eye-level.

A photograph taken by Ugolini's mission shows the paintings in a considerably better state than they are today. Little is now visible of the four figures side by side, other than distinctive haloed vestiges of the Virgin of the Annunciation in the third panel. Her red maphorion falls down over her shoulders and around her down to the ground. Below this she wears a long-sleeved light blue tunic which also falls to her feet and breaks over her shoes. The tunic is elaborately folded and ruffled.

Finally, directly in front of the castle enclosure, another small church occupied the flat ground of the acropolis. Visitors entering the castle would have first noticed its presence. Today only faint levelled traces of its three apses can be seen. The little surviving suggests a domed cross-in-square structure, recalling many of the later Medieval churches of the region such as that of nearby Mesopotam, as well as other churches of the Despotate.

Luigi Ugolini and, more recently, Aleksandër Meksi interpreted the standing fragment of the unfinished early fifth-century triconch dining room in the proposed Triconch Palace as a church. Eleventh-century burials of a family group identified by DNA from its vicinity seemed to clinch this interpretation. Later still, a cluster of thirteenth- to fourteenth-century burials, including a solitary skull set in a packing of stones (similar to one found at Corinth), lends support to the notion of a channel-side chapel hereabouts.[17]

Churches abounded in the landscape around. As in classical times, these cult sites were invariably located to grasp the attention of travellers. Three churches certainly overlooked the town. The first of these is the Late Antique basilica on the hillock on the Vrina Plain in use until the twelfth or thirteenth centuries – did it connote a ferry-point from where one crossed into Butrint? Like the recently excavated basilica at the Masseria delle Quattro Macine near Otranto in Italy, the aisled Medieval church was reduced to its nave and apse. After this, it may well have been transposed to the prominent hilltop of Shën Dëlli where a compact, white-washed monastery exists today. Northwards, overlooking the ferry point below Xarra is the hill of Shën Dimitri, again the site of a Medieval church where a late thirteenth-century hoard of 119 Frankish Morean coins was found.[18] At the lakeside pilgrimage site of Diaporit, the aisled church was long since abandoned by the Middle Ages, but the principal tombs in its apse were exhumed in the thirteenth century. Beyond, occupying a new site in the lea of Çuka e Ajtoit, lies the well-preserved remains of the thirteenth-century monastic church at Çiflik.

In conclusion, the most significant aspect of the Medieval churches lies in their location within the city. The churches appear in almost all the major excavated areas of the city as well as within its immediate hinterland. This could suggest that the town had a considerable population in the later Medieval period, although there is no simple equation between number or size of churches and the number of people present to utilize them. On the other hand, the absence of richly decorated churches such as those that can still be visited in Arta reflects the particular situation of Butrint in the politics of the period. As we have seen, in the early thirteenth century the bishop of Butrint was closely associated with Ioannes Apokaulos, Metropolitan of Naupaktos (1200–32), a staunch advocate of the independence of the Epirote church. It is not known whether Butrint was in Angevin hands during the mid-thirteenth century, but in 1276 it passed back to Byzantium. Nevertheless, two years later, in 1279, it was once more in Despotate hands and was promptly ceded to Charles of Anjou. By 1310 (if not earlier) a Latin bishop had been installed in Butrint. The instability of Butrint and the Angevin presence may account for the absence of the striking churches characteristic of the Despotate. Nonetheless, by refurbishing Early Christian churches in the town there seems to have been a conscious desire to celebrate the memory of earlier Christian architecture in thirteenth-century Epirus.

The Medieval Port and Fishery

The port and townscape of Medieval Butrint are more difficult to pin down than the military and ecclesiastical architecture. Yet, as we have seen, the refurbished fortifications, like the numerous churches, indicate a thriving seaport by the early to mid-thirteenth century. Almost certainly, the main nucleus of the town was gathered around the terraced slopes of the acropolis. In the old sanctuary area, fragments of stone-built dwellings exist, variants of largely complete town-houses that can be visited today in Mistra in the Peloponnese. One such dwelling was excavated by Dhimosten Budina over the remains of the *prytaneion*, the Hellenistic and early Roman council building. Another was found in the area of the erstwhile Roman basilica at the east end of the forum. This included a deep well where large amounts of thirteenth-century maiolica were found as well as Morean coins.

The Butrint Foundation excavations at the Triconch Palace and around the Baptistery revealed a vernacular architecture not dissimilar to the shepherd and fishermen's dwellings recorded by Ugolini. Invariably using either existing Roman walls as foundations or, on occasions, large slabs to support the walls, a dense mass of simple rectangular buildings occupy the area. Where fragments of buildings survive, the archaeology shows that these had timber uprights, dwarf rubble walls supporting wattle and daub upper parts and partitions made with clay or pisé.

The topography of the town remains a mystery. There is no evidence of roads or tracks but several wells, lined with mortared rubble, have been found. This, of course, contrasts with places like Corinth, Mistra and Monemvasia where the urban fabric was well developed. At Butrint, instead, there is a sense, rightly or wrongly, of an urban landscape filled with decayed buildings, some partly recycled into new structures, and interspersed with open rubbish tips and graveyards.

Yet, the apparent poverty of the architecture may be deceptive. The associated deposits are anything but impoverished. The ceramic assemblages are notable first for the presence of Byzantine tablewares – particularly polychrome sgraffito wares best-known from the Aegean as well as ample amounts of thirteenth century Apulian maiolicas.[19] These are superseded by fourteenth- to sixteenth-century north Italian wares,[20] especially early Renaissance sgraffito dishes. East Mediterranean glassware is also prominent. Fish-hooks abound as well.

The clue here may be an exposed wharf alongside the Vivari Channel. Were these undistinguished dwellings the properties of merchants and fishermen whose industry furnished Butrint with its modest moveable wealth? Was the motor of Medieval Butrint privately owned quays along the Vivari Channel, reached by numerous narrow watergates, or was there a large harbour located either in front of the western defences or, with the aqueduct and bridge no longer in place, in the serene reaches of the east bay beyond the northern citadel? As yet, we can only speculate, but the midden archaeology provides an intriguing glimpse of an affluence that, notwithstanding constant changes of administration in the town and unremitting raids from the fifteenth century onwards, was as remarkable as it had been in Late Antiquity.

* * *

Ugolini was fascinated by Butrint's long history, but barely recognized the archaeology of the Medieval town. The Butrint Foundation's project since the 1990s has rectified this. Here, the revival by stages of the Mid-Byzantine Mediterranean can be charted. The ubiquitous presence of south Italian pots is an important factor in this renewal of Ionian trade, as was Butrint's premier asset, fish.

Butrint's prosperity altered incrementally after Constantinople was seized by the Franks in 1203/4. Along with Corfu, it became the principal Mediterranean port for the sub-Byzantine Epirote Despots. Butrint thrived to judge from the new fortress, defences and churches in the turbulent arc of the thirteenth to fifteenth centuries. The ceramics from this era betray an allegiance to places all around the Adriatic Sea, the Morea and the Aegean. These monuments cloak the major features of the townscape: its terraces were formed to confront the high winter water table and the corresponding density of simple dwellings constructed to contend with the conditions in the lagoonal environment. Such conditions did not deter the Venetians at first, familiar as they were from their imperious command of their own lagoon. Perpetual Ottoman skirmishes, on the other hand, were quite another thing. It caused even the steeliest of castellans to re-consider the role of Butrint. And so, long before the town was formally designated as deserted in 1572, it seems likely that, notwithstanding the good revenues to be made from fishing at Butrint, it began to make much greater sense to concentrate the urban features in a more readily managed location, Corfu.

7

Insula Botentro

Corfu's Protector and Right Eye

Toward evening we arrived at a village called Livari, a corruption, it is thought of Vivarium, from the fisheries in the lake, which here finds an outlet into the sea by means of a river. By the people of the place the lake is also called Boïdoperes . . . On the opposite side of the water is a rocky height, with remains of walls, which mark the site of the ancient Buthrotum, the celsam Buthroti urbem *of Virgil. As we were embarking to cross to Corfu, I said to a Turkish official who was standing by, 'Now we are leaving Turkey?' 'Yes,' he replied, 'now you are going to Europe.'*

HENRY FANSHAWE TOZER[1]

Butrint was purchased by the Venetian Empire, together with the island and fortress of Corfu, in 1386, from the Angevin dynasty of southern Italy. For the next 400 years it was to be never more than an outpost of Corfu, though it was of major economic importance for the Venetians' island colony. The fisheries at Butrint certainly provided a substantial proportion of the fish consumed on the island, and the plains to the south and east of the Vivari Channel were an ideal location for the pasturing of livestock and the horses of Corfu's garrison. In addition, the rocky hillsides of the Ksamil peninsula were well suited to the cultivation of the olives that formed a principal component of the Venetian colonial economy from the sixteenth century. Timber, too, was procured from the slopes above Butrint.[2]

According to Andreas Marmora, the Venetian historian of Corfu, Butrint was officially abandoned after 1572.[3] Nevertheless, it continued to be garrisoned and maintained as a fishery and outpost, based upon the fortress on the south side of the Vivari Channel. Reliable documentation relating to the latter has been difficult to obtain and even the date of construction was

FIGURE 7.1 *The image of a lion (the 'lion of Saint Mark') on sherds of a sixteenth-century maiolica jug found during excavations in Butrint.*

uncertain. However, major fortification work took place in the mid-seventeenth century, a period when control of the fishery passed back and forth between the Venetians and the Ottomans.

Venetian Butrint was a four-sided walled enclave at the centre of which was the port, the so-called *insula Botentro*. Many different descriptions exist in the Venetian and Ottoman archives describing its shape. Its bounds are clearest on a cadastral map of 1718. Its northern line ran parallel to but just north of the Hellenistic-period Dema Wall, closing the peninsula between the sea and lake at virtually its narrowest point. From here a line almost bisected Lake Butrint, running to the east side of the fortified refuge of Kalivo and then across Lake Bufi, possibly to the ferry point by Xarra. From here the boundary turned south-westwards to a point where the Pavlass river was bridged at the sharp foot of the Korafit Hills. Then, bisecting Cape Stillo, it ran in a straight east–west line to a protected bay opposite Corfu.

Ancient landmarks formed nodal points of the enclave. The northern line followed the Dema Wall; Kalivo lay alongside the second stretch; and the final point on Cape Stillo terminated in the church of S. Nicola, probably the site of an earlier Hellenistic sanctuary.

An Ottoman document of August 1746 reviews the boundaries of 'Vafrendûs' agreed upon by the Ottomans and the Venetians in 1718. At the time it was decided that the fortress of Butrint would remain Venetian, with some land around it. The border was fixed at the distance that could be travelled in one hour. However, Ottoman violations of the agreement led the Venetian *bailo* in Istanbul to request an official confirmation. This document, addressed to the judge of Delvina and the tax-collectors of the districts (*sancak*s) of Yanya, Avlonya and Delvina, confirms these borders. It mentions monuments (*eser*) on the north side of the lake as a landmark when the boundaries were examined and fixed. There is also mention of an 'old stone bridge' (*atîq tâşküprü*) near the eastern wall of the fortress. Much earlier, in 1387 when there was a threat from Albanian attacks, five *provisores* visited Butrint, recording that it measured 4 miles from the lake to the sea and that in some areas the fortifications were preserved to a height of one *passus*, while in other places they either existed as foundations or not at all. The five *provisores* concluded that the wall did not justify the cost of its repair (1,000 ducats). In 1394 the matter was reviewed again.

The Venetian administration of Corfu and its mainland dependencies were managed by the so-called *Regimen Corphoy*. The belt of fortifications on the *terra firma* opposite the island comprised Butrint, Saigada (also known as Bastia), Parga (from 1401) and Phanari. From time to time all of these suffered attacks from Albanian insurgents. In 1387 the *castellanus* of *Butentro* was permitted to spend 50 *hyperpyra* on the repair of his palace and his house (*habitacionis*). The salt, which the Despots of Ioannina had been extracting from the pans at Saigada down the coast from Butrint, was considered by Venice as unacceptable competition. They destroyed the salt-pan installations in 1387.

The earliest Ottoman presence in present-day southern Albania was in Premedi and Korçë, following the campaigns of 1394 and 1397 under Sultan Beyazid I (1389–1402). The death of Beyazid was followed by a period of chaos in the Ottoman state, during which many Albanian lords recognized Venetian suzerainty. At the beginning of the fifteenth century the Ottomans conquered almost all of Albania and created the province (*sancak*) of Arnavud-ili (1415–17). The provincial governor (*sancakbegi*) resided in Argirikasri (Gjirokastra). The semi-feudal *timar* system was introduced to control the land. This means that land was assigned to certain lords on the condition that they supplied the Ottoman government in Istanbul with military support whenever required. The roughly 300 *timar* regions were in the hands of a limited number of Turkish and Albanian feudal families, who were vassals of the Ottoman state. The rebellion of the famous Skanderbeg did not affect southern Albania, which remained firmly under Ottoman control. The first comprehensive Ottoman tax register (*defter*) for the Sancak of Arvanid dates to the period 1431/2 and mentions a locality *Ayo-Ulas* with its embarkation point of *Vutrando*.

The archives record the almost constant conflicts between the Ottomans and the Venetians, holding resolutely onto their *insula*. Here is a short digest of that conflict as well as the peaceful interludes.

In March 1418 Theodore Mercurius, citizen of Corfu (*Corphoi*), was the new *comestabilis* of the Venetian *castro Vutentro*. The following year, in 1419, a peace treaty was signed between the Venetians and Turks, which contained amongst many issues the signal recognition of the rule of Venice over Corfu and Butrint. In the peace that followed, Cyriacus of Ancona paused at Butrint in 1435, taking note of its antiquities (see Chapter 2).

As early as 1454 Ottoman forces under Ceniz Ziberi appeared at Parga then at Butrint, to be repelled by a combination of Corfiot and Venetian forces. Much of the Ottoman–Venetian war of 1463–79 was fought in Albania. Not surprisingly, then, in 1470 the Ottomans once again postured to attack Butrint and Corfu. In some alarm, the castellan of Butrint set about strengthening the fortifications of the castle and *civitas*. Not everyone was impressed. Michali Pentapoliti of Corfu, a leading leaseholder of the fisheries, lamented that, in response to the Ottoman threat, the grills constraining the fish were opened on the orders of two civil servants to allow a galley to reach the castle. In 1475 the plans to repair the fortifications of the enclave (*Examili*) were revived. This time the experts opined that such works were 'very useful, easy and necessary', not only to protect Butrint but also the island of Corfu (*in conservationem loci Butroti et consequentius insule Corphoi*). Nonetheless, an Ottoman raid occurred in 1494, damaging the fishery of a Corfiot.

As the conflict intensified, so the Sublime Porte in Istanbul strengthened its grip on its westernmost provinces. During this period the region of Elbasan was not added to Arnavud-ili, but was established as a separate *sancak* (1466). In 1479 Avlonya (Vlora) was also made a province in its own right. In the course of the sixteenth century the *timar* system broke down and large estates appeared in the provinces. The ensuing revision of Ottoman taxation in the 'Greek' and 'Albanian' provinces led to civil unrest. During this period, groups of wandering Albanian soldiers became a serious security problem. The Porte managed to restore order to a large extent, but the help of the provincial and local notables (*a'yân*) was indispensable. This confirmed the importance of these notables. The land system was reformed and the *muqata'a* was introduced. Control over these large areas could be leased from the Sublime Porte, the Ottoman government.

The growing conflict was the context for a remarkable fantasy written in about AD 1493 by the Florentine Ugolino Verino.[4] This was an epic poem called the *Carlias*, dedicated to King Charles VIII of France, who that year led his armies to Rome. A central story of the epic describes how Charlemagne went on a crusade to Butrint, where he defeated the Ottomans. A long passage in the poem describes the town in some detail. Of course, Charlemagne never went to Butrint and nor did the town boast splendid piazzas, fountains and palaces, but plainly Verino had some sense from Virgil's *Aeneid* of its erstwhile mythic grandeur.

In his epic, Verino challenges his model (noble, educated) reader by creating imaginary relations not only between Aeneas and Charlemagne, but also between Butrint and other recently lost Angevin and Byzantine towns in what is now Greece. In this way, Butrint was a convenient canvas on which was painted a Mediterranean material past, now reified by the Renaissance.

Venice continued to be concerned to maintain the *Castel de Butintro* in good order, possibly as much because of its historical importance as its strategic value. The enclave was perceived as its protector and right eye (*tutela et ochio dextro*). By the early sixteenth century some 1,300 ducats per annum were allegedly spent on the *castello*, now in bad state of repair. A document of 22 June 1517 shows that the castellans of Butrint were selected from the citizens of Corfu. By this time, though, the threat from the Ottomans combined with the need to combat the water table and constantly repair the fisheries meant that profits had fallen, and the value of the enclave was being questioned.[5]

Worse was to come. In 1537 Sultan Suleiman II, known as the Magnificent, in alliance with King Francis I of France, embarked upon a massive incursion against the Holy Roman Emperor, Charles V. That spring the sultan crossed the Balkans and from Vlora despatched a fleet to take Italy. Meanwhile, a Turkish fleet of 400 ships equipped with 3,000 guns and carrying 25,000 men sailed to the Ionian Sea under the command of the sultan's brother-in-law, Soufti Pasha and Khaired-Din Barbarossa, the celebrated Barbary pirate now High Admiral of the Ottoman navy. In August 1537 the Sultan camped his army at Butrint from where he launched a two-week siege of Corfu.

The historian, Haji Khalifeh, writing in the early nineteenth century, states specifically that the sultan built a bridge of boats from Butrint across the Straits of Corfu. Contemporary sources say nothing of this awesome endeavour. The Straits at the narrowest point, to the south of modern Ksamil in Albania and Agios Stefanos on Corfu, have an especially strong current. Is it possible that Khalifeh was simply attempting to situate Suleiman's expedition alongside that of Xerxes, the Persian King of Kings, who according to Herodotus, crossed the Hellespont on a bridge of boats during his war against Athens in 480 BC?

Corfu repelled the invasion after a protracted siege. But, in the searing aftermath of the withdrawal of Suleiman's forces, Butrint as a settlement cannot have amounted to much more than a fortress emptied of a garrison. This may have prompted the bishop to move his seat to the strategically less conspicuous village of Glyky, near Arta. The siege doubtless did not deter

Corfiot families from refurbishing their fish-houses, but the next two and-a-half centuries were marked by perpetual tension between the Turks and Venetians. Turkish forces were back at Butrint in 1571 when a fleet carrying 8,000 men under Pertan Pasha made an abortive bid to take Corfu. A month later many Corfiots joined Don John of Austria's fleet, which vanquished the Ottoman fleet at the battle of Lepanto on 7 October.

The sea battle at Lepanto brings a Butrint personality briefly into the limelight. Cristoforo Condocali, a major leaseholder at Butrint, armed and commanded one galley that confronted the Ottoman navy in the battle. The Venetian archives contain ample accounts of Condocali's role at Butrint in the aftermath of the brief Ottoman incursion. The context for the written records is almost certainly that the town of Butrint was beyond repair and in 1572 the Prefect of Dalmatia, on a visit here, counselled that it should be abandoned in favour of the fortress (on the Vivari Channel) and the fisheries.

Almost at once the Sancakbeġi of Delvina and Ioannina arrived to prevent any building, and Condocali had to fight them off. For his services he was awarded the title of *cavaliere* on 23 June 1572.

The conflicts between the Venetian leaseholders and the local Ottomans were unending. A sequence of early seventeenth-century unembellished Venetian accounts illustrate the unremitting conditions. In 1606 the Senate instructed a certain Pasqualigo to restore the tower of Butrint, which was reported to be in a ruinous state. On inspection he found that the damage consisted of some broken tiles, caused by the fishermen making a roof-terrace, and some beams damaged by dripping water. He also pointed out that the supervising official of the fishery was obliged to maintain the building and to dig the nearby ditch which separated it from the mainland. In 1654 the Provveditore Generale de Corfu reported rumours that the Turks were planning to take Butrint, which is described as consisting of only one tower.

In January 1656 it was said that the *Bey* had gone to Constantinople to boast of the capture of Butrint and ask for workmen to fortify the old fortress. At that time there were some fifty Turks and two cannons, the largest of which had a range of 1 mile. Some arms were kept in the 'fishermen's tower'. The Turks mounted two guards: one at the tower and the other in the old fortress. It was reported that they had repaired the wall of the old castle.

That same year an anonymous report describes the Turkish capture of Butrint and suggests that the contractor of the fisheries neglected his duty of defence and was in league with the Turks. This account includes a dramatic description of the escape of the fishermen. In October 1656 the garrison of thirty-five Turks seemed much reduced from the earlier 300, while there were about forty fishermen. A galley from Santa Maura (Lefkada), anchored inland, was unable to exit the Vivari Channel because Venetian brigantines were blockading the mouth. There were fears of a renewed Turkish attack on Corfu. Venetian spies suggested that Butrint was so poorly defended that, should Venice wish to take it, they only needed to put a cannon at S. Dimitri and the Turks would abandon it. In December 1656 Venetian spies reported that the Turks were clearing the roads nearby in order to transport cannon from Valona (Vlora) to Butrint.

A drawing from this time, dated to AD 1660, vividly shows the ruinous condition of Butrint, a large swathe of deteriorating walls around the old acropolis castle and lower town, and the compact and isolated Triangular Fortress on the far side of the Vivari Channel. This is how Butrint was to remain until Ugolini's arrival, nearly three centuries later.

With the new century, Sultan Achmet II launched a fresh attempt in 1716 to capture Corfu, bivouacing his armies at Butrint. After a ferocious engagement led by the Austrian general Schulenburg, the Corfiots repulsed the invaders, just as news came that the Sultan's forces had been defeated outside Vienna by Prince Eugene of Savoy. After the sea battle of Lepanto and the twin defeats of Corfu and Vienna in August 1716, Ottoman ambition to take western Europe was checked, changing forever the balance of power in the central Mediterranean.

Following the siege, Corfu's victorious war council met and decided to evict the Ottomans from Butrint. At a subsequent meeting in May 1717, it was described how, having decided to take Butrint for the timber needed for the fleet, Schulenburg occupied it and took measures for its defence. As it happens, not much work had been done because of the spring rains and the difficulty of protecting workers from enemy attack. At one point the demolition of the fort appears to have been considered but the final decision of the meeting was to maintain it and carry out minor works proposed by Schulenburg.

The detailed cadastral survey of 1718 followed directly from this new initiative. A new family, the Gonemi, evidently became the principal leaseholders in the embattled enclave. Giacomo and his brothers had played prominent parts in repulsing the Ottoman siege of August 1716. The family seems to have succeeded in holding onto the fisheries in the face of harsh provocation. But sixty years later, in 1777, a telling report for the Venetian authorities by Pietro Antonio Letter, an engineer by profession, vividly confirms the deplorable deterioration of the Venetian fortifications at Butrint. It proved to be a harbinger of the inevitable. Venetian authority in the Adriatic region, after centuries of conflict with the Ottomans, was now being squeezed by the British and French. In 1797, after the Treaty of Campo Formio, Corfu and with it Butrint passed to the French. The new rulers were viewed by many as liberators. Butrint now belonged to a *nomos* (district) together with Corfu, Paxos and Parga. French rule lasted only two years. Even before they were expelled from Corfu, they had already abandoned Butrint following a fierce clash with the ambitious Ali Pasha of Tepelenë (sensitive to the Sublime Porte's anger at Napoleon's seizure of Egypt). A French infantry captain, J. P. Bellaire, has left a graphic account of the firefight with the Ottomans focused on Vrina (where a house from this era survives today).[6] So ended the story of the Venetian enclave. Henceforth, under the colourful Ali Pasha, Butrint became a monument to the past and a source of good fishing and duck-hunting.[7]

Ali Pasha of Tepelenë was a provincial ruler who took maximum advantage of the weakening of control by the central Ottoman authorities. From the end of the eighteenth century, he brought large parts of present-day Greece and Albania under his control. For the first time Epirus was under the control of one single authority. A ruthless ruler, who undoubtedly deserved his reputation for cruelty, he also improved the infrastructure, notably the road system, making it safer and, as a result, Epirus enjoyed a period of increased prosperity. His lasting legacy was a network of formidable fortresses – including the major examples at Tepelenë, Gjirokastra, and Ioannina, and many minor examples including Preveza and Porto Palermo as well as at the mouth of the Vivari Channel (repurposing an earlier eighteenth-century Venetian house).

During this period the Ottoman authorities began to refer to Epirus as *Toskalık*, the land of (the Albanian tribe of) the Tosks. In 1820 Ali Pasha fell foul of the Porte and was dismissed from his offices. His subsequent rebellion proved to be a catalyst for the Greek War of Independence, but he was murdered in 1821 before the Greek state was proclaimed.

Ali Pasha has a near mythical status in Western literature thanks principally to Lord Byron's poetic description of him, as well as to accounts by other Grand Tourists who visited him. The Great Powers, however, also had a keen appreciation of his importance as a strong leader of a stable region overlooking the central sea route through the Mediterranean. This was the motive for despatching William Martin Leake and François Pouqueville to his court at the height of the Napoleonic War. Through Leake the British gained first-hand knowledge of Ali Pasha's often irascible intentions. Leake also visited much of Epirus, arriving at Butrint, as we have seen, in January 1805 (see Chapter 2).

Using Leake, Ali Pasha wrote directly to King George III asking for guns and ammunition, to be used against the French. The British foreign secretary replied in 1808, providing the military equipment but urging Ali Pasha to mobilize the Albanian chieftains against the French. Not all went smoothly. In 1809 the British seized several of the Vizier's ships, and he retaliated by seizing British properties.

Boundary Issues: Why Is Butrint in Albania?

Butrint became caught up in the southern Albania/northern Epirus crisis on the eve of the First World War. The creation of the republic of Albania was a direct result of the decline of Ottoman power in the Balkans, vigorously exacerbated by Greek nationalism. The Great Powers had attempted and failed to find a solution to empowering the different ethnic communities in the Balkans at the Treaty of San Stefano and the Congress of Berlin in 1878.

Albanian nationalism, for example, certainly came of age in the aftermath of these councils. Greece was actively posturing to incorporate most of southern Albania as part of Epirus in the new Greek state. In 1907, the Albanian leader, Ismail Kemal, in secret meetings with the Greek government, went so far as to concede a border between Albania and Greece running from the Ionian Sea north of Corfu across what was then the *vilayet* of Ioannina. Then, in the Second Balkan War of 1913, the Greek army advanced northwards into Epirus, occupying the region up to a point just south of Vlora.

Various countries now vied for control over the area, Italy and Austria-Hungary being the principal contenders.[8] Greece also laid claim to the area with French and Russian support. At the Ambassadors' Conference of London in 1913, Greece rescinded its claim on Vlora, but insisted on obtaining the area directly opposite Corfu as well as the district of Korçë. Deeply offended, the Italians in May 1913 made it clear that they would seize Saranda (now in Greek military hands) and Vlora if Greece was permitted to control the Straits of Corfu. Such a strategic passage, they argued robustly, could not be controlled by one nation. Earl Grey, the British foreign secretary, came up with a compromise. Greece might retain many of the Aegean islands it had recently acquired from the Ottomans (and, as it happened, an openly expressed aspiration to annexe the Dodecanese islands, then in Italian hands), if it accepted a border running along the south side of Cape Stillo, more or less opposite Corfu Town. This way, the Straits passed through Greece (Corfu) and Albania. All parties acceded to this. The memorandum drawn up by Grey in August 1913 lists Cape Stillo (and Korçë) as ceded to Albania, while by way of compensation several Aegean islands were ceded to the Greeks.

The border was fixed in the Protocol of Florence of 17 December 1913, but a revolt broke out in the area that included Gjirokastra, Saranda and Delvina, as well as Butrint, and a short-lived new state was born. The Republic of Korçë that was proclaimed under its own president, former Greek foreign minister George Zographos, lasted fewer than six months. On 17 May 1914 the inhabitants of the contested area accepted the Protocol of Corfu, giving them certain privileges. This did not assuage the anger of many on either side of the new frontier.

Mindful of the region's Greek antiquity, a young archaeologist was assigned to the new republic's military forces. Demetrios Evangelides, the excavator of the Greek sanctuary at Dodona, was encouraged to investigate the new state for its antiquities. In this short period, he excavated at Saranda, the sanctuary church of Santi Quaranta and the temple at Dobra on the north–south road between Phoenicê and points south. Tellingly, perhaps because it lay in dangerous border lands, Evangelides ignored Butrint.

Evangelides may have been prudent in not investigating Butrint. Very soon the contested troubles of the area brought the new League of Nations to examine the line of Albania's southern boundary. In August 1923 the members of an Italian boundary commission led by General Tellini were

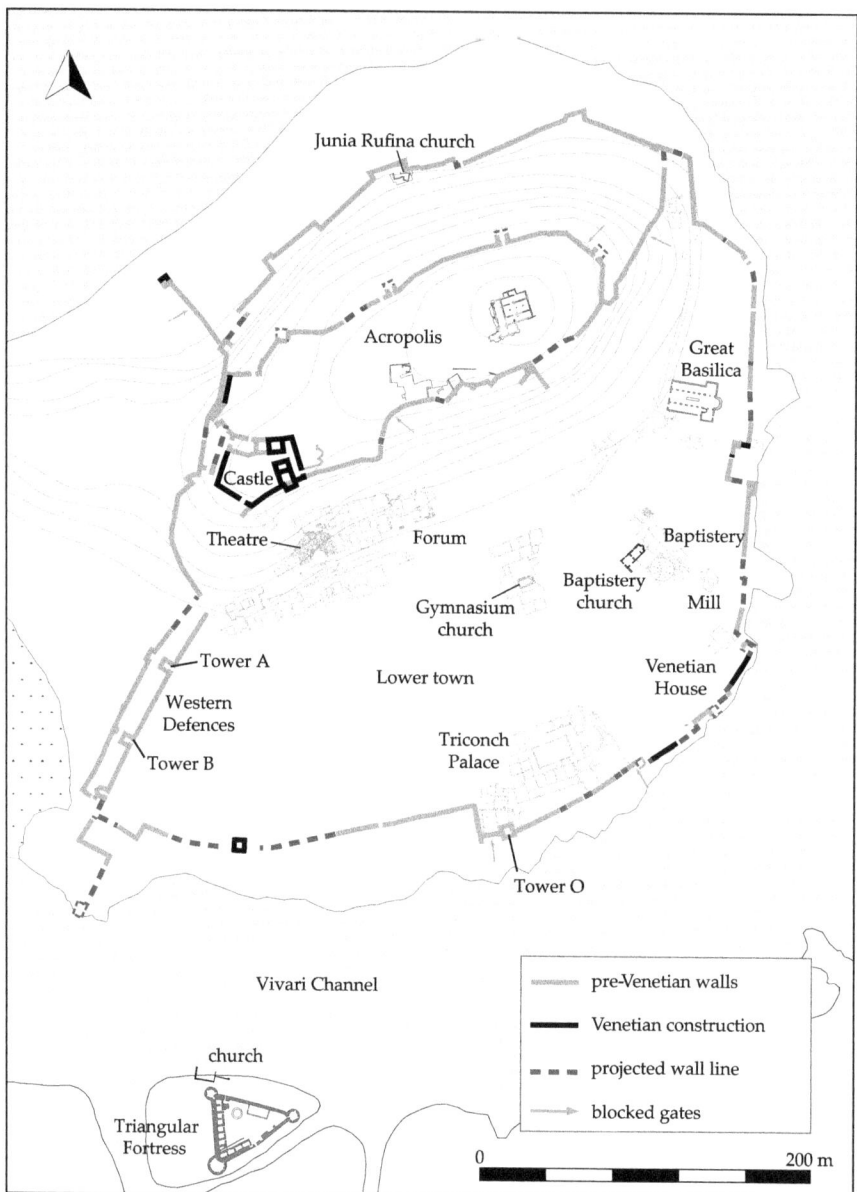

FIGURE 7.2 *A map of fifteenth- to sixteenth-century Butrint in the Venetian period.*

murdered in northern Greece, causing Benito Mussolini to bomb then seize Corfu in search of reparations.[9] The ensuing deliberations brokered by the League resulted in the Protocol of Florence, signed on 27 January 1925. This ratified the 1913 Protocol, leaving Cape Stillo and Butrint just inside Albania, exactly as the Italians had wished.

Life in the Venetian Colony

The archaeology of Butrint's latest periods is mostly military but excavations in the area of the Roman forum by David Hernandez and those in the area of the Triconch Palace shed light on Butrint's twilight centuries as a small Venetian town.[10]

David Hernandez excavated three Venetian houses occupying the site of the erstwhile Roman forum. On the westernmost side a trench exposed the side of house I, revealing a single room with an area of 5.6 × 4.6 metres. A single course of large irregular stones, representing a building's foundations, and the original earthen floor of the house remained *in situ*. The house was constructed in the late fourteenth or fifteenth century judging from seven coins and polychrome sgraffito ware and monochrome glazed ware pottery imported from northern Italy. The latest coin, found in fill touching the floor, is an *akçe* of Süleyman the Magnificent, dating between 1520–66. This silver coin is a unique find, almost certainly belonging to the Ottoman siege of Corfu in 1537 when Butrint was destroyed. Venetian house III lay at the eastern side of the erstwhile forum. The house plan and its overall dimensions could not be determined, but it was evidently large, built on a foundation of sizable irregular stones. Its collapsed roof was found below the house's stone rubble, consisting of a layer of large broken yellow ceramic roof tiles. Its earthen floor was badly burned, and there was ample evidence that the dwelling was destroyed by fire. Fragments of complete ceramic vessels were found on the floor. Ten coins, all minted in Venice, were recovered from the earliest floor level of the house. These coins included two silver Torneselli dating between 1342–1471 (between Doges Andrea Dandolo and Cristoforo Moro) and one is a *soldino* dating between 1368–82 (Doge Andrea Contarini). The presence of proto-maiolica of a type from Taranto and Metaponto coincide with the latest coins, which date the construction of the house to the late fourteenth century. The house had had at least two rooms on the ground floor. The larger of the two, room A, occupied the northwestern side of the building, measuring 6.3 metres in length. A stone masonry hearth paved with thick rectangular tiles occupied the northwestern corner of the house. The hearth/chimney was installed in a later phase of reconstruction in the fifteenth or sixteenth century, with that corner of the house rebuilt in regular coursed masonry. The internal partition wall, separating rooms A and B, belongs to this later phase and was built of *spolia*, which included moulded architectural fragments from ancient buildings. Room A served as a kitchen and storage area. Kitchen utensils and other bronze artifacts were found in this room, including a spoon on the hearth. The iron objects from the room included a blade, the head of a small tool, semi-circular handles, a chain ring, and a hanging hearth chain.

Flotation of the soil from the room's earthen floor yielded large amounts of free-threshing wheat (*T. aestivum/durum*), in addition to einkorns (*T. monococcum*), emmers (*T. dicoccum*), oats (*Avena sativa*), six-row hulled barley (*Hordeum vulgare*), rye (*Secale cereale*), millets (*Panicum/Setaria*), peas (*Pisum sativum*), lentils (*Lens culinaris*), Spanish vetchling (*Lathyrus clymenum*), olives (*Olea europaea*), grapes (*Vitis vinifera*), flax (*Linum usitatissimum*), and various wild berries (*Rubus* sp.; *Sambucus* sp.; *Sorbus* sp.). A large amount of wheat was recovered (c. 38,000 seeds), virtually all of which came from room A. Since pithoi were not present, the wheat appears to have been stored in sacks placed against the northern wall of the kitchen. This archaeobotanical evidence from the kitchen of house III shows that, in the sixteenth century, its household had access to a wide variety of crops, which included cereals and pulses. Other notable crops and fruits were flax, olives, grapes, and berries. Most, if not all, the cereals and pulses would have been cultivated seasonally, probably in small gardens inside and immediately outside the town.

Owing to its size and internal partitions, it is probable that house III was two-storied. The rafters, timber beams, posts, and other wooden elements of the house were lost in the fire. The discovery of a bronze thimble and a bone hairpin in room A may have come from the second floor. These items are associated with sewing and female adornment. However, loom weights and spindle whorls are notably absent from the recovered material. The function of the upper-floor room remains unclear. Perhaps it had a female occupant or served as sleeping quarters. Room A, as a kitchen and storage area, was likely the backroom of the house. If this is correct, then the house's entrance was located on the eastern side, which opened into room B.

The destruction of house III occurred in the first half of the sixteenth century, judging from its latest pottery, which included Italian polychrome sgraffito ware and Italian maiolica. One complete glazed jug painted in red, green, and brown, belonging to the RMR 'Bari Type' imported from southern Italy, is the same type found at the town of Stari Bar, Montenegro, and dated stratigraphically to the first half of the sixteenth century. The large quantities and variety of food indicate that the house was in use immediately before it burned down. On the basis of the house's size, plan, location, and hearth/chimney, as well as its rich bronze and iron objects, coins, and variety of food, its occupants were far from poor.

Construction of houses occurred at the time or soon after Venice's acquisition of Butrint in 1386. The colonial building programme appears to have involved the building of new houses and the refurbishment of older structures into dwellings. This was likely accompanied by a redefinition of property boundaries on the headland.

Little is known about late Medieval domestic buildings in Epirus. In Greece and Italy, urban houses of this period were typically built of stone. The plan of house III is consistent with the linear domestic building designs (rectangular and L-shaped) that were common in the western Balkans in the late Middle Ages (e.g. at Stari Bar in Montenegro). The proximity of the houses in the former area of the Roman forum suggests a fairly tight

FIGURE 7.3 *A view of the sixteenth-century Venetian Tower in the lower town at Butrint.*

clustering of dwellings, each occupying a small plot. House III was located immediately north of the Gymnasium complex (described in Chapter 4) with which it may have been associated. Notably, the bell-tower added to the Gymnasium church (dismantled by Ugolini) and the church beside the Baptistery belong to this colonial period.

Daily life in Venetian Butrint is also illuminated by finds made close to a tower in the town wall within the area of the former Triconch Palace. A remarkable aspect of these finds is the high percentage of coloured tablewares in the Venetian colonial period. The percentage of monochrome glazed wares in one colour far exceeds those of any other period. One reason for the growing inclination to eat from monochrome glazed table utensils was the belief that the copper in the polychrome glazes gave the food a bad taste. Another explanation is that, in an age when pestilence was a constant peril, the serving of food in a clear, hygienic form was considered reassuring. Another aspect of this approach to hygiene was for each diner to have a separate ceramic bowl or dish for each course. Of course, this elaborate changing of plates at the dining table required more varied table services, hence perhaps the volume of broken wares in the rubbish scattered around the tower.[11] Nevertheless, older drinking traditions continued: the Triconch Palace finds indicate that the defenders in the tower drank a diluted wine from maiolica jugs served in delicate Venetian glasses, almost certainly shared by several diners at the table. Indeed, a transparent wineglass with a long delicate stem, which looks similar to the *cristallo* ones found in Butrint, can be seen in the hand of a diner on a Renaissance icon from nearby Corfu. He holds the glass at the base and not at the stem or cup, thus displaying a typical Western drinking habit, favoured by Venice's rich. The transparency of such *cristallo* glasses allowed the colour of the wine to be fully appreciated.

The faunal assemblages from this period also confirm a notable standard of living. Meat from cattle, sheep, goat and pigs was butchered elsewhere and brought as joints to the community, while a small amount of wild animals including deer, wild boar and hare as well as waterfowl in particular, were being consumed. Not surprisingly, the diet of these tower-dwellers was supplemented by fishing. Common species found in the excavations include gilthead, mussels, thorny oysters, murex, cockles, carpet shells and whelks.

Elsewhere in Butrint, the well-head at Junia Rufina was probably still in use, just inside the Lion Gate, as was the chapel beside it. Also in the lower town are two extant stone buildings that date to this period. Both are located close to the Vivari Channel, next to the site of the Baptistery. The largest and most elaborate is a house with a cross-vaulted cellar and living quarters on the first floor. In design it is reminiscent of major townhouses throughout the Venetian empire. The second building, heavily water-worn, may have functioned as a mill, perhaps associated with the tanning described in the archives.

Outside Butrint, the fine third-century vaulted tomb beside the Vivari Channel was transformed into a small chapel, dedicated according to Venetian and French maps to S. Dimitri.[12] The chapel seems to have opened out onto the channel. The footings of a modest brick-built rectangular altar appear to exist against the east wall, above which are traces of later Medieval painting. These are interpreted as a series of panels, irregular in size and sequence, some of which carry figural imagery set in narrow red frames. The most telling feature is a deep red halo, rimmed in white, framing the head. This identifies the figure unambiguously as a Christian saint. This channel-side chapel remained a point of reference long after old Butrint was abandoned in 1572, following the increasingly persistent attacks by the Ottomans on Corfu and its mainland enclave.

Much later, after old Butrint was finally abandoned, it is clear from a Venetian cadastral map of 1718 that houses, which were managing and processing fish, were the principal dwellings here. A small house existed where in *c.* 1807 Ali Pasha built a castle at the mouth of the Vivari Channel.[13] The remains of the Venetian precursor of the castle are few but substantial and indicate that the eighteenth-century house evolved into a small fortress (seemingly without towers). A cadastral map, dating to around 1781 when the Gonemi family was granted a fief in Vrina, depicts a towered enclosure or building. The legend shown on the map reads: 'Casa di abitazione della Famiglia sudetta [that is, Gonemi] con altre case d'intorno per ricovero dei coloni e lavoratori del Feudo Vrina'.[14] This was almost certainly less a military post and more a fortified storage structure, probably for products from the surrounding areas to be taken to Corfu. William Martin Leake

FIGURE 7.4 *Aerial view of Ali Pasha's early nineteenth-century castle.*

remarks that the house was partially ruined during his visit in 1805, at a time when Ali Pasha was negotiating its purchase along with the associated land.

Ali Pasha's early nineteenth-century fort incorporating this earlier house is a small rectangular structure (22 × 30 metres) adrift on the very edge of the marshes. The earliest building within the later fort is a large rectangular tower supported by three barrel-vaulted rooms. The main area of occupation would have been in the upper levels of the tower (now destroyed). Around this tower is a later circuit wall including two round towers on its seaward side and two irregularly sized square towers that overlooked the landward approach. The principal entrance lay to the north where a large, vaulted passageway led to the exterior, opening directly onto the Vivari Channel. The towers had cannon ports, and a wide parapet ran around three sides of the enclosure. It was certainly in use by 1819 when *HMS Glasgow* exchanged salutes with the fort's battery of guns during a conference between Sir Thomas Maitland, the British governor of Corfu and the Ionian islands, and Ali Pasha.

Other less substantial Venetian remains include a modest dwelling on the shore of Alinura Bay, which reoccupied a Late Roman building associated with fishing. A more substantial Venetian settlement lay east of Butrint along the south side of the Vivari Channel at a place called Zarópulo, today called *paleospiti* (old houses). The small settlement dates back to the seventeenth century or earlier and lasted until the later nineteenth century. It appears to have been a channel-side terminus of the old road heading south past the hilltop church of S. Dimitri. Situated close to Lake Bufi, Zarópulo was engaged in fishing as well as procuring timber – principally logs for firewood that was much in demand in Corfu – from the Butrint forest, disputed land on the edge of the Venetian enclave on the slopes of Mount Mile.

Fortress Butrint

Later Venetian Butrint is essentially a story of fortresses. First and foremost, Butrint was a military bulwark in Venetian times occupying a niche – an enclave – in largely Ottoman territory. The military architecture of the colonial phase mattered and was constantly renewed as excavations in the western defences illustrate. In addition, the Water Gate by the Great Basilica (with the old Roman road bridge being a distant memory) and the Acropolis gate to the old Medieval castle were strengthened on several occasions.

The most substantial defensive work is the Triangular Fortress on the south side of the Vivari Channel, constructed in tandem with a formidable channel side tower close to Butrint's western defences.[15] This fortress is an imposing building in the form of an irregular triangle with towers on all three corners, the largest on the south-west side. For much of its history it

FIGURE 7.5 *The seventeenth-century Triangular Fortress.*

stood on one of two islands where the deltaic end of the Pavllas River met the Vivari Channel. The principal entrance to the fort was on its south side. A detailed eighteenth-century survey shows that its entrance was linked to an outerwork or *ravelin* on the other smaller island. The islands and *ravelin* have now disappeared as a result of alluvial changes, land reclamation work and the canalization of the Pavllas river.

Butrint Foundation excavations show that the Triangular Fortress was a new construction *ex novo* opposite the ancient site that evolved over two centuries, not originally an extra-mural later Medieval fort as some scholars have proposed.[16] A drawing in the Venetian archives dated to 1662–4 depicts the Triangular Fortress without towers as '*Forte fatto da turchi nella gola di fiumi sol suo fosso largo passi.*' It is now thought that the towers were added in a fourth phase of the Triangular Fortress in *c.* 1684–1716. The *ravelin* was added later, at some time in the eighteenth century after 1716.

Within the Triangular Fortress, on the western side, the remains of vaulted storerooms supporting artillery platforms can still be seen. The keystone of one of these buildings is decorated with a relief of the Venetian symbol, the Lion of St Mark. These buildings clearly replaced earlier structures. A circular building (perhaps a granary) stands close to the north-west corner. Musket ports at both ground level and the level of the parapet walk pierce the fortress walls. Remains of a brick-built outwork with a row of double musket ports can be seen on the western exterior of the fortress. On the west-facing wall of the fort, and on the two western-most towers, a series of cannon ports protected the approach to the fort from the Vivari Channel.

The fortress remains largely intact and was seemingly in use until General Chabot's troops fired upon it in 1798. Henry Cook's drawing of *c.* 1850 shows it behind a line of buildings occupying the side of the Vivari Channel including a church. Here a periodic market was apparently held on occasions, with fish being despatched inland as far as Ioannina. Similar markets are known to have existed in Albania at Shufada (the delta of Erzeni river), Spinarica (Vjosa river outlet) and Villa Bashtova (at the mouth of the river Shkumbini).

Opposite the Triangular Fortress within Butrint, possibly on top of an early gate, is an elegant Venetian tower standing today to its full height. The entrance to the tower and the lowest floor is more than 3 metres above the exterior ground level, above a large talus or batter. Within the tower a vaulted ceiling supports a second floor. Brick-lined musket ports are present on all four sides of the tower with a cannon port on each floor on the south-facing wall, guarding the Vivari Channel. The Albanian archaeologist Gjerak Karaiskaj attributes the tower to the sixteenth century. Seven similar towers, each the property of great landowners, existed in northern Corfu. Formidably constructed, it is tempting to associate this with Cristoforo Condocali and his efforts to revive Butrint's fortunes after Pertan Pasha launched his attack on Corfu from here in 1571, and it is certainly present on the 1718 cadastral map.

The purpose of the fortifications on either side of the Vivari Channel was clearly to control the lucrative fisheries of Lake Butrint. The cadastral map depicts three lines of fish traps across the channel between these two fortifications, no trace of which survives today. Other fortifications lie close to Butrint. A watchtower overlooks the Vivari Channel, on the south slope of Mt. Sotirës close to the chapel of S. Dimitri (see above). Both Butrint and Corfu are visible from this point and the tower therefore occupied an important signalling position. It comprised a square structure with only one room. A similar tower stood on the hill exposed above the marshes, now occupied by the modern village of Vrina. This is the tower of Jaco, the focus of the firefight between the French led by General Chabot and the forces of Ali Pasha in 1798. Older residents recall its demolition, although nothing is known of its size or construction.[17]

A secondary defensive work in the hinterland of Butrint also merits mention. Situated about 10 kilometres north of Butrint, adjacent to the monastery of St George, the Dema Wall – belonging to the Hellenistic period – was renewed.[18] This ran across the Ksamil peninsula from the shore of Lake Butrint to the Corfu Straits. The wall was only 0.85 metres wide and was of indifferent construction with rectangular towers projecting to the north. It was never a substantial fortification but marked the northern section of the Venetian enclave.

* * *

Butrint in Venetian times was often an embattled enclave, subject to aggressive attacks from local Turkish lords and periodically a base for over-reaching Ottoman sieges of Corfu. Yet, amazingly, for 400 years the Venetians resiliently persisted here, unquestionably because it was so rich in fish. The archaeology offers some insights into the struggle. The military architecture is spare and practical in form. By contrast the colonial dwellings were modest yet their material culture shows a standard of living that, while hard and often aggravating, was verging on the affluent. Presumably this affluence in marine produce is why Butrint was so regularly mapped by Venetian surveyors. It was a wealth that William Martin Leake noted when he visited in 1805, recalling, for example, that the Bishop of Ioannina had a fish-house here. With the cession of the enclave to Ali Pasha of Tepelenë, it became, as the Reverend Fanshawe Tozer later remarked, Turkey. Cook's sketch from the 1850s depicts the community of fisherman gathered around the Triangular Fortress; it had dwindled in size when Ugolini photographed the fortress on his first visit in 1924. By then this was well and truly a liminal place and, as we have seen, this is how it remained, up until Albania re-engaged with Europe in 1991 when Butrint and Corfu effectively embarked upon a reprise of their millennia-old relationship.

8

Tangled Web

Archaeology, Politics and Economic Revival

We the sons of the new age,
Leaving the old to its 'holiness',
Have clenched our fists to fight
In new battles
And to triumph. . . .
We, the sons of the new age,
Scions of a soil drenched in tears
Where the sweat of our brows has been shed in vain,
For our land was the prey to foreigners
Whose fury had to be paid for dearly . . .
We, the sons of the new age,
Brothers born and raised in misery,
When our ultimate and joyful hour
Rang out
We learned to say:
We will not be lost
In the bloody game of human history.
No! No! We will not be forever lost.
We will have victory!
Victory of conscience and of free thought!

MIGJENI[1]

Hunter-Gatherer Stand, Refuge, *Polis*, Healing Sanctuary, Colony, *Municipium*, *Kastron*, Market, Fishery, . . . World Heritage Site

The youthful inter-war poems of Migjeni capture the heroic struggle that has been a persistent theme and very often a bitter reality of Albanian life in the twentieth century. In such circumstances, the inscription of Butrint – albeit Ugolini's Butrint in terms of the area protected – on the UNESCO World Heritage Centre's list in 1992 is something for which we should be grateful. As we have seen, Butrint in fact took many forms in different ages, shaped by the near-constant interaction between the place, its lagoonal landscape and the Mediterranean. Its ever-changing character has undoubtedly contributed to making it eternal. The revised UNESCO inscription of December 1999 takes account of this (see below).

The exposed hilltop overlooking a deep-water lagoon abundant in fish has been an enduring feature of Butrint in its many historical guises. Other than tourism, its main income as a place is still from fish, still caught in a web of rusting, communist traps. Such has been its affluence as a fishery that Corfiots under Venice braved centuries of incursions, first by Albanians then Turks, to exploit the waters here. It is no surprise, then, to discover the lithic instruments of Mousterian manufacture on the beaches surrounding the lagoon. It is no less unsurprising that the hilltop made a suitable refuge or temporary encampment in later Bronze Age times, as the new, metropolitan Corinthian colony of Corfu reached out to the mainland to find sufficient resources to sustain itself.

The next stage in this long history, though, was of signal importance. Blessed with springs that possessed healing qualities, Butrint emerged as the administrative centre of the *koinin* of the Praesebes tribe. Everything points to its continuing closeness to Corfu as a medicinal centre, perhaps an imitation of the long-established Epirote sanctuary at Dodona. Whatever the reason for the perceived healing powers of Butrint's water, it was to be an enduring value measured well into the later Middle Ages when wells like those of Junia Rufina were gracefully renovated.

Julius Caesar, in urgent need of supplies to sustain his bitter struggle against Pompey, viewed the sanctuary through the prism of his own driving ambition. Ringed by largely dried-out marshland, here lay the perfect site to settle veterans as a colony. It was an obvious cornerstone in his strategy to control western Greece and therefore the passage from the Adriatic to the Aegean. With his estate menaced by new Roman colonists, Titus Pomponius Atticus may have regretted this prospect – as might the priests of the sanctuary – but undoubtedly this located Butrint as a place directly before the highest authorities in Rome. Caesar's vision outlived him and, within fifteen years or so, under Augustus' guidance following his epoch-making victory at Actium, provision and purpose were found for the colony. The civic authorities must have been smug when they learnt that Virgil awarded Butrint, rather than the age-old oracle at Dodona, association with the Trojan exiles, Helenus, Andromache and Aeneas himself. It was but a short step to a truly remarkable association with the new imperial court at Rome itself. So, for one or two generations, now linked to the Victory City of Nicopolis rather than in the shadow of Corfu, Butrint prospered. By this time Buthrotum was most definitely not a 'pathetic facsimile of Troy' as one ancient historian reading Virgil's *Aeneid* has deduced.[2] The urban fabric now evolved, sometimes faltered, but was essentially sustained as Caesar's legacy until the later sixth century.

Subsequently, as a Byzantine *kastron* and periodic market, then as a stoutly fortified Medieval town under the Epirote Despots, it was the Roman colonial form (with its ring of Late Roman town walls) that provided its shape. Yet, after AD 600, Butrint was a small enclave, a beachhead in Epirus that at regular intervals came under new political leadership. Its political allegiance almost invariably lay beyond the sea. Certainly, after the Despotate lost it, Butrint had a minimal relationship with its Balkan hinterland. In many ways it was just as it had been before Caesar arrived, when Butrint had been a Corfiot sanctuary. This umbilical relationship persisted long after the town was formally reduced to a fortress and fisheries in 1572, sustained by leading Corfiot families in allegiance to Venice. It persisted until Venice was evicted from the Ionian islands in 1797 and Ali Pasha of Tepelenë and subsequent sub-Ottoman chieftains incorporated it into Epirus. Ali Pasha had clearly understood the strategic significance of Butrint. Control of the old town and the Ionian islands was, as Napoleon described it, 'the key to the Adriatic', yet nevertheless 'the Muslim Bonaparte' (as Ali Pasha has been called) permitted Butrint to be reduced to a fishery and hunting ground effectively on the western limits of Turkey.

In the struggle for Northern Epirus in the fifty years up until the Second Balkan War of 1913, Butrint merits no mention. It was formally attributed to Albania at the Treaty of London in 1913 to some extent because Italy rejected the notion of Greece owning both sides of the Straits of Corfu. In these quixotic circumstances it could so easily have remained as Corfu's outpost on the Epirote mainland. Yet this seemingly arbitrary decision also brought the place great advantages. Being Albania's southwestern-most point, as Luigi Maria Ugolini discovered, it lay in a virtually forgotten landscape.[3] Little changed, too, after the Second World War, when it was out-of-bounds to all but the few villagers of the region and Tirana's trusted élite. As such the Butrint we see today is special because it is a microcosm of Mediterranean history, locked in an exceptional twentieth-century time warp.

Butrint encapsulates a Mediterranean story. In many ways that was why, notwithstanding the Virgilian story, we may suspect that Ugolini deserted Phoenicê, a classic Epirote site, in favour of investigating Butrint. But it is Corfu rather than Troy in miniature. It is a story that continues to be part of the common destiny of this quintessential Mediterranean island city. Today, with the advent of the so-called globalized Mediterranean, this relationship persists thanks – in the historian David Abulafia's provocative opinion – to two inventions: 'the aeroplane and the bikini'.[4]

Changing Perceptions

If you look around our country and our cities you will see how much energy individuals have spent to increase the quality of life. You would be amazed if you had any idea of how it was ten years ago. But now we have to start – and we have already started – to build a sense of belonging to the space that is in between 'my house' and 'the other's house'.[5]

None of us when we began the Butrint Foundation project in 1994 perceived Albania to be part of Turkey as the Reverend Fanshawe Tozer had in 1869, when he crossed to Corfu. The ethos of Albania was a European venture even if the then-Western image in the media was the antithesis of Europeanness as conceptualized by the European Union.

Like so many before us, we arrived from Corfu, having taken the ferry from Brindisi. The mountains, the sunsets, 'the splendid sheet of water', as Edward Lear called Lake Butrint were seemingly untouched by the twentieth century. A balm of mature woodland, initially approached through an avenue of eucalyptuses, now made Ugolini's excavations more enchanting. Discrete concrete signs and the crazy paved path through the archaeological site provided the only hint of the sixty years that had transpired since Ugolini's early demise. Butrint had survived the era of communism, its surreal blanketing of the Albanian countryside in concrete bunkers and the ubiquitous use of severe cement. In the misty early mornings, with the iridescent dawn light reflecting off the Vivari Channel, the ancient town might have been time-warped in the age of Ugolini and his mission. But, of course, it was not.

Butrint, in fact, was in great jeopardy.[6] Albania was plainly not Turkey; it was a Balkan country that had barely shaped an identity before it was sealed in a hapless Stalinist escapade. In the early 1990s the newly elected government, proud of Butrint's UNESCO World Heritage status, was being flattered with architects' concepts to exploit the ancient town as the nexus of a ring of vacation villages, each served by golf courses, marinas, supermarkets and even helicopter pads.

Looking back, the Albanians, unshackled after state imprisonment, leapt at the opportunities. It was quite understandable. Notwithstanding the absence of good beaches, entrepreneurs from many different European backgrounds tendered to transform the olive terraces and marshlands beyond Butrint into the same undifferentiated townscape that has deprived adjacent Corfu of the exquisite beauty that enchanted Edward Lear and Lawrence Durrell in different centuries.

The Butrint Foundation found itself defending Albania from its own intentions. Was this wise, we may ask in retrospect? After all, the transition to a market economy overwhelmed Albania like an earthquake. More than a million of its population – approximately one-third – emigrated in the first three years after communism ended. Most escaped by boat or walked through the mountains to evade Greek border guards, embarking on odysseys, experiences mostly unknown to West Europeans since 1945. Meanwhile, the country, having wrecked the last elements of its agriculture and industry in a muddled bid to cauterize its communist past, was steeped in abject poverty. The average income was no more than a pitiful $2–3 per day. Into this lethal vacuum, fuelled by limited capacity and sub-communist misinformation, came the aid agencies and businessmen who offered tantalizing elixirs. Soon everyone would be rich.

The visit of James Wolfensohn, President of the World Bank, to Butrint in October 1995, paradoxically encouraged both developers and the Butrint Foundation. A conference sponsored by the World Bank in Tirana in May 1996 largely concentrated upon an orgy of development around Butrint. Only Albania's financial 'pyramid' crisis and ensuing civil uprising from January to March 1997, leading to the resignation of President Berisha's government, put a brake on the plans. No-one, after all, was going to visit Albania for years to come.

Following the civil uprising an UNESCO emergency mission to Butrint in October 1997 recommended that the World Heritage Site should be managed by a coordinating body that sought to carefully develop it as a resource. Particular emphasis, the mission believed, should be given to protecting its surrounding cultural landscape. The new Albanian government swiftly recognized the economic benefits of this approach. In 1998–9, following public meetings launched by the Butrint Foundation and with the support of Edi Rama, then the Minister of Culture, a new project was launched to deploy Butrint as a major cultural destination for eco-tourism – a place where Albania's new identity would be on display. Central to this was a programme to enlarge the bounds of Butrint, safeguarding its lagoonal landscape.

Not all the government was convinced. As late as July 1999 the then Albanian Prime Minister was claiming that a tourist airport would be built at Butrint. Nevertheless, the Butrint Foundation's proposals were supported by UNESCO who in December 1999 formally enlarged the inscription from 20 hectares to 29 square kilometres, and by Rama's Ministry of Culture, Youth and Sports which created the Butrint National Park with its own management office. The new park followed more or less the boundaries of the late Medieval Venetian enclave, *the Insula Botentro*.

With the National Park established, mostly in response to the Butrint Foundation's intercession, UNESCO provided funds for the development of local community programmes and an educational programme; the World Bank has provided a substantial grant to support the institutional development of the Park; the European Union has voted support for infrastructural development in order to attract, control and assist in visitor management and

FIGURE 8.1 *View of the Triconch Palace after conservation, 2005.*

site security; and the Shinto Foundation, Worldmate, has refurbished the village school at Vrina at the southern entrance to the park.

Against all odds, Albania has a modern eco-sensitive project providing its first World Heritage site (the towns of Gjirokastra and Berat were designated in 2005 and 2007 respectively) with a protected setting. The 20,000 foreign visitors registered in 2004 have ballooned to 300,000 in 2023, of whom at least 50,000 were Albanians and Kosovans. The reflexive collaboration between the Albanian Ministry of Culture, Youth and Sports (with national legislative authority) and foreign NGOs (non-governmental organizations) (working with the bureaucracies of the major international agencies) has

FIGURE 8.2 *Visitors looking at the Roman forum and Theatre.*

proved a critical alliance in achieving a genuinely new and important future for this historic tract of Mediterranean coastline.

Ostensibly, Butrint appears to be a safe resource, garnering substantial ticket revenue from international and national tourists. The new Park authority (as of 2000) has managed concerts and an international theatre festival here, enhancing the national recognition for the archaeological site. Butrint, moreover, is now considered a model for other Albanian archaeological sites such as Apollonia, Durrës and Lezha. But, by being special, Butrint's undeveloped surrounding coast and lagoon is once again being menaced by extraordinary development. This existential threat has prompted Prime Minister Edi Rama to support the making of a new foundation – the Butrint Management Foundation – an alliance between the Ministry of Culture and the Albanian–American Development Foundation – to take over the management of the site in 2024 and have a strategic plan for its long-term future.

Future Directions

For Grand Tourists, from Ciriaco d'Ancona to the Reverend Fanshawe Tozer, Butrint was largely an enigmatic relic of the age of Aeneas. It belonged to a classical Mediterranean story. Paradoxically Ugolini altered that. His great enterprise transformed Butrint into the premier archaeological site of the new republic. Albania as a country was fifteen years old when he started his excavations and anxious only that he should not steal statues that belonged to it, not Italy. Enver Hoxha's communist government of 1944–91 saw it differently. Archaeology, like history, was at the service of the nation.[7] Accordingly, for a country that was politically isolated – indeed mistrustful of its Mediterranean neighbours – Butrint was of marginal interest in comparison to the ancient cities of Apollonia and Byllis where the Illyrians had been prominent. Of course, attempts were made to enlarge Butrint's part in the Illyrian myth of nation-building, consequently downplaying the role of the Greek tribes. Greatest emphasis was placed upon Butrint as a defiant bulwark. Here was a place that was continuously re-fortified (several times, as it happened in the face of prospective Albanian incursions). It exactly mirrored Albania's fixation with the number of times (allegedly forty-six) that the country had been invaded in history – a fixation that led to the zealous construction in the 1970s of 600,000 concrete bunkers to defend the people from sea and air invasion by Western powers.

Butrint became important once again when, after cutting relations with the Chinese in the 1970s, the Albanian government in need of hard currency tolerated limited tours terminating at Butrint. Yet even the tourists were treated to a curious history that took no account, for example, of Julius Caesar, the lagoon history, or indeed, much of the post-classical Byzantine, Epirote and Venetian periods. No wonder, then, that when the Butrint Foundation project began, there was genuine hope amongst Albania's archaeologists that, with Western resources and technology, Enver Hoxha's myths might be proved. Butrint, so the thinking went, might be ascribed to Illyrian ancestry rather than Greek and, while the role of the Romans was acknowledged, the impact of the Slavs in terminating the Roman history might be identified. Instead, a new generation of Albanian archaeologists has appreciated that this story is not one of isolation and endless attack by outside forces, but one rooted – as the Butrint Museum now illustrates – in the endlessly fascinating rhythms of Mediterranean history.

Looking forward, the perplexing problem is not the direction of archaeological research, but the use of the site itself. In common with many UNESCO World Heritage Sites, Butrint is in great danger. The reason is simple: the seduction of place. As the Italian novelist, Italo Calvino wrote in *Invisible Cities* (1974): '. . . cities believe themselves to be the work either of the mind or of chance, but neither the first nor the second suffices to maintain the walls'.[8] Butrint did not just happen. As we have seen, it is a palimpsest of millennia, culminating in Ugolini's imaginative explorations and reconstruction. We must therefore assume that this ancient town – like modern Tirana – is malleable, and that we, citizens, administrators, architects, planners, historians and visitors – can do something to make its management better rather than worse. Like a modern town, the fabric is

FIGURE 8.3 *Telemack Llahana (left) and Lords Sainsbury (centre) and Rothschild (centre right) discuss conservation with the author (right) at Butrint, 1995.*

mottled, fissured, discontinuous and determined by antecedence. It has always been changing, often to a tempo influenced by its environment.

Globalization in the form of UNESCO and contributing agencies such as the World Bank has altered the balance of affairs at Butrint. The price of this intervention is an impending loss of immediacy at the site and a growing sense of insecurity fuelled by the transformation of the neighbouring tourist village at Ksamil, which boasted one hotel in 1991 and now boasts 108! This investment in tourism is counter-balanced by the visitor ticket revenue. Herein, we might conclude, is a balance worth supporting, especially if the revenue is reinvested in the ancient town as UNESCO and the World Bank have commended. But Butrint will always be prey to developers while its immediate environs remain – as they do – only loosely protected by domestic law. The image of a place rich in classical treasures harnessed to global vacation benchmarks is too tempting to ignore. Destroy the magic of the place (Butrint's key quality identified by Albanians in the Management Plan workshop held at Saranda in April 1998) and its identity will disappear. Butrint will still have a complex and often fascinating Mediterranean history, but it will no longer be special. On the other hand, continue to concentrate development away from Butrint and protect its Homeric landscape including Cape Stillo, as the Butrint Foundation has proposed in partnership with the global agencies, and its magical spirit will endure. Is this utopian – the construction of a new Butrint that serves not only Albania but also the Mediterranean?

The first town at Butrint was almost certainly a Greek *polis*. The Greeks, as it happened, used the same word for a dice-and-board game that, like modern backgammon, depends upon a mixture of fortune and rules. Skill is shown by the manner of improvisation after every throw of the dice. So, we might conclude, we are all agents as well as visitors in the matter of our archaeological sites. This is especially true for those ancient places listed as World Heritage Sites. For three millennia Butrint has been at a geo-political crossroads. Its fate has been determined from all compass directions. Today, the large numbers of foreign tourists visiting Butrint underscores our international responsibilities towards this special site.

Although firmly rooted in a corner of Albania, Butrint looks to all of us to ensure it remains eternal.

FIGURE 8.4 *The Butrint team, 2002.*

NOTES

Preface

1 Ugolini 1937; Gilkes and Miraj 2000.
2 Braudel 1972.
3 Norwich, preface to Ceka 1999.
4 Hodges 2006.

Chapter 1

1 Virgil, *Aeneid* III, 291–3: trans. David West 2003.
2 Durrell 1978, 16–17.
3 Soustal 2004, 26.
4 Soustal 2004, 23.
5 Pavlides et al. 2001; Sakkas et al. 2022.
6 For an introduction to the environmental context of Butrint see: Lane 2004; Morellón et al. 2016.
7 Bescoby 2013, 26–9.
8 Hammond 1967, 432.
9 Konispoli cave: see Schuldenrein 2001; for Luigi Cardini's research about the early prehistory of Albania as part of the Italian Archaeological Mission in the 1930s, see Francis 2005. See also Galaty and Bejko 2023, 423–4; 444.
10 Giorgi and Bogdani 2012 for an overview; see also Hernandez and Hodges 2020b, 295–303; for the Molossian towns, see Dausse 2007.
11 Hammond 1967, 45.
12 Raynor 2017; Domínguez 2018.
13 Hammond 1967, 44.
14 Leake 1837, 95.
15 Pouqueville 1820, 34–5.
16 For an accessible introduction to Ali Pasha, see Fleming 1999.
17 Guy 2012.

18 For an introduction to the issues involved in establishing the national boundaries of Albania, see Kondis 1997 and Guy 2012. Barros 1965 remains a good introduction to the so-called Corfu incident in 1923.
19 Ugolini 1937; see also Gilkes and Miraj 2000; Gilkes 2003a; 2003b; 2003c.
20 Hammond 1983.
21 Newby 1984, 133.

Chapter 2

1 Dupré 1825, 10.
2 Soustal 2004, 26 (according to letter III in L. Mehus, *Kyriaci Anconitani Itinerarium*, 1742); Hammond 1967, 709–12; Bodnar 1960, 28, 43.
3 On the archaeology of later Venetian Butrint, see Hernandez 2019, as well as Gwynne, Hodges and Vroom 2014.
4 Lane 2004, 33–5.
5 Lane 2004, 34, fig. 3.7.
6 Lane 2004, 34.
7 Leake 1835, 105.
8 Pouqueville 1820, 34–5.
9 Dupré 1825, 10.
10 See the portrait of Luigi Maria Ugolini by Igino Epicoco: Hodges 2020, fig. 2.4.
11 'Poetically clad in ivy', Ugolini 1927, 169; Hodges 2020, 6.
12 Leake 1835, 99; see Hodges 2020 on the visit the previous year by S. S. Clarke in 1923.
13 Gilkes 2003c.
14 Ugolini 2003, 206, figs 8.13, 8.14; Hansen 2007, 51, fig. 4.9; Gilkes 2003c, 14.
15 Hansen 2007, 51.
16 See Skeates 2023 for a more critical assessment of Ugolini.
17 Gilkes and Hodges 2020 for an edited version of the interview with Dhimosten Budina; see also De Maria and Giorgi 2005; and Korkuti 2005. See Budina 1971a; 1971b; 1972; Budina, Drini and Pollo 1988.
18 Hodges 2009.
19 Kadare 1973, translation by Diana Ndrenika.
20 Hoxha 1980, 376–7.
21 Ceka 1976; Karaiskaj 1976; 2009; Meksi 1983; Lako 1981.
22 Hodges 2017; Hodges, Bowden and Lako 2004; Hansen and Hodges 2007; Bowden and Hodges 2011; Hansen, Hodges and Leppard 2013; Bowden 2020; Greenslade 2019; Hernandez and Hodges 2020a; Hodges and Molla 2025.
23 See, for example, Hernandez 2017; 2019.

Chapter 3

1. Virgil, *Aeneid* III, 352: trans. West 2003.
2. Ugolini 1927, 169; Hodges 2020, fig. 1.5.
3. See Lima 2013; 2020; Hernandez and Hodges 2020b, 294–5; cf. Galaty and Bejko 2023, 444.
4. Morellón et al. 2016.
5. Francis 2005; see Galaty and Bejko 2023 for an overview of Albanian prehistory.
6. Galaty and Bejko 2023, 444.
7. Respectively Korkuti et al. 1998; Forsén and Tikkala 2011.
8. Arafat and Morgan 1995, 33–7; Hernandez 2017a, 247.
9. Arafat and Morgan 1995, 28; see also 33–7.
10. Hammond 1967, 499; Hernandez 2017a, 213.
11. Hammond 1967, 499; Hernandez 2017a, 213.
12. Hernandez 2017a, 218.
13. Ceka 1976; 2013; cf. Hernandez and Hodges 2020b, 296–303.
14. Hernandez 2017a, 230–3.
15. Hernandez 2017a, 232, fn 112.
16. Arafat and Morgan 1995, 37.
17. Hernandez 2017a.
18. Hernandez 2017a, 254–6.
19. Hernandez 2017a, 220–1; table 2; Hernandez and Hodges 2020b, 295–6.
20. Hernandez and Hodges 2020b, 303–4.
21. Hernandez and Hodges 2020b, 296–300.
22. Suha 2009; 2016.
23. Hernandez and Hodges 2020b, fig. 25.5.
24. See the limited excavations described in Hernandez and Hodges 2020a, 124–35; 296–300.
25. Hammond 1967, 629–35.
26. My thanks to David Hernandez for showing me these excavations. On the manumissions from the Tower of Inscriptions see Cabanes, Drini and Hatzopoulos 2007.
27. Ginouvès et al. 1994.
28. Hernandez and Çondi 2018; Melfi 2007.
29. Melfi 2007, 23.
30. Melfi 2007, 20.
31. Melfi 2007; 2012.
32. Ugolini 1937; see now: Hernandez 2017b; Hernandez and Çondi 2018, 632–4.
33. Cf. De Maria and Mancini 2019.

34 Cabanes, Drini and Hatzopoulos 2007, 71–2, n.7; 289.
35 Giannotta 2005.
36 See Wilkes 2003 for the details of the Theatre; see also Gilkes 2003b.
37 Hernandez 2017b; Hernandez and Çondi 2018, 632–4.
38 See, however, Aleotti, Gamberini and Mancini 2020 for a proposed re-dating of the votive deposit.
39 Cabanes, Drini and Hatzopoulos 2007.
40 Cabanes, Drini and Hatzopoulos 2007, 153.
41 Hernandez unpublished; my thanks to David Hernandez for sharing this study. See also Hernandez and Hodges 2020b, 303–4.
42 Ugolini 2020; Islami 2020; see also Bogdani and Aleotti 2024.
43 Çondi 1984.
44 Bowden and Përzhita 2020.
45 Bowden and Përzhita 2020; Deniaux 2007; Hansen 2007; 2011.

Chapter 4

1 Bettini 1997, 18.
2 Abdy 2012.
3 Deniaux 2007; see also Rizakis 1996.
4 Hansen 2007; 2011.
5 See Zachos 2024 on the so-called 'Victory Monument' at Nicopolis.
6 Alcock 1993, 132–40; Zachos 2015.
7 Bartman 1999, 169–70.
8 Hernandez 2017b; Hernandez and Çondi 2018.
9 Hammond 1967, 692; see De Maria, Bogdani and Giorgi 2017 on the routes connecting Phoenicê to Onchesmos and Butrint.
10 Bescoby 2013, 27–9.
11 Leppard 2013.
12 Wilson 2013.
13 Hernandez and Çondi 2018.
14 Pojani 2007; Hansen 2007.
15 Gilkes 2003b is the full publication of Ugolini's manuscript about his excavation of the Theatre (with commentaries) found in the Museo della Civiltà Romana, Rome in 1998; Ugolini 2003, 198–205.
16 Marin and Vickers 2004.
17 Hernandez, Hodges, Islami and Schofield 2020; see also Boardman 1997.
18 Bescoby 2019.
19 Romano 2003; see also Alcock 1993, 137–40; 166–9.

20 Bescoby 2019; Greenslade and Hodges 2019a, 359–61.
21 Ricciardi 2007; Greenslade 2019, 303–21.
22 Greenslade 2019, 303–21.
23 Greenslade and Hodges 2019a; Alcock 1993, 19–24.
24 Hansen 2007; 2011.
25 Hernandez and Mitchell 2013.
26 Reynolds 2020.
27 Crowson 2020.
28 Bowden and Përzhita 2020; see also Bowden 2018; Bowden and Përzhita 2014.
29 Ugolini 1937, fig. 76; Hansen 2007, 52, fig. 4.10.
30 Ugolini 1937, fig. 76; Hansen 2007, 52, fig. 4.10.
31 Bowden and Hodges 2011.
32 Bescoby 2013.
33 Greenslade 2019, 128–48.
34 Abdy 2012.

Chapter 5

1 Whittow 2013, 134.
2 Soustal 2004, 20–2.
3 Bowden 2011.
4 Bowes 2010, 98.
5 Bowden 2011, 303–6.
6 Mitchell 2011, 252.
7 Mitchell 2011, 252.
8 Greenslade 2019, 131–46; Greenslade and Hodges 2019b, 365–9.
9 Bowden 2020, 258; see also Mitchell 2020.
10 Ugolini 1936.
11 Personal communication, David Hernandez.
12 Andrews et al. 2004; Karaiskaj 2009; see now Hodges and Molla 2025.
13 Meksi 1983; Molla 2013.
14 Meksi 1983; Mitchell 2004.
15 Bowden and Përzhita 2004a.
16 Mitchell 2008.
17 Bowden and Mitchell 2004, 111–13; Greenslade, Leppard and Logue 2013, 65–7, fig. 4.27.
18 Greenslade and Hodges 2019b, 369–72. See also Mitchell 2019, 350–1.
19 Bowden and Përzhita 2004b.

20 Harper 2017.
21 Bowden 2020, 258–9; Bowden and Hodges 2012.
22 Bowden 2020, 259.
23 Durrell 1945, 75.

Chapter 6

1 Ducellier 1981, 652.
2 Soustal 2004, 20–2. See also Nicol 1957; Molla 2019.
3 Venice: Gasparri and Gelichi 2024.
4 Constantinople: Harris 2019.
5 Rome: Krautheimer 1980.
6 Hodges and Molla 2025.
7 Greenslade and Hodges 2019c.
8 Hodges 2011, 319–23; Hodges 2015.
9 Hodges 2015.
10 Soustal 2004, 23.
11 Papadopoulou 2020, 101.
12 Greenslade, Leppard and Logue 2013.
13 Molla, Paris and Venturini 2013; Karaiskaj 2009.
14 Meksi 1983; Molla 2013.
15 Bowden and Mitchell 2004.
16 Sebastiani et al. 2013.
17 Hodges 2011, 353.
18 Papadopoulou 2020, 102–3.
19 Vroom 2004.
20 Vroom 2004; cf. Bowden 2020, 260–8.

Chapter 7

1 Tozer 1869, 232–3.
2 Soustal 2004, 25–6; Davies 2013.
3 Marmora 1672.
4 Gwynne, Hodges and Vroom 2014.
5 Davies 2013 describes the Venetian history of Butrint; her essay is based on a longer unpublished report in the Butrint archives at Waddesdon Manor.
6 Andrews et al. 2004, 148.

7 Fleming 1999 provides a good introduction to this extraordinary man; see also Dupré 1820.
8 Guy 2012 describes the protracted negotiations lasting from 1913 until 1923.
9 Barros 1965.
10 Hernandez 2019.
11 Gwynne, Hodges and Vroom 2014, 221–30.
12 Hernandez and Mitchell 2013, 189–92.
13 Carvajal and Palanco 2013.
14 'The house of the family (Gonemi) with other houses for their workers in the commune of Vrina'.
15 Bevilacqua et al. 2015.
16 Davies 2013; Parangoni, Gilkes and Bescoby 2020; see also Bevilacqua et al. 2015.
17 Davies 2013; Parangoni, Gilkes and Bescoby 2020; Andrews et al. 2004, 148.
18 Hodges 2014.

Chapter 8

1 Migjeni [Millosh Gjergj Nikolla] (1911–38), 'The Sons of the New Age', translated Robert Elsie, 1991, 29.
2 Farrell 2021, 282.
3 Hodges 2020.
4 Abulafia 2011, 636.
5 Rama 2003, 206.
6 Hodges 2017, 79–112.
7 Bowden and Hodges 2004.
8 Calvino 1974, 44.

FURTHER READING

This book draws upon two principal sources of material: the unpublished archives pertaining to the work of the Butrint Foundation (1994–) now archived at Waddesdon Manor, Waddesdon, Buckinghamshire, UK; and, of course, recent publications describing the archaeology and history of Butrint and the Central Mediterranean region.

The unpublished archives include material belonging to the Albanian Institute of Archaeology in Tirana and the Museo della Civiltà Romana in Rome. These are being made into an electronic resource by the Butrint Foundation, thanks to a generous grant from the Drue Heinz Trust and the Rothschild Foundation. A volume based on the archives of the Italian Archaeological Mission on the prehistory has been assembled in Karen Francis, *Explorations in Albania, 1930–39. The notebooks of Luigi Cardini*, London (2005). For Luigi Maria Ugolini's unpublished excavations of the Hellenistic Theatre and associated sanctuary see Oliver J. Gilkes (ed.) *The Theatre at Butrint*, London (2003).

The Butrint Foundation has published a series of reports with Oxbow Books, Oxford: R. Hodges, W. Bowden and K. Lako (eds), *Byzantine Butrint: Surveys and Excavations 1994–99* (2004); I. L. Hansen and R. Hodges (eds) *Roman Butrint: An Assessment* (2007); W. Bowden and R. Hodges, *Butrint 3: Excavations of the Triconch Palace* (2011); I. L. Hansen, R. Hodges and S. Leppard (eds), *Butrint 4: The Archaeology and Histories of an Ionian Town* (2013); S. Greenslade (ed.) *Butrint 6: Excavations on the Vrina Plain. The Lost Roman and Byzantine Suburb. 3 Vols.* (2019); W. Bowden (ed.) *Butrint 5: Life and Death at a Mediterranean Port. The Non-ceramic Finds from the Triconch Palace* (2020); D. R. Hernandez and R. Hodges (eds) *Butrint 7: Beyond Butrint* (2020).

Ugolini's work at Butrint is fundamental to our present understanding. He published a general study of Butrint, *Butrinto. Il mito d'Enea. Gli Scavi* (1937), as well as three monographs on Albanian archaeology: *Albania Antica I: richerche archeologiche* (1927); *Albania Antica II, l'acropoli di Fenice* (1932); and *Albania Antica III, l'acropoli di Butrinto* (1942).

The general theme of this book is drawn from Peregrine Horden and Nicholas Purcell, *The Corrupting Sea: A Study of Mediterranean History*, Oxford (2000); see also David Abulafia (ed.) *The Mediterranean in History*, London (2003) and *The Great Sea*, Oxford (2011). A comprehensive review of the region from the earliest times to the present is M. Sakellariou (ed.)

Epirus: 4000 Years of Greek History and Civilization, Athens (1997). See also T. J. Winnifrith's *Badlands – Borderlands: A History of Southern Albania/Northern Epirus*, London (2002).

The setting of Butrint as well as its early history is admirably surveyed in N. G. L. Hammond, *Epirus*, Oxford (1967). The history and archaeology of Corfu are described in Andreas Mustoxidi, *Delle Cose Corciresi* (1848) republished by Società per lo Studio della Storia Grecia, Athens (2000). A useful modern survey is Nondas Stamatopoulos, *Old Corfu: History and Culture*, Corfu (1978).

For general accounts of Albanian archaeology see: Neritan Ceka, *Ilirët*, Tirana (2014). For the later Illyrian and Roman archaeology see John Wilkes, *The Illyrians*, London (1992). On the later Roman period see William Bowden, *Epirus Vetus: The Archaeology of a Late Antique Province*, London (2003). On recent excavations at the Phoenicê see: Sandro de Maria and Shpresa Gjongecaj (eds) *Phoinike I*, Florence (2002), and *Phoinike II*, Bologna, (2004).

On the Slavs see Florin Curta, *The Making of the Slavs*, Cambridge (2001). On the early Middle Ages see Michael McCormick, *Origins of the European Economy*, Cambridge (2001). The classic study of the Epirote Despotate is by Donald Nicol: *The Despotate of Epirus, 1267–1479*, London (1984); see also Alain Ducellier, *La Façade Maritime de l'Albanie au Môyen Age*, Thessalonika (1981) on the later Medieval and Venetian port. On the Venetian era in Albania see: P. Xhufi, *Arbërit e Jonit. Vlora, Delvina dhe Janina në shekujt XV–XVII*, Tirana (2016).

K. E. Fleming, *The Muslim Bonaparte: Diplomacy and Orientalism in Ali Pasha's Greece*, Princeton (1999) is a good introduction to Ali Pasha of Tepelenë. See also William Martin Leake, *Travels in Northern Greece*, London (1835) [reprinted by Elibron Classics (2000) – www.elibron.com]; F. C. H. L. Pouqueville, *Voyage en Moree à Constantinople et en Albania*, Paris (1805) [reprinted by Elibron Classics (2000)]. Tourism in the region is elegantly summarized in Robert Eisner, *Travelers to an Antique Land: The History and Literature of Travel to Greece*, Ann Arbor (1991). An engaging introduction to the artist, Edward Lear, who visited and drew Butrint can be found in: Philip Sherrard, *Edward Lear: The Corfu Years*, Athens (1988)

On the modern history of Albania see Miranda Vickers, *The Albanians*, London (1997); for the 1913 Treaty of London as it affected Butrint, see: Basil Kondis, *Greece and Albania 1908–1914*, Thessalonika (1976) and Nicola C. Guy, *The Birth of Albania: Ethnic Nationalism, the Great Powers and the Question of Albanian Independence, 1912–21*, London (2019).

On the cultural heritage issues at Butrint, see Richard Hodges, *The Archaeology of Mediterranean Placemaking: Butrint and the Global Tourist Industry*, London (2016).

GLOSSARY

Actus (quadratus): a square unit of land equivalent to about 35 square metres.
Amphora: a ceramic transport vessel usually for oil or wine.
Asclepius/Aesculapius: the ancient god of medicine. The son of Apollo and Coronis. He became so skilful a healer that he could revive the dead, whereupon he was slain by Zeus. The cult of the god may have originated in Thessaly, though the best-known sanctuary was at Epidauros in Asia Minor. The cult spread to Italy, where it became popular following a plague in Rome during 293 BC.
Augustales: local priests appointed for the worship of deified emperors.
Bagenetia or Vagenetia: the Middle Byzantine name for the province in which Butrint was located.
Bailo: a local officer commanding a castle in Medieval times.
Basilica: a Roman-period administrative building, and later, a Christian church.
Bey: a local Ottoman landowner.
Bifora: a window divided in two by a central pillar.
Bothros: a sacred pit in Greek times.
Cape Stillo: the peninsula south of Butrint, overlooking the east side of the Straits of Corfu, subject of international discord in 1913.
Capitaneus: a local officer commanding a castle in Medieval times.
Castellan: a local officer commanding a castle in Venetian times.
Castello: a Medieval castle.
Castellum divisorium: reservoir served by a Roman aqueduct.
Catachumeneum: the hall in which the bishop instructed candidates before baptism.
Cavea: the part of a Roman theatre where the audience sat. Generally divided into two or three zones, upper (*summa cavea*), middle (*media cavea*), and lower (*ima cavea*).
Cella: enclosed inner room of a temple.
Chaonia: the later Hellenistic territory with its capital at Phoenicê in which Butrint was located.
Civitas: a Roman or Medieval town or centre.
Comestabilis: a captain or official in charge of Venetian Butrint.
Compitum: a crossroads shrine in the Roman forum, the civic centre.
Confessio: a Late Antique or Medieval relic-deposit.
Consignatorium: the room in which, following the Roman rite, neophytes were anointed and confirmed by the bishop immediately after their baptism.
Çuka e Ajtoit: an archaic and Hellenistic hilltop settlement, 10 kilometres east of Butrint, believed to be ancient Kestrine.
Cuneus (pl. cunei): wedge-shaped section of seating in a Roman theatre (equivalent to the Greek *kerkis*).
Curia: a meeting place for the town administrators or senators.
Cyclopean: a distinctive wall type of large irregular blocks.

Defter: Ottoman tax document.
Diazoma (pl. diazomata): semi-circular gangway separating the zones of the *koilon* in a Greek theatre (equivalent to the Roman *praecinctio*).
Domus: a Roman town-house or (patrician) household.
Duovirs: magistrates – usually appointed in pairs – to be judges for the Roman town.
Emboropanegyri: a Medieval fair or market.
Enkomion: praise for a person or thing.
Epirote Despots: a secessionist sub-Byzantine kingdom of Epirus and the Ionian islands created in 1204/5 after the fourth crusade captured Constantinople and deposed the Byzantine emperor.
Eurioa: ancient town in Epirus, inland from Parga, later known as Glyky.
Follis: a low value Byzantine coin, usually of copper alloy.
Insula(e): a section or block of a Roman town.
Kalivo: a large, fortified hilltop east of Butrint overlooking Lake Butrint, a later Bronze Age settlement and possible Hellenistic refuge created by King Pyrrhus.
Kantharos: a large two-handled vessel for wine.
Kastron: a Byzantine castle.
Koinon: an administrative sub-territory in the Hellenistic period.
Magistri: elected Roman officials.
Maiolica: coloured, glazed Italian later Medieval wares.
Manumissions: official documents – in Butrint's case, stone inscriptions – giving slaves their freedom.
Naos: the inner chamber of a Greek or Roman temple.
Nomisma: a Byzantine gold coin.
Nymphaeum: a Greek or Roman fountain dedicated to the nymphs.
Opus sectile: a pavement composed of different coloured cut marble pieces.
Orchestra: semi-circular area at the foot of the cavea between the seating and the stage.
Parodos: unroofed lateral entrance leading into the orchestra of a Greek theatre (equivalent to the Roman *aditus maximus*).
Paroikoi: parishes administered by the Greek church.
Peraia: in the third or second century BC, the word signified the mainland territory or enclave attached to a Greek island colony.
Phoenicê: (also called Phoinike and Finiq) 30 kilometres north of Butrint, the Chaonian capital and Roman hilltop town.
Pisé: a wall principally made of clay.
Polis: a Greek city, often an independent state.
Praesebes: a tribe within the Hellenistic territory of Chaonia, its principal administrative centre being Butrint.
Pronaos: the porch area of a Graeco-Roman temple.
Prostates: senior officials of the Hellenistic era.
Proteichisma: a double line of fortifications, imitating the Byzantine land walls of Constantinople.
Provisories: Venetian-period administrator.
Prytaneion: a public building, sometimes a meeting hall, in certain Greek cities, regarded as the centre of the community, in which official hospitality was extended to distinguished citizens and strangers.
Pulpitum: the stage of a Roman theatre, sometimes referred to as the *proscaenium*.
Puteal: a wellhead.

Sancak: an Ottoman province.
Saranda: the port 20 kilometres north of Butrint, ancient *Onchesmos*, also known as Santi Quaranta or the Forty Saints, briefly re-named as Zogaj by King Zog, then Porto Edda by Mussolini in 1939.
Scaenae frons: the front of the scene building facing the audience. It usually had an architecturally elaborate façade and contained the three doorways through which the actors came on stage.
Sgraffito: Medieval ceramic with distinctive incised and glazed decoration.
Skyphos: flat, open cup of the Greek period.
Stata Mater: literally, Mother who stops or stabilizes – a god to prevent fires.
Stoa: covered public space with a substantial open internal area, known as or used as a portico in Roman cities.
Strategos: a senior Greek magistrate, originally a military commander.
Stratelates: the local administrator of a *kastron*.
Thesauros: a safe-box.
Triclinium: a large formal dining room with couches for diners.
Triconch: a room with three apses.
Vicus: a small Roman town.
Villa maritima: an elegant Roman villa located on the coast.
Vivari Channel: the wide channel connecting Lake Butrint to the Straits of Corfu (and the Ionian Sea).
Vomitorium: vaulted and sometimes stepped entrance passage, permitting access to the seating of a theatre, amphitheatre or circus.
Voussiors: the tile or stone segments that form an arch.

DRAMATIS PERSONAE

Ali Pasha, of Tepelenë (1740–1822) – an Albanian ruler who served as an Ottoman pasha of the Pashalik of Ioannina but maintained a large degree of independence.
Aeneas – the Trojan hero of Virgil's *Aeneid* who, after many adventures, founds Rome.
Agrippa, Marcus Vipsanius (63–12 BC) – Augustus' admiral at the Battle of Actium in 31 BC, married the daughter of Titus Pomponius Atticus, Caecilia Attica (probably born in 51 BC).
Andromache – wife of the Trojan prince, Hector, taken as a concubine by Neoptolemus to Epirus with Hector's brother, Helenus. Eventually marries Helenus.
Atticus, Titus Pomponius (110–32 BC) – a Roman banker and patron of letters, best known for his correspondence and friendship with Marcus Tullius Cicero. Owner of many estates including one near Butrint.
Augustus, Emperor (63 BC–AD 14) – as Octavian he was the adopted son and heir of Julius Caesar, who after winning victory over Mark Antony at the Battle of Actium founded the Roman Empire.
Budina, Dhimosten (1930–2004) – communist-period archaeologist responsible for Butrint and its territory from the 1950s until 1990.
Caesar, Julius (100–44 BC) – Roman general, politician and author who won the civil war against Pompey but, on becoming a dictator, set in motion the events that ended the Roman Republic.
Cardini, Luigi (1898–1971) – an Italian prehistorian who was a member of the inter-war Italian Archaeological Mission at Butrint.
Ceka, Neritan (1941–) – son of Hasan Ceka, 'the father of Albanian archaeology', who has excavated and studied many sites in Albania principally associated with the Illyrians.
Cicero (106–43 BC) – Marcus Tullius Cicero was a Roman statesman, scholar and writer who played a major political role in the events that led to the establishment of the Roman Empire. A close friend of Titus Pomponius Atticus.
Clarke, S. S. (1897–1924) – a research student at the British School at Athens, who visited the Butrint area in May 1923.
Çondi, Dhimetër (1948–) – trained by Dhimosten Budina, a member of the team working at Butrint and the surrounding area since the 1970s.
Cyriacus of Ancona (1391–1452) – member of a merchant family from Ancona who became a distinguished antiquarian and humanist. Visited Butrint in 1435.
Durrell, Lawrence (1912–90) – novelist and travel-writer who lived on Corfu in the inter-war period and visited Butrint often.
St Elias the Younger (822/23–903) – born John Rachites at Enna, central Sicily, travelled extensively around the Mediterranean with his companion, Daniel. Arrested as a Moslem spy at Butrint in 881.

Guiscard, Robert (1015–85) – born in Normandy, he conquered southern Italy and Sicily, before invading the Byzantine Empire. Conquered Butrint in 1084.
Hammond, N. G. L. (1907–2001) – a British professor of ancient Greek history, and former student of the British School at Athens, who visited Butrint in 1930.
Helenus – brother of Cassandra and Hector of Troy, taken as a slave to Epirus by Neoptolemus where he was permitted to found Buthrotum. Later married Andromache, who bore him a son, Kestrine.
Hoxha, Enver (1908–85) – leader of the communist party of Albania, and dictator, from 1944 until his death.
Karaiskaj, Gjerak (1941–) – Albanian architectural historian, specializing in fortifications including those at Butrint.
Kavanagh, Arthur MacMurrough (1831–89) – Irish politician with poorly formed arms and legs who visited Butrint in 1862.
Kestrine – son of the Trojan exiles, Andromache and Helenus.
Khrushchev, Nikita (1894–1971) – First Secretary of the Communist Party of the Soviet Union, 1953–64, visited Albania including Butrint in May 1959.
Lako, Kosta (1949–2021) – member of the Saranda office of the Albanian Institute of Archaeology, specialist in Late Roman archaeology, excavated the defences of Butrint as well as the Triconch Palace.
Leake, William Martin (1777–1860) – a soldier, spy, diplomat, author and antiquarian. He served as an army officer reporting on Mediterranean seaports; visited Butrint in 1805.
Lear, Edward (1812–88) – painter and poet, who travelled extensively around the Mediterranean and, being based on Corfu, visited and drew Butrint on several occasions in the 1850s.
Meksi, Aleksandër (1939–) – an architectural historian and archaeologist who studied the Great Basilica and Baptistery at Butrint in 1982; later Prime Minister of Albania's first democratically elected government, 1992–7.
Pan – the Greek god of shepherds and flocks, and companion of nymphs, who (apparently) died close to Butrint.
Pouqueville, François (1770–1838) – a French diplomat, spy and writer who visited Butrint in 1805.
Pyrrhus, King (319/18–272 BC) – King of the Molossians, and later Epirus; strong opponent of early Rome who invaded southern Italy, probably responsible for building the Hellenistic Theatre at Butrint.
Rama, Edi (1964–) – painter who became Minister of Culture in 1998, and Prime Minister in 2013; responsible for creating the Butrint National Park.
Rothschild, Jacob, Lord (1936–2024) – 4th Baron Rothschild, financier and philanthropist, who established the Butrint Foundation with Lord Sainsbury in 1993.
Sainsbury, John, Lord (1927–2022) – President of Sainsbury's grocery supermarkets and politician, who established the Butrint Foundation with Lord Rothschild in 1993.
Ugolini, Luigi Maria (1895–1936) – Italian prehistorian and classical archaeologist who directed the Italian Archaeological Mission in Albania, 1924–36, first visiting Butrint in 1924 and excavating there from 1928.
Virgil (70–19 BC) – born Publius Vergilius Maro, he became the court poet of Imperial Rome, his most celebrated work being the *Aeneid*, which includes a section on Aeneas traveling to Butrint to meet Andromache and Helenus.
Zog, Ahmed (1895–1961) – Albanian politician proclaimed king in 1928 and deposed by an Italian invasion in 1939.

BIBLIOGRAPHY

Abdy, R. (2012) Monuments, myth and small change in Buthrotum (Butrint) during the early Empire. In F. López Sánchez (ed.) *The City and the Coin in the Ancient and Medieval Worlds*, 91–101. Oxford: Archaeopress.
Abulafia, D. (2003) (ed.) *The Mediterranean in History*. London: Thames and Hudson.
Abulafia, D. (2011) *The Great Sea*. Oxford: Oxford University Press.
Aleotti, N., Gamberini, A. and Mancini, L. (2020) Sacred space, territorial economy, and cultural identity in Northern Epirus (Chaonia). In E. Giorgi and G. Lepore (eds) *Boundaries Archaeology: Economy, Sacred Places, Cultural Influences in the Ionian and Adriatic Areas: Panel 7.3*, 45–63. Heidelberg: Propylaeum.
Alcock, S. E. (1993) *Graecia Capta: The Landscapes of Roman Greece*. Cambridge: Cambridge University Press.
Andrews, R., Bowden, W., Gilkes, O. and Martin, S. (2004) The Late Antique and Medieval fortification of Butrint. In R. Hodges, W. Bowden and K. Lako (eds) *Byzantine Butrint: Excavations and Surveys 1994–1999*, 126–50. Oxford: Oxbow Books.
Arafat, K. and Morgan, C. (1995) In the footsteps of Aeneas: Excavations at Butrint, Albania 1991–2. *Dialogos, Hellenic Studies Review* 2, 25–40.
Barros, J. (1965) *The Corfu Incident of 1923: Mussolini and the League of Nations*. Princeton: Princeton University Press.
Bartman, E. (1999) *Portraits of Livia: Imaging the Imperial Woman in Augustan Rome*. Cambridge: Cambridge University Press.
Bescoby, D. (2013) Landscape and environmental change: New perspectives. In I. L. Hansen, R. Hodges and S. Leppard (eds) *Butrint 4: The Archaeology and Histories of an Ionian Town*, 22–30. Oxford: Oxbow Books.
Bescoby, D. (2019) The Roman land organisation of the Butrint hinterland. In S. Greenslade (ed.) *Butrint 6: Excavations on the Vrina Plain Volume I: The Lost Roman and Byzantine Suburb*, 18–25. Oxford: Oxbow Books.
Bettini, M. (1997) Ghosts of exile: doubles and nostalgia in Vergil's *parva Troia* (*Aeneid* 3. 294ff). *Classical Antiquity* 16, 8–33.
Bevilacqua, M. G., Pierini, R., Pierotti, M. and Ruschi, P. (2015) The Triangular Fortress of Butrint, Albania: New studies for the conservation and the valorisation. In P. Rodríguez-Navarro (ed.) *Defensive Architecture of the Mediterranean: XV to XVIII Centuries 2*, 33–9. València: Editorial Universitat Politècnica de València.
Boardman, J. (1997) *The Great God Pan: The Survival of an Image*. New York: Thames and Hudson.

Bodnar, E. W. (1960) *Cyriacus of Ancona and Athens (collection Latomus 43)*. Brussels/Berchem: Latomus.
Bogdani, J. and Aleotti, N. (2024) Le necropoli di Çuka e Ajtoit. Vecchie e nuove ricerche a confronti. *Atlante Tematico Di Topografia Antica* 34, 139–60. https://doi.org/10.48255/2283-6357.ATTA.34.2024.7
Bowden, W. (2011) Urban change and the Triconch Palace site in the 5th to 7th centuries. In W. Bowden and R. Hodges (eds) *Butrint 3: Excavations at the Triconch Palace*, 302–18. Oxford: Oxbow Books.
Bowden, W. (2018) The villas of the eastern Adriatic and Ionian coastlands. In G. Métraux and A. Marzano (eds) *Roman Villas in the Mediterranean Basin*, 377–98. Cambridge: Cambridge University Press.
Bowden, W. (2020) *Butrint 5: Life and Death at a Mediterranean Port. The Non-Ceramic Finds from the Triconch Palace*. Oxford: Oxbow Books.
Bowden, W. and Hodges, R. (2004) Balkan Ghosts? Nationalism and the question of rural continuity in Albania. In N. Christie (ed.) *Landscapes of Change: The Evolution of the Countryside from Late Antiquity to the Early Middle Ages*, 195–222. Aldershot: Scolar Press.
Bowden, W. and Hodges, R. (2011) *Butrint 3: Excavations at the Triconch Palace*. Oxford: Oxbow Books.
Bowden, W. and Hodges, R. (2012) An 'Ice Age settling on the Roman Empire': Post-Roman Butrint between strategy and serendipity. In N. Christie and A. Augenti (eds) *Urbes Extinctae*, 207–41. Aldershot: Ashgate.
Bowden, W. and Mitchell, J. (2004) The Christian topography of Butrint. In R. Hodges, W. Bowden and K. Lako (eds) *Byzantine Butrint: Excavations and Surveys 1994–99*, 104–25. Oxford: Oxbow Books.
Bowden, W. and Përzhita, L. (2004a) Archaeology in the landscape of Roman Epirus: Preliminary report on the Diaporit excavations, 2002–3. *Journal of Roman Archaeology* 17, 413–33.
Bowden, W. and Përzhita, L. (2004b) The baptistery. In R. Hodges, W. Bowden and K. Lako (eds) *Byzantine Butrint: Excavations and Surveys, 1994–99*, 176–201. Oxford: Oxbow Books.
Bowden, W. and Përzhita, L. (2014) The Roman villa and early Christian complex at Diaporit. In L. Përzhita, I. Gjipali, G. Hoxha and B. Muka (eds) *Proceedings of the International Congress of Albanian Archaeological Studies (Tirana 2013)*, 469–84. Tirana: Centre for Albanian Studies.
Bowden, W. and Përzhita, L. (2020) The Diaporit Villa in Context. In D. R. Hernandez and R. Hodges (eds) *Butrint 7: Beyond Butrint*, 192–207. Oxford: Oxbow Books.
Bowes, K. (2010) *Houses and Society in the Later Roman Empire*. London: Duckworth.
Braudel, F. (1972) (trans. S. Reynolds) *The Mediterranean and the Mediterranean World in the age of Philip II*. New York: Harper & Row.
Budina, D. (1971a) Hartës arkeologjike të bregdeiti Jon dhe e pellgut të Delvinës. *Iliria* 1, 275–342.
Budina, D. (1971b) L'appartence éthnique illyrienne des tribus épirotes. In *Les Illyriens et la Genèse des Albanais*, 111–31. Tirana: Universitè de Tirana.
Budina, D. (1972) Harta arkeologjike e lungës së Drinosit. *Iliria* 3, 343–79.
Budina, D., Drini, F. and Pollo, G. (1988) *Butroti: Permbledhje Studimesh*. Tirana: Akademia e Shkencave e RPSSH, Qëndra e Kërkimeve Arkeologjike.

Cabanes, P., Drini, F. and Hatzopoulos, M. (2007) *Corpus des Inscriptions Grecques d'Illyrie Méridionale et d'Épire 2. Inscriptions de Bouthrôtos*. Athens: École Française d'Athènes.
Calvino, I. (1974) *Invisible Cities*. London: Random House.
Carvajal, J. C. and Palanco, N. (2013) The Castle of Ali Pasha at Butrint. In I. L. Hansen, R. Hodges and S. Leppard (eds) *Butrint 4: The archaeology and Histories of an Ionian Town*, 289–308. Oxford: Oxbow Books.
Ceka, N. (1976) Fortifikimi antik i Butrintit dhe i territorit të Prasaibëve. *Monumentet* 12, 27–48.
Ceka, N. (1999) *A Guide to Butrint*. London: The Butrint Foundation.
Ceka, N. (2013) *The Illyrians to the Albanians*. Tirana: Migjeni.
Çondi, Dh. (1984) Fortesa-vilë në Malathre (La forteresse-villa a Malathre). *Iliria* 2, 131–52.
Crowson, A. (2020) A possible Roman villa at the Customs House. In D. R. Hernandez and R. Hodges (eds) *Butrint 7: Beyond Butrint*, 143–6. Oxford: Oxbow Books.
Davies, S. (2013) Late Venetian Butrint: 16th–18th centuries. In I. L. Hansen, R. Hodges and S. Leppard (eds) *Butrint 4: The Archaeology and Histories of an Ionian Town*, 280–8. Oxford: Oxbow Books.
De Maria, S. and Giorgi, E. (2005) Un colloquio sul lavoro di Dhimosten Budina a Phoinike. In S. De Maria and S. Gjongecaj (eds) *Phoinike III. Rapporto Preliminare Sulle Campagne di Scavi e Ricerche 2002–2003*, 13–17. Bologna: Ante Quem.
De Maria, S. and Mancini, L. (2019) Territori e paesaggi sacri nella Caonia ellenistica e romana. In Adolfo J. Domínguez (ed.) *Politics, Territory and Identity in Ancient Western Greece: Epirus and Acarnania (Diabaseis 8)*, 193–247. Pisa: Edizioni ETS.
De Maria, S., Bogdani, J. and Giorgi, E. (2017) Ricerca e tutela in un territorio di frontiera. L'Epiro del Nord fra età ellenistica e presenza di Roman. In *Paesaggi mediterranei di età romana. Atti del convegno internazionale Bari-Egnazia, 5–6 maggio*, 49–63. Bari: Edipuglia.
Deniaux, E. (2007) La structure politique de la colonie romaine de Buthrotum. In I. L. Hansen and R. Hodges (eds) *Roman Butrint: An Assessment*, 33–9. Oxford: Oxbow Books.
Dausse, M.-P. (2007) Les Villes Molosses. In D. Berranger-Auserve (ed.) *Épire, Illyrie, Macédoine. Mélanges offerts au Professeur Pierre Cabanes*, 197–233. Clermont-Ferrand: Presses universitaires Blaise Pascal.
Domínguez, A. J. (2018) New Developments and Traditions in Epirus: The Creation of the Molossian State. In A. J. Domínguez (ed.) *Politics, Territory and Identity in Ancient Epirus (Diabaseis 8)*, 1–42. Pisa: Edizioni ETS.
Ducellier, A. (1981) *La Façade Maritime de l'Albanie au Moyen Âge*. Thessalonika: Institute for Balkan Studies.
Dupré, L. (1825) *Voyages à Athènes et à Constantinople*. Paris: Dondey/Dupré.
Durrell, L. (1945) *Prospero's Cell*. London: Faber & Faber.
Durrell, L. (1978) *The Greek Islands*. London: Faber & Faber.
Farrell, J. (2021) *Juno's Aeneid*. Princeton: Princeton University Press.
Fleming, K. E. (1999) *The Muslim Bonaparte*. Princeton: Princeton University Press.
Forsén, B. and Tikkala, E. (2011) (eds) *Thesprotia Expedition II: Environment and Settlement Patterns, Papers and Monographs of the Finnish Institute at Athens 16*. Helsinki: Suomen Ateenan-Instituutin.

Francis, K. (2005) (ed.) *Explorations in Albania, 1930–39: The Notebooks of Luigi Cardini, Prehistorian with the Italian Archaeological Mission, British School of Athens Supplementary Volume 37*. London: British School at Athens.

Galaty, M. L. and Bejko, L. (2023) Conclusion. In M. L. Galaty and L. Bejko (eds) *Archaeological Investigations in a Northern Albanian Province: Results of the Projekti Arkeologjik i Shkodrës (PASH), Vol. 1: Survey and Excavation Results; Vol. 2: Artifacts and Artifacts Analysis*, 423–47. Ann Arbor: University of Michigan Press.

Gasparri, S. and Gelichi, S. (2024) *Le Isole del Rifugio. Venezia prima di Venezia*. Rome: Laterza.

Giannotta G. (2005) Il teatro di Phoinike: materiali e stratigrafie per la cronologia delle fasi. In S. De Maria and S. Gjongecaj (eds) *Phoinike III: Rapporto preliminare sulle campagne di scavi e ricerche 2002–3*, 82–7. Bologna: Ante Quem.

Gilkes, O. J. (2003a) The voyage of Aeneas: Myth, archaeology and identity in interwar Albania. In S. Kane (ed.) *The Politics of Archaeology and Identity in a Global Context*, 31–49. Boston: Archaeological Institute of America.

Gilkes, O. J. (2003b) (ed.) *The Theatre at Butrint: Luigi Maria Ugolini's Excavations at Butrint 1928–1932, Albania Antica IV, British School at Athens Supplementary Volume 35*. London: The British School at Athens.

Gilkes, O. J. (2003c) Luigi Maria Ugolini and the Italian Archaeological Mission to Albania. In O. J. Gilkes (ed.) *The Theatre at Butrint: Luigi Maria Ugolini's Excavations at Butrint 1928–1932, Albania Antica IV, British School at Athens Supplementary Volume 35*, 3–21. London: The British School at Athens.

Gilkes, O. J. and Hodges, R. (2020) Dhimosten Budina (1930–2004): 'Architect' of the Butrint Archaeological Park. In D. R Hernandez and R. Hodges (eds) *Butrint 7: Beyond Butrint*, 310–17. Oxford: Oxbow Books.

Gilkes, O. J. and Miraj, L. (2000) The myth of Aeneas: The Italian archaeological mission in Albania 1924–43. *Public Archaeology* 1, 109–24.

Ginouvès, R., Guimier-Sorbets, A.-M., Jouanna, J. and Villard, L. (1994) *L'eau, la santé et la maladie dans le monde grec, Actes du colloque organisé à Paris (CNRS et Fondation Singer-Polignac) du 25 au 27 novembre 1992 par le Centre de recherche « Archéologie et systèmes d'information » et par l'URA 1255 « Médecine grecque »* (BCH suppl 28). Athens, L' École Française d'Athènes.

Giorgi, E. and Bogdani, J. (2012) *Il Territorio di Phoinike in Caonia: Archeologia del Paesaggio in Albania Méridionale; Scavi di Phoinike; Serie Monografica 1*. Bologna: Ante Quem.

Greenslade, S. (2019) (ed.) *Butrint 6: Excavations on the Vrina Plain Volume I: The Lost Roman and Byzantine Suburb*. Oxford: Oxbow.

Greenslade, S. and Hodges, R. (2019a) The Roman suburb on the Vrina Plain and its issues. In S. Greenslade (ed.) *Butrint 6: Excavations on the Vrina Plain Volume I: The Lost Roman and Byzantine Suburb*, 358–64. Oxford: Oxbow Books.

Greenslade, S. and Hodges, R. (2019b) From villa to church, *c.* AD 250–550? In S. Greenslade (ed.) *Butrint 6: Excavations on the Vrina Plain Volume I: The Lost Roman and Byzantine Suburb*, 365–78. Oxford: Oxbow Books.

Greenslade, S. and Hodges, R. (2019c) The aristocratic oikos on the Vrina Plain, Butrint, *c.* AD 830–1200. In S. Greenslade (ed.) *Butrint 6: Excavations on the Vrina Plain Volume I: The Lost Roman and Byzantine Suburb*, 379–88. Oxford: Oxbow Books.

Greenslade, S., Leppard, S. and Logue, M. (2013) The acropolis of Butrint reassessed. In I. L. Hansen, R. Hodges and S. Leppard (eds) *Butrint 4: The Archaeology and Histories of an Ionian Town*, 47–76. Oxford: Oxbow Books.

Guy, N. (2012) *The Birth of Albania*. London: Bloomsbury.

Gwynne, P., Hodges, R and Vroom, J. (2014) Archaeology and Epic: Butrint and Ugolino Verino's *Carlias*. Papers of the British School at Rome 82, 199–235.

Hammond, N. G. L. (1967) *Epirus: The Geography, the Ancient Remains, the History and the Topography of Epirus and Adjacent Areas*. Oxford: Clarendon Press.

Hammond, N. G. L. (1983) Travels in Epirus and south Albania before World War II. *Ancient World* 8, 13–46.

Hansen, I. L. (2007) The Trojan connection: Butrint and Rome. In I. L. Hansen and R. Hodges (eds) *Roman Butrint: An Assessment*, 44–61. Oxford: Oxbow Books.

Hansen, I. L. (2011) Between Atticus and Aeneas: The making of a colonial elite at Roman Butrint. In R. J. Sweetman (ed.) *Roman Colonies in the First Century of Their Foundation*, 85–100. Oxford: Oxbow Books.

Hansen, I. L. and Hodges, R. (2007) (eds) *Roman Butrint: An Assessment*. Oxford: Oxbow Books.

Hansen, I. L., Hodges, R. and Leppard, S. (2013) (eds) *Butrint 4: The Archaeology and Histories of an Ionian Town*. Oxford: Oxbow Books.

Harper, K. (2017) *The Fate of Rome: Climate, Disease and the End of an Empire*. Princeton: Princeton University Press.

Harris, J. (2019) *Constantinople: Capital of Byzantium*. London: Bloomsbury.

Hernandez, D. R. (2017a) Bouthrotos (Butrint) in the Archaic and Classical periods: The Acropolis and Temple of Athena Polis. *Hesperia* 86, 205–71.

Hernandez, D. R. (2017b) Buthrotum's sacred topography and the imperial cult, I: The west courtyard and pavement inscription. *Journal of Roman Archaeology* 30, 38–63.

Hernandez, D. R. (2019) The abandonment of Butrint: From Venetian enclave to Ottoman backwater. *Hesperia* 88, 365–419.

Hernandez, D. R. and Çondi, Dh. (2018) The agora and forum at Butrint: A new topography of the ancient urban center. In J.-L. Lamboley, L. Përzhita and A. Skenderaj (eds) *L'Illyrie Méridionale et l'Épire dans l'Antiquité -VI*, 629–46. Paris, Diffusion De Boccard.

Hernandez, D. R. and Hodges, R. (2020a) (eds) *Butrint 7: Beyond Butrint*. Oxford: Oxbow Books.

Hernandez, D. R. and Hodges, R. (2020b) Dominion, territory, environment and the corrupting sea. In D. R. Hernandez and R. Hodges (eds) *Butrint 7: Beyond Butrint*, 292–309. Oxford: Oxbow Books.

Hernandez, D. R. and Mitchell, J. (2013) The western cemetery: Archaeological survey of Roman tombs along the Vivari Channel. In I. L. Hansen, R. Hodges, and S. Leppard (eds) *Butrint 4: The Archaeology and Histories of an Ionian Town*, 182–201. Oxford: Oxbow Books.

Hernandez, D. R., Hodges, R., Islami, S. and Schofield, L. (2020) Pan at Butrint. In D. R. Hernandez and R. Hodges (eds) *Butrint 7: Beyond Butrint*, 277–91. Oxford: Oxbow Books.

Hodges, R. (2006) *Eternal Butrint: A UNESCO World Heritage Site in Albania*. London: General Penne.

Hodges, R. (2009) Nikita Khrushchev's visit to Butrint – May 1959. *Expedition* 51, 24–6.

Hodges, R. (2011) From Roman *insula* to medieval quarter? In W. Bowden and R. Hodges (eds) *Butrint 3: Excavations at the Triconch Palace*, 319–26. Oxford: Oxbow Books.

Hodges, R. (2014) The Dema Wall. *Annual of the British School at Athens* 113, 1–5.

Hodges, R. (2015) 'A God-guarded city'? The new Medieval town of Butrint. *Byzantine and Modern Greek Studies* 39, 191–218.

Hodges, R. (2016) *The Archaeology of Mediterranean Placemaking: Butrint and the Global Heritage Industry*. London: Bloomsbury Academic.

Hodges, R. (2020) A colonial indifference to Butrint, 1923–24: S.S. Clarke's 'survey' of the hinterland of Buthrotum. In D. R. Hernandez and R. Hodges (eds) *Butrint 7: Beyond Butrint*, 2–9. Oxford: Oxbow Books.

Hodges, R. and Molla, N. (2025) *Butrint 8: The Middle Byzantine Archaeology of Butrint, Its Enclave, Saranda and Santi Quaranta*. Oxford: Oxbow Books, forthcoming.

Hodges, R., Bowden, W. and Lako, K. (2004) (eds) *Byzantine Butrint: Excavations and Surveys 1994–1999*. Oxford: Oxbow Books.

Horden, P. and Purcell, N. (2000) *The Corrupting Sea*. Oxford: Blackwell.

Hoxha, E. (1980) *The Khruschevites*. London: Workers' Publishing House, 376–7.

Islami, S. (2020) Çuka e Aitoit: The 1979 Survey and Excavations. In D. R. Hernandez and R. Hodges (eds) *Butrint 7: Beyond Butrint*, 76–109. Oxford: Oxbow Books.

Kadare, I. (1973) *Dimri i vetmisë së madhe* (The Winter of the Great Loneliness). Tirana: Naim Fräsheri.

Karaiskaj, G. (1976) Fortifikimet mesjetare pranë kanalit të Vivarit në Butrint dhe restaurimi i tyre. *Monumentet* 11, 147–58.

Karaiskaj, G. (2009) *The Fortifications of Butrint*. London: The Butrint Foundation.

Kondis, B. (1997) Epirus as part of the Greek state: The inter-war period. In M. B. Sakellariou (ed.) *Epirus: 4000 Years of Greek History and Civilization*, 387–8. Athens: Ekdotike Athenon.

Korkuti, M. (2005) Dhimosten Budina, una vita dedicate all'antice Caonia. Scritti 1959–1990. In S. De Maria and S. Gjongecaj (eds) *Phoinike III. Rapporto Preliminare Sulle Campagne di Scavi e Ricerche 2002–2003*, 18–22. Bologna: Ante Quem.

Korkuti, M., Davis, J. L., Bejko, L., Galaty, M. L., Muçaj, S. and Stocker, S. R. (1998) The Mallakastra Regional Archaeological Project: First Season, 1998. *Iliria* 28, 253–73.

Krautheimer, R. (1980) *Rome: A Portrait of a City*. Princeton: Princeton University Press.

Lako, K. (1981) Rezultatet e gërmineve arkeologjike në Butrint në vitet. *Iliria* 11, 93–154.

Lane, A. (2004) The environs of Butrint 1: The 1995–96 environmental survey. In R. Hodges, W. Bowden and K. Lako (eds) *Byzantine Butrint: Excavations and Surveys 1994–1999*, 27–46. Oxford: Oxbow.

Leake, W. M. (1835) *Travels in Northern Greece*. London: J. Rodwell.

Leppard, S. (2013) The Roman bridge of Butrint. In I. L. Hansen, R. Hodges and S. Leppard (eds) *Butrint 4: The Archaeology and Histories of an Ionian Town*, 97–104. Oxford: Oxbow Books.

Lima, S. (2013) Butrint and the Pavllas River Valley in the Late Bronze Age and Early Iron Age. In I. L. Hansen, R. Hodges and S. Leppard (eds) *Butrint 4: The Archaeology and Histories of an Ionian Town*, 31–46. Oxford: Oxbow Books.

Lima, S. (2020) The Late Bronze Age pottery from Mursi, Albania. In D. R. Hernandez and R. Hodges (eds) *Butrint 7: Beyond Butrint*, 245–65. Oxford: Oxbow Books.

Marin, E. and Vickers, M. (2004) *The Rise and Fall of an Imperial Shrine: Roman Sculpture from the Augusteum at Narona*. Split: Arheološki Muzej.

Marmora, A. (1672) *Della Historia di Corfù Descritta*. Venice: Il Curti.

Melfi, M. (2007) The sanctuary of Asclepius. In I. L. Hansen and R. Hodges (eds) *Roman Butrint: An Assessment*, 17–32. Oxford: Oxbow Books.

Melfi, M. (2012) Butrinto: da santuario di Asclepio a centro federale. In G. de Marinis, G. M. Fabrini, G. Paci, R. Perna and M. Silvestrini (eds) *I Processi Formativi ed Evolutivi della Città in Area Adriatica, British Archaeological Reports International Series 2419*, 23–31. Oxford: Archaeopress.

Meksi, A. (1983) Bazilika e madhe dhe baptistery i Butrintit. *Monumentet* 25, 47–75.

Migjeni (Millosh Gjergj Nikola) (1991) *Free verse* (translated by Robert Elsie). Tirana: 8 Nentori Publishing House.

Mitchell, J. (2004) The mosaic pavements of the Baptistery. In R. Hodges, W. Bowden and K. Lako (eds) *Byzantine Butrint: Excavations and Surveys 1994–99*, 202–18. Oxford: Oxbow Books.

Mitchell, J. (2008) *The Butrint Baptistry and Its Mosaics*. London: The Butrint Foundation.

Mitchell, J. (2011) The mosaic pavements and painted walls of the domus. In W. Bowden and R. Hodges (eds) *Butrint 3: Excavations of the Triconch Palace*, 231–76. Oxford: Oxbow Books.

Mitchell, J. (2019) The mosaic pavement of the basilica. In S. Greenslade (ed.) *Butrint 6: Excavations on the Vrina Plain Volume I: The Lost Roman and Byzantine Suburb*, 336–57. Oxford: Oxbow Books.

Mitchell, J. (2020) The small finds. In W. Bowden (ed.) *Butrint 5: Life and Death at a Mediterranean Port*, 106–217. Oxford: Oxbow Books.

Molla, N. (2013) The Great Basilica: A reassessment. In I. L. Hansen, R. Hodges and S. Leppard (eds) *Butrint 4: The Archaeology and Histories of an Ionian Town*, 202–14. Oxford: Oxbow Books.

Molla, N. 2019 'The Despotate of Epirus: the Archaeology of a Late Byzantine State.' Doctoral thesis, Università di Siena. http://hdl.handle.net/11365/1075416.

Molla, N., Paris, F. and Venturini, F. (2013) Material boundaries: The city walls of Butrint. In I. L. Hansen, R. Hodges and S. Leppard (eds) *Butrint 4: The Archaeology and Histories of an Ionian Town*, 260–80. Oxford: Oxbow Books.

Morellón, M. F., Anselmetti, S., Ariztegui, D., Brushulli, B., Sinopoli, G., Wagner, B., Sadori, L., Gilli, A. and Pambuku, A. (2016) Human-climate interactions in the central Mediterranean region during the last millennia: The laminated record of Lake Butrint (Albania). *Quaternary Science Reviews* 136, 134–52.

Newby, E. (1984) *On the Shores of the Mediterranean*. London: William Collins.

Nicol, D. (1957) *The Despotate of Epirus*. Oxford: Clarendon Press.

Norwich, J. J. (1999) Foreword. In N. Ceka, *A Guide to Butrint*. London: The Butrint Foundation.

Papadopoulou, P. (2020) The middle and late Byzantine, medieval and early modern coins. In W. Bowden (ed.) *Butrint 5: Life and Death at a Mediterranean Port. The Non-Ceramic Finds from the Triconch Palace*, 95–105. Oxford: Oxbow Books.

Parangoni, I., Gilkes, O. J. and Bescoby, D. (2020) Trial excavations at the Triangular Fortress, 2014. In D. R. Hernandez and R. Hodges (eds) *Butrint 7: Beyond Butrint*, 147–54. Oxford: Oxbow Books.

Pavlides, S., Kociu, S., Mukelli, P., Hyseni, A. and Zouros, N. (2001) Archaeological evidence for seismic activity at Butrinti (SW Albania) and Neotectonics of the area. *Bulletin of the Geological Society of Greece* XXXIV: 311–19.

Pojani, I. (2007) The monumental togate statue from Butrint. In I. L. Hansen and R. Hodges (eds) *Roman Butrint: An Assessment*, 62–77. Oxford: Oxbow Books.

Pouqueville, F. H. C. L. (1820) *Travels in Epirus, Albania, Macedonia and Thessaly*. London: Sir Richard Phillips and Co.

Rama, E. (2003) Resolving the contradictions. In N. Ascherson and A. Marshall (eds) *The Adriatic Sea: A Sea at Risk*. Athens: Religion, Science and Environment symposium.

Raynor, B. (2017) Alexander I of Molossia and the creation of Apeiros. *Chiron* 47, 243–70.

Reynolds, P. (2020) *Butrint 6: Excavations on the Vrina Plain. Volume 3: The Roman and Late Antique Pottery from the Vrina Plain Excavations*. Oxford: Oxbow Books.

Ricciardi, R. (2007) Two Roman monuments: proposals for function and context. In I. L. Hansen and R. Hodges (eds) *Roman Butrint: An Assessment*, 165–74. Oxford: Oxbow Books.

Rizakis, A. D. (1996) Les colonies romaines des côtes occidentales grecques. Populations et territoires. *Dialogues d'Histoire Ancienne* 22, 255–324.

Romano, D. R. (2003) City planning, centuriation and land division in ancient Corinth. In C. K. Williams and N. Bookidis (eds) *Corinth: The Centenary 1896–1996*, 279–301. Princeton: The American School of Classical Studies at Athens.

Sakkas, V., Kapetanidis, V., Kaviris, G., Spingos, I., Mavroulis, S., Diakakis, M., Alexopoulos, J. D., Kazantzidou-Firtinidou, D., Kassaras, I., Dilalos, S., et al. (2022) Seismological and Ground Deformation Study of the Ionian Islands (W. Greece) during 2014–2018, a period of intense seismic activity. *Applied Sciences* 12: 2331.

Schuldenrein, J. (2001) Stratigraphy, sedimentology and site formation at Konispol Cave, southwest Albania. *Geoarchaeology* 16.5, 559–602.

Sebastiani, S., Gooney, D., Mitchell, J., Papadopoulou, P., Reynolds, P., Vaccaro, E and Vroom, J. (2013) The Medieval church and cemetery at the well of Junia Rufina. In I. L. Hansen, R. Hodges and S. Leppard (eds) *Butrint 4: The Archaeology and Histories of an Ionian Town*, 260–80. Oxford: Oxbow Books.

Skeates, R. (2023) Review of *Malta Antica, vols 1–4*. *European Journal of Archaeology* 26, 251–68.

Soustal, P. (2004) The historical sources for Butrint in the Middle Ages. In R. Hodges, W. Bowden and K. Lako (eds) *Byzantine Butrint: Excavations and Surveys 1994–99*, Oxford: Oxbow Books, 20–6.

Suha, M. (2009) The fortification walls of Agios Donatos. In B. Forsén (ed.) *Thesprotia Expedition I: Towards a Regional History, Papers and Monographs of the Finnish Institute at Athens 15*, 119–31. Helsinki: Suomen Ateenan-Instituutin.

Suha, M. (2016) The walls of Elea: Some thoughts concerning their typology and date. In B. Forsén, N. Galanidou and E. Tikkala (eds) *Thesprotia Expedition III:*

Landscapes of Nomadism and Sedentism, Papers and Monographs of the Finnish Institute at Athens 22, 311–40. Helsinki: Suomen Ateenan-Instituutin.
Tozer, H. F. (1869) *Researches in the Highlands of Turkey*. London: John Murray.
Ugolini, L. M. (1927) *Albania Antica 1: Ricerche Archeologiche*. Rome: Società Editrice d'Arte Illustrata.
Ugolini, L. M. (1932) *Albania Antica 2: L'Acropoli di Fenice*. Rome: Scalia Editore.
Ugolini, L. M. (1936) Il cristianesimo e l'organizzazione ecclesiastiche a Butrinto. *Orientalia Christiana Periodica* 2, 309–29.
Ugolini, L. M. (1937) *Butrinto. Il Mito d'Enea: Gli Scavi*. Rome: Istituto Grafico Tiberino.
Ugolini, L. M. (1942) *Albania Antica 3: L'Acropoli di Butrinto. Il Sacello di Asclepio*. Rome: Scalia Editore.
Ugolini, L. M. (2003) The sculpture from the Theatre. In O. J. Gilkes (ed.) *The Theatre at Butrint: Luigi Maria Ugolini's Excavations at Butrint 1928–1932, Albania Antica IV, British School at Athens Supplementary Volume 35*, 195–245. London: The British School at Athens.
Ugolini, L. M. (2020) Monte Aetòs (Çuka e Aitoit): Scavi. In D. R. Hernandez and R. Hodges (eds) *Butrint 7: Beyond Butrint*, 49–59. Oxford: Oxbow Books.
Vroom, J. (2004) The Medieval and post-Medieval fine wares and cooking wares from the Triconch Palace and the Baptistery. In R. Hodges, W. Bowden and K. Lako (eds) *Byzantine Butrint: Excavations and Surveys 1994–1999*, 278–92. Oxford: Oxbow.
West, D. (2003) (ed.) *The Aeneid*. Harmondsworth: Penguin Books.
Whittow, M. (2013) How much trade was local, regional and inter-regional? In L. Lavan (ed.) *Local Economies: Production and Exchange of Inland Regions in Late Antiquity*, 133–66. Leiden: Brill.
Wilkes, J. (2003) The Greek and Roman Theatres of Butrint: A commentary and reassessment. In O. J. Gilkes (ed.) *The Theatre at Butrint: Luigi Maria Ugolini's Excavations at Butrint 1928–1932, Albania Antica IV, British School at Athens Supplementary Volume 35*, 107–80. London: The British School at Athens.
Wilson, A. (2013) The aqueduct of Butrint. In I. L. Hansen, R. Hodges and S. Leppard (eds) *Butrint 4: The Archaeology and Histories of an Ionian Town*, 77–96. Oxford: Oxbow Books.
Zachos, K. (2015) *An Archaeological Guide to Nicopolis: Rambling through the Historical, Sacred, and Civic Landscape*. Athens: DIPCA- Scientific committee of Nicopolis.
Zachos, K. (2024) (ed.) *The Victory Monument of August at Nicopolis: The Tropaeum of the Sea Battle of Actium*. Athens: Research Association of Nicopolis.

INDEX

Acheron 64
Achilles 3, 43
acropolis, Butrint viii, ix, 1, 3, 10, 16, 17, 20, 22, 27, 32, 35, 36, 37, 38, 39, 40, 41, 42, 44, 45, 46, 47, 48, 50, 56, 69, 87, 89, 92, 94, 101, 102, 110, 126, 128, 129, 130, 131, 132, 134, 135, 136, 137, 145, 154
acropolis, Mycenae xi, 22
Actium, Battle of 25, 61, 62, 63, 69, 78, 79, 158, 181
Adriatic Sea 1, 18, 60, 64, 92, 117, 129, 138
Aegean Sea 5, 122, 123, 138, 147
Aeneas xi, 1, 3, 14, 21, 59, 61, 63, 88, 143, 159, 163, 181
Aeneid xi, 1, 35, 44, 61, 143, 159, 181, 182
Agamemnon 89
agora at Butrint 38, 50, 53, 54, 66, 68
Agrippa, Marcus Vipsanius 61, 62, 63, 68, 181
Agrippina the Younger 64
Ahenobarbus, L. Domitius 63, 64
Albanian American Development foundation (AADF) 33, 163
Albanian–Soviet Mission 55
Alexander the Great 11, 42, 43
Al-Idrisi 129
Ali Pasha of Tepelenë 5, 11, 12, 19, 20, 32, 145, 146, 152, 153, 156, 159, 181
Ambracian Gulf 62
amphora 177; Corinthian 41, 42; Otranto 122, 123, 124, 125, 129; Roman 87, 99, 114
amulet 100
Anamali, Skënder 28
Andromache 28, 159, 18, 182

Angevins, the 120, 130, 131
Antigonea 29, 43
Apokaukus, Ioannes 137
Apollo 25, 53, 63, 78, 177
Apollo Agyieus 78
Apollonia xiii, 4, 22, 25, 28, 29, 38, 40, 42, 48, 53, 56, 86, 163, 164
Apulia 104, 119, 138
aqueduct at Butrint 62, 66, 67, 76, 77, 85, 103, 138, 177
Arafat, K. W. 38, 169
Arcadia 47, 72
Arta 131, 132, 136, 143
Artemis, 38
Asclepian sanctuary 25, 27, 29, 50, 51, 52, 63, 74, 75
Asclepieion 54, 107, 177
Asclepieion Gate 74
Asclepieion treasury, *see* treasury
Asclepius, temple of 27, 50, 51, 53, 54, 84, 92, 127
Attica 41
Attica, Caecilia 61, 181
Atticus, Titus Pomponius 20, 57, 60, 61, 63, 64, 71, 82, 158, 181
Augustales 64, 74, 177
Avaro-Slavic ware 122

Balkan wars 147, 159
Baptistery at Butrint 13, 23, 27, 32, 92, 94, 101, 102, 103, 104–5, 114, 115, 134, 135, 137, 151, 152, 182
Baptistery mosaic pavement 23, 100, 105–10
Baptistery, Lateran at Rome 110
Baptistery of St. Ambrose, Milan 105, 108
Baptistery, Ravenna 97, 104, 105, 109, 117

Basilica, Palaiopolis 38, 106, 121
Basilica, Léchaion at Corinth 107
Bellum Civiles (by Julius Caesar) 60
Benedict of Peterborough (Roger of Howden) 129
Benitses 84
Berat xiii, 162
Bertinoro 21, 22
Bettini, Maurizio 59, 170
Bibulus, M. Calpurnius 60
Bishop Arsenios of Corfu 64, 126
Bishop Eugenius 92
Bishop Eusebius of Caesarea 75
Bishop Jovianus of Kerkyra (Corfu) 105
Bishop Matthew of Butrint 92
Bistrice, river (Lumï Bistrica) 7
Blavatski, Vladimir 28
Bondisa 4
Boni, Giacomo 27
Bowden, William xvi, 100, 175
Bowes, Kim 94
Bronze Age 6, 11, 17, 32, 36, 37, 38, 43, 45, 158, 178
Budina, Dhimosten 28, 29, 31, 32, 45, 73, 137, 181
Budrout 4
Buondelmonti, Cristoforo 15
Buthroti 139
Buthroti, Stephanus, episcopus 92
Buthrotos 91
Buthrotum xi, 1, 15, 20, 22, 44, 59, 60, 64, 73, 74, 84, 139, 159, 182
Buthrotum Municipium 14, 158
Butrint Bay 4, 7, 18, 19, 131, 141
Butrint Foundation xi, xiii, xiv, xvi, 1, 32, 33, 36, 45, 46, 56, 75, 79, 80, 81, 86, 87, 102, 104, 114, 118, 134, 137, 138, 155, 160, 161, 166, 175, 182
Butrint Lake xiii, 1, 3, 6, 7, 8, 10, 11, 20, 22, 30, 36, 37, 39, 40, 44, 47, 48, 55, 56, 59, 64, 66, 77, 81, 82, 83, 84, 101, 113, 129, 131, 139, 140, 156, 160, 178, 179
Butrint Management Foundation (BMF) 33, 163
Butrint National Park 2, 6, 17, 32, 161, 162, 163, 182
Butrinto 12, 15, 21, 119

Butrinto, Il Mito d'Enea (by Luigi Maria Ugolini) 11, 14, 21, 28, 65, 175
Byllis 53, 164
Byron, Lord George 12, 146

Cabanes, Pierre 52, 54, 169, 170
Caesar, Julius 5, 10, 46, 48, 57, 59, 60, 68 71, 75, 88, 116, 158, 159, 164, 181
Calvino, Italo 164
Camotti, Giovanni 18
Cape Stillo 21, 32, 36, 37, 141, 147, 148, 166, 177
Cardini, Luigi 11, 27, 36, 37, 167, 175, 181
Carlias (by Ugolino Verino) 142
Carte Physique Historique De La Grèce 18
castellum divisorium 67, 85, 103, 129
cavea 23, 177, 178
Ceka, Hasan 25, 28, 31, 181
Ceka, Neritan 31, 40, 181
centuriation 76
Ceschi, Carlo 26, 69, 70
Chaeronea, Battle of 5
Chaonia/Chaonian 1, 10, 42, 43, 45, 46, 47, 48, 52, 56, 177, 178
Chartulararon de Bagenetia 118
chora at Butrint 40, 41, 42
Cicero, Marcus Tullius 5, 20, 46, 57, 60, 61, 91, 181
Città Morta (by G. d'Annunzio) 89
Cleopatra 5, 61
coins
    Hellenistic 51; Medieval 136, 137; Middle Byzantine 125, 126, 129, 130; Roman 60, 66, 82, 99, 124; Venetian 150
Compitum 74, 177
Çondi, Dhimetër 29, 32, 181
Constantinople 5, 19, 65, 91, 96, 101, 102, 117, 120, 121, 122, 130, 138, 140, 178
Cook, Henry 79, 155, 156
Corcyra (Corfu) 4, 5, 40
Corfu xii, 1, 3, 4, 5, 8, 9, 10, 12, 14, 15, 18, 20, 22, 32, 38, 39, 40, 41, 42, 46, 47, 48, 55, 59, 60, 61, 63, 64, 81, 84, 108, 116, 117, 118, 119,

120, 121, 123, 131, 132, 133, 136, 139, 141, 142, 143, 144, 145, 147, 148, 149, 152, 153, 154, 155, 156, 158, 159, 160, 179
Corfu, Straits of 1, 3, 6, 7, 39, 59, 66, 71, 81, 98, 102, 130, 156, 159
Corinth/Corinthian 4, 5, 38, 40 41, 42, 46, 51, 76, 78, 79, 103, 107, 110, 136, 137, 158
Coronelli, Vincenzo 18
Coronis 53, 54, 176
Croatia 68
Crociera Virgiliana (Virgilian cruise) 25
Crusaders 117, 119
Çuka e Ajtoit 22, 28, 29, 36, 37, 41, 42, 45, 47, 55, 56, 64, 67, 75, 80, 129, 132, 136, 177
Cyriacus d'Ancona 3, 15, 16, 143, 181

Dalmatia 15, 38, 82, 105, 117, 144
Dandolo, Doge Enrico 129
D'Annunzio, G. 189
Delvina 25, 29, 118, 141, 144, 147
Dema Wall 40, 47, 129, 140, 141, 156
Deniaux, Elizabeth 60
Diaporit 32, 56, 81, 82, 84, 87, 92, 97, 113–15, 136
diazoma 53, 54, 178
Dimri i vetmise së madhe (by Ismail Kadare) 29
Dionysius 11, 44, 50, 52, 71, 85
Dodona 10, 11, 43, 50, 53, 61, 147, 158, 159
domus 86, 87, 94, 95, 96, 97, 99, 111, 112, 178
Doukellis, Pano 32
Drinos Valley 29
Dupré, Louis 15, 19, 20
Durrell, Lawrence 1, 116, 160, 181
Durrës 1, 4, 5, 38, 42, 60, 102, 117, 119, 120, 129, 163
Dyrrhachium 1, 4, 5, 60, 102, 117, 119, 120
Dzimâra (Himara) 4

Echetus 5
Emperor Alexius III 129
Emperor Andronius 129
Emperor Augustus (*see also* Octavian) xi, 5, 61, 62, 63, 66, 68, 74, 82, 88, 91, 158 181
Emperor Constantine 65, 75, 91
Emperor Decius 64
Emperor Galba 63
Emperor Gratian 65
Emperor Hadrian 69, 84
Emperor Isaac II 129
Emperor Justinian 91, 92, 114, 115, 120
Emperor Leo I 92
Emperor Manuel Comnenus 129
Emperor Nero 63, 64, 66
Emperor Theodosius 69
Emperor Theodosius II 91
Emperor Tiberius 61, 63, 73, 75
Empress Livia 63
Epicoco, Igino 26, 70
Epicurus 61
Epidamnos (Durrës) 1, 5, 38, 42, 48
Epidauros 54, 177
Epirote Despots 5, 17, 117, 120, 130, 131, 133, 136, 137, 138, 141, 159, 178
Eretrians 41
Euboea 38
Euroia 118
Evangelides, Demetrios 147

farms
  Bronze Age 36; Hellenistic 11, 56; 1960s 8
Fâsko 4
flint implements 11, 36, 37
folles, Byzantine 128
forum at Butrint xvi, 23, 29, 32, 41, 48, 63, 64, 66, 67, 68, 69 71, 73, 74, 82, 84, 85, 86, 87, 92, 94, 96, 102, 105, 123, 128, 134, 137, 149, 150, 163, 177
Fulvius, Gnaeus 48

Gardiki Bay 38, 131
gates (*see also* Asclepieion Gate, Lake Gate; Lion Gate; Scaean Gate; Tower Gate) Bronze Age/Hellenistic 45; Hellenistic 48, 49; Late Roman 102, 132; Medieval 138
Germanicus Caesar 63, 68

Geroviglia 20
Getty Grant Program 13
Gjirokastra xiii, 4, 12, 29, 43, 64, 118, 141, 146, 147, 162
Glykys Limen 64
Goddess of Butrint 23, 24, 25, 63
Gonemi family 145, 152, 173
Grand Tourists 18, 20, 163
Great Basilica at Butrint 31, 32, 67, 92, 101, 102, 103–4, 105, 110, 114, 115, 126, 128, 130, 132, 133, 135, 154, 182
Great Powers 12, 148, 158
Guilleminot, Comte 18
Guiscard, Robert 119, 181
Gymnasium at Butrint 25, 31, 32, 66, 85, 86, 94, 101, 134, 135, 151

Hadzis, Kati 32, 41
Hammond, N. G. L. 11, 14, 38, 39, 40, 64, 66, 102, 182
Hekataios 40
Helenus 15, 28, 59, 61, 63, 88, 159, 181, 182
Hernandez, David xvi, 41, 42, 48, 54, 67, 69, 73, 149
hiereus Philistos 51
Hierocles 91
Himara (*see also* Dzimâra) 4, 119, 129
HMS Firefly 18
HMS Glasgow 153
Holocene deposits 6, 8, 9
Hoxha, Enver 29, 30 31, 40, 164, 182

Idrografia Generale del Mare Adriatico 18
Illyria/Illyrians xiii, 4, 11, 30, 31, 38, 39, 40, 47, 48, 164, 181
Invisible Cities (by Italo Calvino) 164
Ioannina 4, 11, 12, 61, 119, 141, 144, 146, 147, 155, 158, 181
Ionian Islands/region/Sea xii, 1, 4, 5, 6, 9, 10, 18, 22, 32, 40, 41, 47, 60, 62, 63, 73, 123, 129, 138, 143, 147, 153, 159, 178, 179
Islami, Selim 28, 31
Istituto Luce (Rome) 23, 25

Italian Archaeological Mission xiv, 11, 14, 17, 21–8, 32, 36, 40, 101, 134, 135, 136, 160, 167, 181, 182
Itinerarium Maritimum 64

Judgement of Paris 42
Julian the Apostate 65
Julio-Claudian imperial family 63, 74, 79, 82
Junia Rufina well at Butrint 23, 84, 101, 128, 135, 152, 158

Kadare, Ismail 29
Kakavia xii
Kalivo 6, 7, 22, 29, 32, 36, 37, 43, 44–7, 55, 80, 140, 141, 178
Kanoni 38, 40
kantharos 107, 108, 134, 178
Karaiskaj, Gjerak 31, 155, 182
Karavasta 8
Kassiope 118, 131
Kassope 10, 62
Kavanagh, Arthur MacMurrough 20, 21, 182
Kefalonia 119
Kestrine (Çuka e Ajtoit) 28, 36, 80, 177, 182
Khrushchev, Nikita xiii, 4, 28, 29–30, 80, 182
koinon 43, 54, 55, 178
Konispoli xiii, 4; Konispoli Cave 11, 167
Korafit Hills 7, 141
Korbat mbi mermer (by Teodor Laço) 24
Korçë 28
Korypho (Corfu) 5
Ksamil Bay 4, 8, 14, 21, 30, 40, 42, 47, 102, 139, 143, 156, 165; Tomb 41–2

Lablôna 4
Laço, Teodor 24
Lake Armur 7
Lake Bufi 7, 8, 140, 154
Lake Butrint, *see* Butrint Lake
Lake Gate at Butrint 103, 132
Lako, Kosta xvi, 29, 31, 32, 182
L'Albania Antica (by Luigi Maria Ugolini) 27, 175
Lanciani, Rodolfo 27

land reclamation 7, 155
League of Nations 12, 147, 148
Leake, Colonel William Martin 12, 19, 22, 35, 146, 153, 156, 182
Lear, Edward 20, 21, 131, 132, 160, 182
Lebena 51
Lefkada 12, 144
Lepanto, battle of 144, 145
Leukas 42, 62
Levallois flakes 37
Lezha 163
Libanius 65
Lion Gate at Butrint 23, 30, 40, 41, 48, 79, 84, 101, 102, 132, 135, 152
Livári, Livari 20, 139
Llahana, Telemack 165

Macedonia 4, 36, 42, 48, 107, 118, 120
macellum at Butrint 86, 94
maiolica 137, 138, 140, 149, 150, 151, 178
Maitland, Sir Thomas 20, 153
Malathrea 47, 56
Mali Gjerë (mountain range) 7
Mansell, Commander A. L. 18
manumission 23, 50, 54, 55, 178
Marconi, Pirro 27
Mark Antony 5, 61, 181
Mediterranean Pilot, The 4, 18
Meksi, Aleksandër 31, 103, 107, 133, 136, 182
Melfi, Milena 51
Merchant's House at Butrint 94
Metaponto 38, 149
Milan 104, 105, 108
Mile mountain range 6, 7, 72, 73, 154
Minerva Augusta 68
Ministry of Culture, Youth and Sports, Albanian 32, 161, 162, 163
Ministry of Foreign Affairs, Italian 22, 25, 27
Mistra 130, 137
Mitchell, John xvi, 100
Molossian tribe 11, 42, 55, 182
Molossius, Alexander 42

Mon Repos, Corfu 38
Monaco, Dario Roversi 25
Morgan, Catherine 38
Monte Aetos (*see also* Çuka e Ajtoit and Kestrine) 22, 36
Montenegro 150
Mursia xiii, 7, 32, 36, 37, 47, 55, 75
Museo della Civiltà Romana, Rome 27
mussels 7, 152
Mussolini, Benito 11, 12, 22, 24, 148, 179
Mustilli, Domenico 27
Mycenaean Age 36, 37, 55, 72

Nanaj, Astrid 29, 32
Napoleon Bonaparte 18, 19, 145, 159
Napoleonic era 5, 18, 19, 38, 146
Narona 69
Naupaktos 118, 119, 137
Nea Taktika 133
Nemean Ode 10
Newby, Eric 14
Nicopolis 4, 15, 61, 62, 64, 78, 79, 80, 85, 90, 91, 92, 102, 103, 104, 106, 118, 159
Nike, Greek goddess of victory 78, 79
Nocera 104
Normans, the 117, 119, 129, 181
Norwich, John Julius xii
Notitia of the Iconoclasts 118
nymphaeum at Butrint 83, 94, 101, 134, 178

Octavian (*see also* Emperor Augustus) 5, 61, 181
Odysseus 3, 73
Odyssey, the 5
Ohrid 118, 119
On the Shores of the Mediterranean (by Eric Newby) 14
Onchesmos (*see also* Saranda) 80, 102, 170n.9, 179
Oricum 40
Ostia, Ostia Antica 74, 76
Otranto 117, 122, 124, 136
Otranto, Straits of 73

Ottoman xii, 8, 12, 14, 17, 19, 32, 117, 118, 120, 138, 140, 141, 142, 143, 144, 145, 146, 147, 149, 152, 154, 156, 159, 177
Ovid 41, 63

Packard Humanities Institute xiv, xvi
Palaeolithic vii, 11, 27, 36, 37
Palaia Epeiros (Old Epirus) 91
Palaio Frourio (Old Fortress, Corfu) 5
Palaiopolis (Corfu) 38, 106, 121
Paleokastritsa 123
Palestine 105
Pan 71–5, 182
Parga 15, 120, 141, 145, 178
parodos 52, 178
Partitio Romaniae 116
Patras 62, 64, 78
Paulus, Consul Aemilius 11
Pavlass, river (Lumï Pavla) 7, 44, 155
Paxos 4, 73, 145
pebble-tools 37
peraia 39, 42, 46
Peloponnese 15, 72, 117, 126, 130, 137
Periander 4
peristyle house at Butrint 77, 84, 95, 96
Persephone 24
Persian Wars 5
Peutinger Table 4, 64
Philip II of Macedonia 5, 42
Philistos 51
Phoenicê xiv, 10, 22, 25, 27, 29, 42, 45, 47, 52, 56, 64, 78, 80, 92, 147, 159, 177, 178
Pietrabbondante 53
Pindar 10
Pleistocene 6, 8
Plutarch 43, 73, 75
polis 17, 40, 42, 47, 121, 158, 166, 178
Polybius 11, 47
Pompeii 53, 81, 86
Pompey the Great 5, 46, 48, 57, 60, 158, 181
Pouqueville, François 12, 19, 20, 146, 182
Porto Palermo 12, 146

Praesebes 43, 49, 54, 80 158, 178
praetorium at Butrint 102, 134
Preveza 8, 146
Procopius 9, 114
prostates 43, 54, 178
proteichisma at Butrint 102, 131, 178
prytaneion at Butrint 50, 53, 84, 137, 178
Pyrrhus, King 5, 42, 43, 45, 47, 179, 182

Ragusa 117
Rama, Edi 161, 163, 182
Ravenna 97, 104, 105, 109, 117
Romano, David Gilman 76
Rothschild, Lord Jacob xii, xvi, 165, 182

S. Costanza 104
S. Demetrios 80
S. Giovanni a Canosa 104
S. Maria Maggiore, Rome 104
Sainsbury, Lord John of Preston Candover xii, xvi, 165, 182
Santi Quaranta (Saranda) 147, 179
Saranda (see also *Onchesmos*) xii, xiii, 4, 7, 10, 14, 19, 24, 29, 30, 80, 102, 118, 147, 166, 179
Sazen Island 64
Scaean Gate at Butrint 35, 36, 48, 49, 135
scaenae frons at Butrint 23, 27, 69, 70, 179
Schliemann, Heinrich xi
Schulenberg, J. M. von der 145
seals, Byzantine 124, 125
sgraffito ware 138, 149, 150, 179
Shën Dëlli 136
Shën Dimitri 136
Sicily 1, 97, 123, 181
Simois 20
Skhodra 14, 22
skyphos 38
Slavs 116, 118, 164; Slavic attacks 92
Smyth, Captain W. H. 18
snakes (*see also* vipers) 29
Soviet Union 29, 182
Spain 1, 66
Stari Bar 150

St Elias the Younger 118, 126, 182
St Terinus 64, 134
Stabiae, villa at 78
Stalin, Josef/Stalinist 29, 160
statues 23, 24, 26, 51, 63, 69, 85, 164
Strabo, C. Julius 38, 59, 63, 73
strategos 43, 53, 179
Sultan Achmet II 145
Sultan Beyazid I 141
Sultan Suleiman II, the Magnificent 143
Syria 105

Taranto 38, 149
Tectonic Paroxysm, Early Byzantine 10
Tepelenë 12, 146
Tertullian 108
Teuta, Queen 47, 48
Thamus, Captain 73
Theatre at Butrint xiii, 3, 11, 23, 25, 26, 27, 29, 32, 43, 50, 51, 52, 53, 54, 62, 63, 64, 69, 70, 74, 84, 110, 131, 134, 163, 177, 178, 179
thesauros at Butrint 51, 179
Thessalonika 1, 4, 36, 53, 96, 118, 119
Thessaly 4, 36, 53, 177
Thrassamund, King 113
Thucydides 4, 40, 46
Tirana xii, xiii, 4, 14, 24, 28; University of Tirana 71; National Museum, 159, 161, 164
Tower Gate at Butrint 49, 53, 54, 67, 76, 85, 94, 103, 132
Tower of Inscriptions at Butrint 50, 55
trapeza 51
treasury at Butrint 22, 50, 51, 53
Treaty of Campo Formio 145
Treaty of London (1913) 3, 12, 159
Treaty of San Stefano 148
Trebonius 84
Triangular Castle/Fortress at Butrint 3, 7, 20, 32, 42, 76, 145, 154, 155, 156
Triconch Palace at Butrint 32, 86, 87, 93, 94–100, 102, 104, 115, 123, 126, 127, 128, 129, 130, 131, 136, 137, 149, 151, 162, 179

Trojans 44
Troy xi, xii, 15, 22, 35, 36, 37, 41, 44, 45, 59, 61, 63, 88, 90159, 182

Ugolini, Luigi Maria xi, xiv, 14, 15, 16, 21, 22, 23, 24, 25, 26, 27, 28, 29, 31, 32, 35, 36, 44, 45, 48, 50, 51, 54, 55, 62, 63, 64, 65, 69, 70, 73, 78, 80, 81, 84, 89, 100, 101, 104, 109, 110, 111, 130, 131, 134, 136, 137, 138, 145, 151, 156, 159, 160, 164, 182
UNESCO (World Heritage Site) xii, xiii, xiv, 1, 14, 32, 158, 160, 161, 164, 165

Venice 1, 12, 27, 117, 120, 125, 141, 141, 142, 143, 144, 149, 150, 152, 158, 159
Verige Bay villa 82
Verino, Ugolino 142
Vettraino brothers 25
vipers (*see also* snakes) 26
Virgil xi, xiv, 1, 3, 11, 22, 25, 27, 35, 36, 41, 44, 48 59, 61, 63, 88, 89, 139, 143, 159, 181, 182
Vispania (granddaughter of Titus Pomponius Atticus) 61
Vivari Channel 1, 3, 4, 7, 16, 22, 25, 28, 41, 47, 49, 52, 53, 55, 56, 65, 66, 67, 68, 71, 77, 78, 80, 81, 84, 85, 86, 94, 95, 96, 97, 99, 102, 111, 126, 129, 130, 132, 138, 139, 144, 145, 146, 152, 153, 154, 155, 156, 160, 179
Vivarium 139
Vlach shepherds 4, 35, 44
Vlora 4, 11, 40, 64, 119, 142, 143, 145, 147
Vonitsa 4
Vrina xiii, 7, 152, 156, 162, 173
Vrina Plain 17, 32, 33, 57, 66, 67, 75–9, 92, 99, 111–13, 123, 124, 126, 129, 136, 145

western defences at Butrint 94, 121, 122, 123, 128, 131, 138, 154
Wolfensohn, James 163

Xarra xiii, 36, 37, 55, 66, 67, 75, 77, 132, 136, 140
Xerxes 143

Zadar 117
Zarópulo 154

Zenobius Bostroensis 91
Zeus 54, 177
Zeus Soter, temple at Butrint 49, 53, 54
Zog, King 24, 25, 179, 182
Zographos, George 147